# Exploring the Migration Industries

This book concentrates on the role of commercialised intermediary actors in migration. It seeks to understand how these actors shape migration and mobility patterns through the services they offer.

In addressing the role that migration industries play in migration, the book uses diverse examples such as labour market brokers and recruitment agencies from Eastern Europe to the United Kingdom; Latvian migration to Norway; super-rich lifestyle brokers; international students agents; the Global Mobility Industry for corporate expatriates; skilled migrant intermediaries; and those providing services to West African migrants coming to Europe or Indonesians leaving for Malaysia. Through these examples, the contributors examine the actors in migration industries, showing how they respond to and shape migration trends. They also consider how migration industries operate, manoeuvre and interact with government policy on migration management. Finally, the book looks at how migration industries enable certain forms of migration through enticement, facilitation and control, translating into specific migration trajectories and im/mobility.

Providing examples from across the world, this book analyses how charities, businesses, subcontractors, informal recruitment agencies, and other actors help to shape migration processes, and it will be of interest to those studying not only the causes of migration, but also the migration process itself.

This book was originally published as a special issue of the *Journal of Ethnic and Migration Studies*.

**Sophie Cranston** is Lecturer in Human Geography at Loughborough University, UK. Her research interests include skilled international migration, the Global Mobility Industry and the relationship between youth mobility and global identities.

**Joris Schapendonk** is Assistant Professor in the Department of Geography, Planning and Environment at Radboud University, The Netherlands; and Researcher at the Nijmegen Centre for Border Research. His research concentrates on African im/mobility trajectories and European borders.

**Ernst Spaan** is Assistant Professor of International Public Health at the Radboud Institute for Health Sciences, The Netherlands. His research interests concern population and development, international migration systems, environmental change impacts on health and livelihoods, and health systems reform in developing countries.

# Research in Ethnic and Migration Studies

Series editor:
Paul Statham, Director, Sussex Centre for Migration Research (SCMR), University of Sussex, UK

The *Research in Ethnic and Migration Studies* series publishes the results of high-quality, cutting-edge research that addresses key questions relating to ethnic relations, diversity and migration. The series is open to a range of disciplines and brings together research collaborations on specific defined topics on all aspects of migration and its consequences, including migration processes, migrants and their experiences, ethnic relations, discrimination, integration, racism, transnationalism, citizenship, identity and cultural diversity. Contributions are especially welcome when they are the result of comparative research, either across countries, cities or groups. All articles have previously been published in the *Journal of Ethnic and Migration Studies* (*JEMS*), which has a rigorous peer review system. Collective volumes in this series are either the product of Special Issues published in the journal or published articles that the Editor has selected from individual submissions.

**Titles in the series:**

For a full list of titles please visit
https://www.routledge.com/Research-in-Ethnic-and-Migration-Studies/book-series/REMS

# Exploring the Migration Industries

New Perspectives on Facilitating and
Constraining Migration

*Edited by*
**Sophie Cranston, Joris Schapendonk
and Ernst Spaan**

Routledge
Taylor & Francis Group

LONDON AND NEW YORK

First published 2019
by Routledge
2 Park Square, Milton Park, Abingdon, Oxon, OX14 4RN

and by Routledge
52 Vanderbilt Avenue, New York, NY 10017

First issued in paperback 2020

*Routledge is an imprint of the Taylor & Francis Group, an informa business*

Introduction, Chapters 1-4, 6 © 2019 Taylor & Francis
Chapter 5 © 2017 Sophie Cranston. Originally published as Open Access.
Chapter 7 © 2017 Joris Schapendonk. Originally published as Open Access.
Chapter 8 © 2017 Ernst Spaan and Ton van Naerssen. Originally published as Open Access.

*British Library Cataloguing in Publication Data*
A catalogue record for this book is available from the British Library

ISBN 13: 978-0-367-66152-6 (pbk)
ISBN 13: 978-0-367-18983-9 (hbk)

Typeset in Minion Pro
by RefineCatch Limited, Bungay, Suffolk

**Publisher's Note**
The publisher accepts responsibility for any inconsistencies that may have arisen during the conversion of this book from journal articles to book chapters, namely the possible inclusion of journal terminology.

**Disclaimer**
Every effort has been made to contact copyright holders for their permission to reprint material in this book. The publishers would be grateful to hear from any copyright holder who is not here acknowledged and will undertake to rectify any errors or omissions in future editions of this book.

# Contents

# Citation Information

The chapters in this book were originally published in the *Journal of Ethnic and Migration Studies*, volume 44, issue 4 (March 2018). When citing this material, please use the original page numbering for each article, as follows:

**Introduction**
*New directions in exploring the migration industries: introduction to the special issue*
Sophie Cranston, Joris Schapendonk and Ernst Spaan
*Journal of Ethnic and Migration Studies*, volume 44, issue 4 (March 2018), pp. 543–557

**Chapter 1**
*Oiling the wheels? Flexible labour markets and the migration industry*
David McCollum and Allan Findlay
*Journal of Ethnic and Migration Studies*, volume 44, issue 4 (March 2018), pp. 558–574

**Chapter 2**
*Facilitating labour migration from Latvia: strategies of various categories of intermediaries*
Oksana Žabko, Aadne Aasland and Sylvi Birgit Endresen
*Journal of Ethnic and Migration Studies*, volume 44, issue 4 (March 2018), pp. 575–591

**Chapter 3**
*Enabling, structuring and creating elite transnational lifestyles: intermediaries of the super-rich and the elite mobilities industry*
Sin Yee Koh and Bart Wissink
*Journal of Ethnic and Migration Studies*, volume 44, issue 4 (March 2018), pp. 592–609

**Chapter 4**
*Adapting to change in the higher education system: international student mobility as a migration industry*
Suzanne E. Beech
*Journal of Ethnic and Migration Studies*, volume 44, issue 4 (March 2018), pp. 610–625

**Chapter 5**
*Calculating the migration industries: knowing the successful expatriate in the Global Mobility Industry*
Sophie Cranston
*Journal of Ethnic and Migration Studies*, volume 44, issue 4 (March 2018), pp. 626–643

**Chapter 6**

*Intermediaries and destination reputations: explaining flows of skilled migration*
William S. Harvey, Dimitria Groutsis and Diane van den Broek
*Journal of Ethnic and Migration Studies*, volume 44, issue 4 (March 2018), pp. 644–662

**Chapter 7**

*Navigating the migration industry: migrants moving through an African-European web of facilitation/control*
Joris Schapendonk
*Journal of Ethnic and Migration Studies*, volume 44, issue 4 (March 2018), pp. 663–679

**Chapter 8**

*Migration decision-making and migration industry in the Indonesia–Malaysia corridor*
Ernst Spaan and Ton van Naerssen
*Journal of Ethnic and Migration Studies*, volume 44, issue 4 (March 2018), pp. 680–695

For any permission-related enquiries please visit:
http://www.tandfonline.com/page/help/permissions

# Notes on Contributors

**Aadne Aasland** is Researcher at the Norwegian Institute for Urban and Regional Research (NIBR) at Oslo Metropolitan University, Norway. His main research interests are welfare and migration, with a special focus on Russia and the Baltic countries.

**Suzanne E. Beech** is Lecturer in the School of Geography and Environmental Sciences at Ulster University, UK. Her research lies at the intersections between social and cultural geography, focusing on young people, migration and mobility, and international higher education.

**Sophie Cranston** is Lecturer in Human Geography at Loughborough University, UK. Her research interests include skilled international migration, the Global Mobility Industry and the relationship between youth mobility and global identities.

**Sylvi Birgit Endresen** is Associate Professor in the Department of Sociology and Human Geography at the University of Oslo, Norway.

**Allan Findlay** is Professor at the Centre for Population Change, Geography and Geosciences at the University of St Andrews, UK. His research and teaching interests focus on international migration and population mobility.

**Dimitria Groutsis** is Program Director of the Dalyell Scholars Stream and Associate Professor in the Discipline of Work and Organisational Studies at the University of Sydney Business School at the University of Sydney, Australia.

**William S. Harvey** is Professor of Management at the Business School at the University of Exeter, UK. He conducts research on reputation, talent management and leadership across multiple sectors.

**Sin Yee Koh** is Senior Lecturer in the School of Arts and Social Sciences at Monash University, Malaysia. Her work is positioned at the intersections of migration studies, urban studies and postcolonial geography.

**David McCollum** is Senior Lecturer at the Centre for Population Change, Geography and Geosciences at the University of St Andrews, UK. His research and teaching interests centre on issues relating to migration, labour markets, and welfare and mixed methods research.

**Joris Schapendonk** is Assistant Professor in the Department of Geography, Planning and Environment at Radboud University, The Netherlands; and Researcher at the Nijmegen Centre for Border Research. His research concentrates on African im/mobility trajectories and European borders.

**Ernst Spaan** is Assistant Professor of International Public Health at the Radboud Institute for Health Sciences, The Netherlands. His research interests concern population and development, international migration systems, environmental change impacts on health and livelihoods, and health systems reform in developing countries.

**Diane van den Broek** is Associate Professor in the Discipline of Work and Organisational Studies at the University of Sydney Business School at the University of Sydney, Australia.

**Ton van Naerssen** is Associate Researcher at the Nijmegen Centre for Border Research (NCBR) at the Institute for Management Research at Radboud University, The Netherlands.

**Bart Wissink** is Associate Professor in the Department of Public Policy at the City University of Hong Kong, China. His research interests include enclave urbanism, urban controversies, social networks and the neighbourhood, contemporary art and the city, cities that care, and critical urban studies.

**Oksana Žabko** is Project Director and Researcher at the Baltic Institute of Social Sciences, Latvia. Her research interests are system of taxes and benefits (social aspects), job satisfaction and motivation, migration, sampling methods and sample formation in quantitative research, and assessment of data validity and reliability.

# New directions in exploring the migration industries

Sophie Cranston ⏺, Joris Schapendonk and Ernst Spaan

**ABSTRACT**
This Special Issue explores the directions through which we can take research on the migration industries. In this introduction, we review existing research on migration industries to look at how this explores questions on how migration industries foster, assist and constrain migration. In doing so, we argue that these questions have primarily been approached from three different perspectives: structuralist, labour market and mobilities, but these perspectives often speak past rather than to one another. In highlighting how these approaches can work together, the question that the Special Issue explores becomes how do the migration industries function and when/where/how do they intersect with other domains of migration. In highlighting the contributions that each paper in the special issue makes to answering this question, we show how an understanding of the migration industries is not just a research field in itself, but can strengthen our understanding of migration.

Migration industries work to shape mobility patterns and mobile identities through the services that they offer (Cranston 2016), from before migrants move (Alpes 2012), to their journeys abroad (Spaan and Hillmann 2013), and after they have arrived (Glick-Schiller 2009). As part of a growing rise in non-state intervention into migration, they are operated by, among others, charities, businesses, sub-contractors and informal agencies. Together the services offered by migration industries contribute to an intensified transnational character of the facilitation as well as control of migration (Nyberg-Sørensen 2012).

Through this special issue, we argue that a focus on migration industries allows us not only to gain empirical insights into the mechanisms by and through which people move, it also provides us with an analytical lens to better unpack the social, economic and geographical complexities of migration processes. Beyond this, understanding the migration industries helps us understand contemporary articulations of the interactions between the economy, nation states, non-governmental organisations and the movement of people.

An examination of the migration industries not only tell us about the commercialisation of migration, but how we can move beyond the methodological and conceptual logics of the nation-state (Wimmer and Glick-Schiller 2002) by investigating business networks and in/formal institutions that specialise in transcending borders. To do so, we seek to bring together a fragmented set of research that loosely researches processes associated with the migration industries (e.g. Andersson 2014; Cranston 2016; Gammeltoft-Hansen and Nyberg-Sørensen 2013; Garapich 2008; Hernández León 2008; Lindquist 2010; Nyberg-Sørensen 2012; Spaan 1994; Xiang and Lindquist 2014) to further develop the ways in which migration industries can be considered a field of research (Gammeltoft-Hansen and Nyberg-Sørensen 2013)

Within this set of literature, there has been a variety of terminology used to describe the actors involved within migration 'industries', such as 'business' or 'infrastructure'. For example, in thinking about trafficking, Salt and Stein (1997) highlighted the ways in which migration can be seen as 'business', arguing for a need to think about the actors involved in the 'institutionalized networks with complex profit and loss accounts, including a set of institutions, each of which stands to make a commercial gain' (468). However, it has also been argued that due to the different ways in which actors work to facilitate and control migration, this means that the term 'infrastructure' is more appropriate than 'industry': 'migration industry primarily constructs migration as a form of business and pays less attention to the fact that migration brokers are not simply selling opportunities for migrating overseas, but are also dealing with various components of infrastructure' (Xiang and Lindquist 2014, S133). However, we see the 'dealing with infrastructure' also as a migration industry, that is 'industry' captures the ways in which the processes of migration become an economy; the production and circulation of knowledge, the offering of services and so on. One could challenge the notion that intermediaries offer their services for monetary returns only; services and resources are exchanged, for example, for prestige of political support as well (Faist 2014; Spaan 1999). As to the scope of migration industry, this is predominantly defined as encompassing the facilitation and control of migration, rendering services related to the various phases of (voluntary or forced) migration, from mobilising resources for the actual migration, services needed to circumvent regulatory barriers to crossing borders or for settling in at destinations. Migration industry however performs broader functions, for example, enticement (Spaan and Van Naerssen 2018; Beech 2018), promotion of cosmopolitan lifestyles (Koh and Wissink 2018) but also market expansion through knowledge creation on migration and migrants (Cranston 2018). In this way, we adopt Spener's (2009) understanding of migration industries as a figure of speech to describe the 'ensemble' (Hernández León 2008, 2013) of actors and actions involved. We argue that it is the labour involved in managing, facilitating and controlling migration that makes this an industry. The ways in which we see the involvement of non-profit social networks (see Garapich 2008) means we cannot simply understand this as a business.

The prominence of the discussions of the terminology used to describe the migration industries shows that this is an emerging field. The existing work on migration industries highlights a lack of detailed understanding of the migration industries, a 'gaping theoretical hole concerning the position, contribution and relations of profit-driven actors in the social organization of international migration' (Hernández León 2013, 24). This absence contributes to a dearth in our understanding about how migration industries intersect with migration, what has been described as the 'black box' in migration research (Lind-quist, Xiang, and Yeoh 2012). In this introductory paper, we take up these gaps within the literature to explore what the migration industries are, how migration industries work and how they relate to other dimensions of migration facilitation and migration control. In the next section, we examine the field of research on migration industries and how it intersects with other developments in the study of migration. We argue that these approaches look to understand migration industries by exploring the question: *how is migration fostered, constrained, shaped and assisted?* In looking at how this question comes to be answered from three perspectives – structuralist, labour market and mobilities approaches – we argue that although these approaches have the potential to highlight the intersections between migration and migration industries, in speaking past one another they often miss the larger, more important questions. Instead, we argue that in conversa-tion, the question that migration industries researchers can address is: how do the migration industries function and when/where/how do they intersect with other domains of migration. How this special issue addresses these questions will be the focus of the final section.

## Structrualist approaches

Firstly, from a structuralist approach, scholars have explored the commercialisation of migration – how migration is mediated by businesses as diverse as brokers, security com-panies, transporters and recruitment agencies (Gammeltoft-Hansen 2013; Nyberg-Sørensen 2012; Spaan 1994). It is from this literature that we get the notion of 'migration industry' where attempts are made to address the scope and complexity of the phenom-enon as highlighted above. It is, however, less well understood how these commercial actors relate to other facilitators of migration, for example, 'the social networks' of migrants or the State. In how far should migration industry be considered functionally and conceptually separate from migrants' social networks? Is migration industry to be seen as meso-level structure, connecting migrants and institutions at national and inter-national level?

Evidently, international migration is a time-consuming and costly endeavour, given the spatial, juridical, economic and social barriers, and required access to resources. These include tangible and intangible assets, such as land or information, that can be trans-formed into capital. Included within this are second order resources (Boissevain 1974), that is, access to strategic actors that control needed resources. Social capital, accrued through social networks, thus facilitates access to resources needed for furthering ones aims, such as migration. Social capital has been defined as 'resources embedded in a social structure which are accessed and/or mobilized in purposive actions' (Lin 1999, 35). Investing in social networks is assumed to result in some form of (expected) return, such as jobs (Lin 2001, 19–21). The crucial role of networks, built on reciprocal ties of kinship, co-ethnicity or community, for fostering migration has been convincingly argued (Lomnitz 1977; MacDonald and MacDonald 1974; Massey et al. 1987). However, social network theory fails to sufficiently take into account the wide range of other actors and institutions, external to the migrant's personal network, that impact on the migration process (Krissman 2005). Within migrant social networks commercialised, bureaucratic transactions replace or work alongside reciprocal relations. Harney (1977), studying

Italian migration to North America in the early twentieth century, showed how migrants, lacking sufficient knowledge and skills, turn to intermediaries for transport, required documentation and money. These brokers, embedded in migrant communities, seek out migrants for profit, hence the term 'commerce of migration,' what Salt and Stein (1997, 468) later referred to the global migration business. In highlighting how migration is structured, they expanded the scope of actors and institutions that facilitate migration, but restricted the conceptual boundary to those that gain *commercially* from engaging with migration. However, as Goss and Lindquist (1995, 336) argued, a routinisation of social practice related to migration evolves, reflecting goals of individual and institutional agents. They advocate the mid-level concept of migrant institutions, as having more explanatory power than social networks. Hugo (1996) and Castles, de Haas, and Miller (2013), utilising the term *migration industry*, similarly position it as meso-structure, mediating between the micro-level social networks and the state level and international institutions shaping migration flows, through policy and political economy. However, this structure is not fixed, but may appear to the migrant as rather fluid (Schapendonk 2018).

Therefore, the migration industries literature shows us that while migrants rely on their networks for mobilising resources for the actual migration and for gaining access to housing and jobs at destination, it is the migration industries' role in negotiating of borders that is pivotal, within the context of restrictive migration policies and border control. Some studies have focused on the illegal dimension, that is, the human smuggling industry (Kyle and Koslowski 2001; Laczko and Thompson 2000; Spener 2004); however, a more comprehensive approach to migration industry shows a structural interweaving of the informal and formal in migration facilitation and control. An ever expanding range of migration intermediaries, *function within and without* the legal structures set up by the State (Hugo 1996). This literature shows us that if we accept the premise that migration industry centres on the commodification of migration, the preconditions for its evolving are neo-liberalism favouring free market for services and a public governance structure characterised by opening up opportunities for private business and out-sourcing of public functions in migration management and control. Governments have deliberately shifted certain functions and services toward private entities to rationalise governance and externalise costs and risks related to the matching of supply and demand for migrant labour (Menz 2013). Simultaneously, the post 9/11 world and current refugee crises has fostered policies of securitisation of the nation-state and stricter migration regulation and control (Lemberg-Pedersen 2013). The ensuing barriers to migration have created a demand for services aimed at surmounting such barriers, services that are sanctioned by government or take on a more illegal form–Nyberg Sørensen and Gammeltoft-Hansen (2013, 6–7) defined migration industry as 'the array of non-state actors who provide services that facilitate, constrain or assist international migration'. However, cases of collusion between brokers and state representatives facilitating migration flows (Lindquist 2010; Spaan 1999), calls for inclusion of public sector actors in the conceptualisation of migration industry. Faist (2014, 44–45) rightly points out that the State (as well as civil society) is involved in labour brokerage, in line with a broader conceptualisation of migration industry as the 'various public and private agencies and actors [that] provide for such information, products and services relating to migration, thereby promoting, facilitating and organizing the process of migration' (Spaan and Hillmann 2013, 64).

To conclude this section, research from a structuralist approach suggests that commercialisation as juxtaposed to reciprocity and solidarity seems to be a defining criterion for what constitutes migration industry. Within social networks sustaining migration, solidarity is commodified, when actors capitalise on their in-group membership and position, by providing migration services for monetary gain (Hernández León 2013, 29). Migration industry has evolved into a global business, encompassing professional private and public entities, but also intermediaries, with varying degrees of professionalism, emanating from social networks, be it friends, relatives or other community members (Lindquist 2010; Spaan 1994). Moving on from this, we can see that migration industry and social networks are not substitutes, but, are rather entwined and operate simultaneously, as manifested in the cooperation of recruitment agencies with individuals acting as informal sub-agents within migrant social networks (Harvey, Groutsis and van den Broek 2018; Spaan and Van Naerssen 2018).

## Labour market intermediaries

Research that looks at labour migration has explored the role that labour market brokers play in 'channelling' this form of migration (Groutsis, van den Broek, and Harvey 2015; McCollum and Findlay 2015). This is what others have described as being a way into understanding the 'black box' of studies in migration where the focus becomes not the experiences or mapping of migration, but 'how mobility is made possible and organized by brokers, most notably in the process of recruitment and documentation' (Lindquist, Xiang, and Yeoh 2012, 9). The primary focus here is on the facilitation of migration processes, how intermediaries help to move migrants as opposed to processes of bordering that other approaches focus on. The role that migration plays within labour markets has been the subject of academic attention for as long as migration for work has been the subject of popular anxiety on a spectrum of the availability of jobs, wages, brain drain and global talent. Set within neoclassical 'push-pull' discussions of migration, this research focused on 'the factors that encourage and discourage the movement of economically active people between countries' (Boyle and Halfcree 1998, 83). We can quite clearly see that migration industries act as a factor within the movement of labour forces, both legal and illegal (Salt and Stein 1997). Scholars who look at migration industries from a labour market perspective draw primarily upon two bodies of work.

First, research looking at labour market intermediaries – temporary staffing agencies, contractors, recruitment agents, headhunters – highlighted the role that these industries play in the structuring and experiences of contemporary labour markets. For example, from a Marxist perspective, research on temporary staffing agencies showed the relationship between employers, the outside companies that staffing was outsourced to, and the workers themselves, in how they produced an insecure, flexible workforce (Peck, Theodore, and Ward 2005). Other research focused more on the selection of employees by headhunters, looking at how elite power structures reproduce themselves (Faulconbridge et al. 2009).

Second, research that looks at migration also looked at the role that labour market 'brokers', 'intermediaries' or 'agents' play in 'channelling' labour migration decisions, again 'push' and 'pull' factors. The idea of channels was derived by research looking at different ways by which Scottish emigrants moved abroad, identifying internal labour markets of MNCs, international recruitment agencies and other mechanisms (Findlay and Garrick 1990). Channels then were described in character as 'by channelling information and resources, hav[ing] an influence in moulding the process of international migration' (Findlay and Li 1998, 682). This work therefore represented an important shift in thinking about migration, with the use of channels being used in work that seeks to move beyond individual accounts of why people migrate, to look at the role that (global) networks play within this (e.g. Poli 2010). However, with some exceptions, the research carried out in this area focused on the social networks that worked to facilitate migration. As Ryan et al. (2008) highlight, migrant's social networks are complex, taking on different forms such as friendship groups or community centres, carrying out roles from childcare, to emotional support, to help finding work.

These sets of research were both asking similar questions about the role that institutions play in structuring labour markets and labour market outcomes. For migrants who move for work, these institutions are those that we can call the migration industries. What this presented then was a shift in the scale of understanding migration industries, one that looked to explore the ways in which the demand and supply of migrant labour is produced and facilitated. To date, we can see two key sets of research that have brought these considerations together. First, Lindquist in looking at private recruitment brokers that facilitate migration from Indonesia to Asia and the Middle East examines 'how mobility is made possible and organized by brokers, most notably in the process of recruitment and documentation' (Lindquist, Xiang, and Yeoh 2012, 9), illustrating the ways in which local, national (state) and global processes intersect together to produce labour market outcomes (Lindquist 2010). Second, Findlay, McCollum and other's research on A8 migration to the U.K., which illustrates both how 'migration industries' work to structure labour migration patterns (Findlay and McCollum 2013) and also migrant identities (Findlay et al. 2013). This latter research project is also presented in the McCollum and Findlay paper in this special issue.

Therefore, although research on migration industries from a labour market perspective is still somewhat piecemeal, we can see that it makes two key contributions to our understandings of migration industries. First, it moves us beyond looking solely at the role that labour market intermediaries play in the structuring of migration patterns, to looking at how migrant identities are produced in different ways through migration industries, from representations to practices (Beech 2014; Cranston 2016; Shubin, Findlay, and McCollum 2014). Second, it includes migrant 'infrastructures': other domains of migration such as people, networks and institutions that are not necessarily directed by profit. However, in opening up these other lines of theoretical and empirical research, questions still specifically remain about the function of migration industries themselves: how and why do migration labour market intermediaries operate? These are questions that are taken up by the papers by Harvey, Groutsis and van den Broek (2018); McCollum and Findlay (2018) and Žabko, Aasland and Endresen (2018).

## Migration industries and im/mobilities

The third development is that which draws upon the mobilities turn (Cresswell 2006, 2010; Ernste, Martens, and Schapendonk 2012; Sheller and Urry 2006), which challenges sedentarist understandings of the social and sees migration as being a journey that is produced on the move, but not necessarily bound up by discrete beginnings and ends (Mainwaring and Brigden 2016; Schrooten, Salazar, and Dias 2016). This literature is in part directed by research that explores what happens on the move as a way by which we can understand how the meaning of mobility is produced (Cresswell 2006), but also controlled (Glick-Schiller and Salazar 2013). Importantly, this literature works to reconceptualise how we understand migration, highlighting how it is an ongoing process rather than an event (Schapendonk and Steel 2014).

This strand of debate has resulted in at least two important openings for research on migration industries. The first is rather empirical and implies a move beyond a focus on the facilitation of traditional forms of labour migration towards a focus on more flexible forms of movement. As King (2015, 2369) noted recently, there are many other space-time rhythms of movements that challenge our conventional notion of migration, such as student and lifestyle-related mobility. Moreover, migrants that have reached their destinations may be involved in onward movements (Van Liempt 2011) return visits (Ley and Kobayashi 2005) and transnational practices (Sinatti and Horst 2014) that require other forms of facilitation and are subjected to other forms of control. To understand our world on the move, we need to be sensitive to the multiple mobility processes and the actors and networks that facilitate them. This may eventually result in a semantic shift from 'migration industry' towards 'mobility industry', as is also argued by Koh and Wissink (2018). The fact that all these human mobilities deviate from the prototypical long-term immigrant, encourages us to think about what Allison Hui calls 'migrant exceptionalism'. This notion points to the assumption that migrants are somehow 'extraordinary mobile subjects, discrete from other (concurrent) subject positions and central units within methodologies' (Hui 2016, 10).

The second opening for migration industry literature is conceptual as it concerns the fact that mobilities studies are particularly sensitive to the power dynamics and differentiated meanings attached to human movement. With this starting point, a focus on migration industries enables us to gain vital insights related to the question why some people are able to transcend borders, while others remain involuntarily immobile in their countries of origin (Carling 2002) or get stuck in transit (Collyer 2007). As stated by Faist (2014), brokerage creates and perpetuates power asymmetries and social inequalities. Moreover, it helps us to understand how the migration industry provokes different experiences of mobility, as well as immobility, across lines of class, legal status, age and gender (Conlon 2011). In relation to this, there exists an increasing number of studies that empirically focus on the migrant journey, most notably on the perilous journeys of irregular migrants and asylum seekers (e.g. Belloni 2016; Khosravi 2011; Mainwaring and Brigden 2016; Schapendonk and Steel 2014). These studies underline that mobility processes may include multiple thresholds (Van der Velde and Van Naerssen 2015) as well as multiple forms of facilitation and control. In the same light, there are calls to concentrate on the materialities of the journeys themselves, including the transportation mechanisms used by migrants and their facilitators (Burrell 2008; Walters 2015). This is not only important to relate the migration industry to the actual travel experiences they produce, but also because vehicles are 'mobile zones of governance and contestation' (Walters 2015, 5). This mix of differentiated mobility experiences, materialities and governance is inherently intertwined with the business of bordering, which may on its turn form a highly mobile landscape (Andersson 2014; see Schapendonk 2018).

Thus, instead of focusing on single actors that facilitate the moments of departure or arrival of migrants, the mobility turn invites us to follow carefully the dynamics of facilitation and control during mobility processes. In so doing, we become sensitive to the ways how identities, aspirations and travel needs may shift along the path of movement, and how this creates new markets for migration facilitation and control. Furthermore, we gain further insights into the question of how migrant's mobility processes are impacted by the various ways different actors of facilitation and control liaise, bypass each other, or work in a continuum of practices. This helps us to move away from the notion that the migration industry exists of clearly demarcated and static sub-domains, separating state actors from brokering services and non-profit actors (see also Spaan and Van Naerssen, 2018).

## Migration industries, migration and new directions

This short review of literature on institutions that can be considered the migration industries illustrates the diversity and complexity of the ways in which different aspects of different types of migration can be commercialised. This is a point that we take forward in this special issue. The migrants that feature in this special issue are Indonesian, Latvian, Indian, African and East European labour migrants moving to or in Malaysia, Norway, Italy and the U.K.; they are the transnational super-rich in China; the corporate expatriate, students and asylum seekers. We see them at different stages of the migration process, negotiating whether to move or being 'dealt' with as their migration is undesirable to the host state.

This means the migration industries that feature in this special issue are also similarly diverse, they are facilitators and controllers of migration processes, they have been outsourced by the state, they act to produce knowledge about migration and they work to reproduce certain lifestyles. In this way, we argue that we cannot be prescriptive when thinking about the contours and limits about what constitutes the industry of migration industries. Therefore, this issue shows that instead of trying to singularly define what the migration industries are, the more productive question is to ask what work does an understanding of migration industries do? The special issue looks at how we can answer these questions from three different, although overlapping, angles.

First, the special issue offers insights into the ways in which we conceptualise migration industries in light of recent migration trends. The papers by Will Harvey, Dimitria Groutsis and Diane Van den Broek; David McCollum and Allan Findlay and Oksana Žabko, Aadne Aasland and Sylvi Birgit Endresen provide insights into the nexus between labour migration and labour market intermediaries. This research helps us to understand their function as migration industries. Žabko, Aasland and Endresen, in looking at Latvian migration to Norway, look at the strategies that intermediaries utilise in order to overcome stricter regulatory practices by the state on immigration. Harvey, Groutsis and Van den Broek, addressing a gap in the literature by focusing on skilled migrant intermediaries, highlight the role that they play in addressing these migratory flows through reputational effects. McCollum and Findlay, focusing on Eastern European migration to the U.K., illustrates the relationships between different actors, namely recruiters and employers. This research helps us understand the mechanisms through which migration industries work, the strategies that they utilise both to facilitate migration processes by working with or against the government and also to produce and maintain commercial gain. It is for this reason that McCollum and Findlay argue that a greater attention needs to be paid to the ways in which we think about differences and connections between actors in the migration industry. For example, this is a point that the papers by Žabko, Aasland and Endresen and Harvey, Groutsis and Van den Broek address by illustrating ways in which social networks can be conceptualised in relation to migration industries. In doing so, the papers show how these migration industries work to shape migration flows and experiences, for example, in thinking about why skilled migrants move to particular locations or how they work to reproduce insecurity in the migrant labour force.

Thinking about the ways in which the migration industries have an impact upon our understanding of migration or mobility is the explicit focus of the papers by Sin Yee Koh and Bart Wissink; Joris Schapendonk and Ernst Spaan and Ton Van Naerssen. For example, Spaan and Van Naerssen illustrate the role that migration industries play in Malaysian migrant's trajectories, how the manoeuvering of migration industries, within the changing context of government policies, 'market' demands and public discourse, generate new niches for migration. This therefore illustrates how migration industries play a role in migrant decision-making, particularly with regards to location, shaping the flows of who goes where. Koh and Wissink approach this question from a different angle showing how the intermediaries of the super-rich work to structure privileged migration for this group of people. Drawing upon literature in the mobilities paradigm, the paper shows how these intermediaries do not just facilitate super-rich lifestyles, but produce them. Joris Schapendonk's paper highlights the ways in which African migrants to Europe navigate the migration industry, looking at how these migrants use the industry as ways in which to improvise and negotiate their mobility or immobility. Looking at these industries is, as Koh and Wissink highlight in their conclusion, a way through which we can understand the production of different types of migrants.

While all of these papers show the entanglements between migration industries and migrants themselves, other papers focus more explicitly on the operation of migration industries in themselves. Suzanne Beech, looking at higher education agents in the U.K., looks at the ways in which this migration industry negotiates visa controls, highlighting the ways in which agents work to shape the mobility flows of this group of migrants. This paper, therefore illustrates the way in which the state has an effect on the changing fortunes in the operation of the migration industries. In a different view of the economy, Sophie Cranston's paper utilises a cultural economy perspective arguing that the Global Mobility Industry, in making corporate expatriate mobility known, works to produce a need for itself within the global economy. Collectively then by focusing on different types of mobility and different actors within the migration industries, we can focus on the linkages between theoretical and empirical approaches to ways in which migration industries can be understood.

## New directions

The special issue therefore shows the value of moving our understanding of migration forward, to considering the role that migration industries play, theoretically, empirically and methodologically in our understanding of migration. That is, we see research on the migration industries as not just as a research field in itself, but as a vehicle for understanding contemporary processes of migration. Theoretically, as the papers of Schapendonk and Koh and Wissink in the special issue illustrate, looking at the intersections between migration and the migration industries allows us to revisualise migration as not just a move from here to there, but a changing journey over both space and time. Therefore, an appreciation of the role that migration industries play within processes of migration will also help studies of migration move away from the methodological nationalism that has been a subject of critique (Wimmer and Glick-Schiller 2002). Looking at migration industries helps highlight that our research on migration needs to go beyond the nation – both in looking at non-governmental agencies that intersect with migrant lives and their often global impulses and also how we can make sense of the journeys that migrants take. This is in part an empirical question, it gets us to think how ideas and practices associated with migration circulate in spaces that we do not necessarily directly associate with the movement of people. Part of this, is, as the special issue shows, is a revisualisation of the sites in which we carry out research on migration/ migration industries. For example, we see research sites as diverse as human resource management, education agents, the migration corridor between Indonesia and Malaysia and U.K. recruitment agents. It shows that to understand migration, we cannot simply locate our research with migrants, but have a need to think more widely about the actors that intersect with their journeys.

However, in setting a future agenda for research on the migration industries, we argue that researchers should not just think about the actors that work to facilitate or control migration, but think about the wider context into which research on migration industries can be placed. That is, the value of understanding migration industries can be seen as wider than migration. As the papers in the special issue show, understanding the migration industries tells us stories about the evolving role of the state, the day-to-day operation of globalisation and how we can understand the economy. For example, an appreciation of migration industries helps us understand both the ways in which borders are produced and navigated – we see this in Žabko, Aasland and Endresen's paper as well as Beech's paper. Migration industries therefore can be seen as part of a much wider trend of the outsourcing of state functions (Roberts 2014). However, through this special issue we argue that migration industries can be seen as more than simply a reflection of a neoliberalising world economy. The special issue illustrates the value of opening up research on migration industries to a variety of different theoretical understandings of the economy, helping us locate migration industries as part of informal, knowledge economies. Research on migration industries has, to date, primarily been from a political geography or sociology perspective. The paper by Harvey, Groutsis and van den Broek shows us how a management perspective can contribute to the way in which we appreciate the migration industries as business, with the role of reputation being important. Cranston's paper also highlights how migration industries can be seen as a manifestation of the knowledge economy. The different ways in which the economy of migration industries can be understood is a reflection on how migration industries are themselves part of the 'business' of migration in different forms.

The thinking about the 'business' of migration also has both political and policy implications. For example, thinking critically about migration industries helps us to appreciate how some 'small' questions, such as the use of recruitment agents from the U.K. to Poland in McCollum and Findlay's paper, can help us appreciate some of the bigger questions that migration poses, such as the production of the insecurity of labour migrants. Or both Koh and Wissink and Cranston's paper illustrate how privilege is (re)produced for already privileged migrants. In addition, the papers in this special issue show the role that migration industries play in both acting as agents for the state and assisting migrants to circumvent the state. As migration is, arguably, one of the defining issues of our time, reflected in both a rise of Far Right parties globally and increasingly protectionist immigration policies, this shows a need to understand not just the nexus between migration and the state, but migration, the state and migration industries. For example, Harvey, Groutsis and van den Broek's paper illustrate how migration intermediaries play a role in attracting the skilled migrants that are often seen as desirable for states and Beech's paper highlights the role that punitive visa regulations have upon the higher education market in the U.K. In moving forward with research on migration industries then there is a case for highlighting how this research can contribute to policy-making, in thinking about challenging the current anti-migration political climate.

## Acknowledgements

This set of paper derives from two sessions at the RGS-IBG on Exploring the Migration Industries. We would like to thank all of the participants in these sessions as well as the attendees for the useful discussion. We would also like to thank all of the reviewers for the papers for helping us strengthen the arguments being made.

## Disclosure statement

No potential conflict of interest was reported by the authors.

## ORCID

*Sophie Cranston* 🔟 http://orcid.org/0000-0001-7068-7029

## References

Alpes, M. 2012. "Bushfalling at All Cost: The Economy of Migratory Knowledge in Anglophone Cameroon." *African Diaspora* 5 (1): 90–115.

Andersson, R. 2014. *Illegality Inc. Clandestine Migration and the Business of Bordering Europe.* Oakland: California Press.

Beech, S. 2014. "Why Place Matters: Imaginative Geography and International Student Mobility." *Area* 46 (2): 170–177.

Beech, S. E. 2018. "Adapting to Change in the Higher Education System: International Student Mobility as a Migration Industry." *Journal of Ethnic and Migration Studies* 44 (4): 610–625. doi:10.1080/1369183X.2017.1315515.

Belloni, M. 2016. "My Uncle Cannot Say No if I Reach Libya: Unpacking the Social Dynamics of Border-Crossing Among Eritreans Heading to Europe." *Human Geography* 9 (2): 47–56.

Boissevain, R. 1974. *Friends of Friends: Networks, Manipulators and Coalitions.* Oxford: Basil Blackwell.

Boyle, P., and K. Halfcree. 1998. *Exploring Contemporary Migration.* Harlow: Pearson, Prentice Hall.

Burrell, K. 2008. "Materialising the Border: Spaces of Mobility and Material Culture in Migration from Post-socialist Poland." *Mobilities* 3 (3): 353–373.

Carling, J. 2002. "Migration in the Age of Involuntary Immobility: Theoretical Reflections and Cape Verdean Experiences." *Journal of Ethnic and Migration Studies* 28 (1): 5–42.

Castles, S., H. de Haas, and M. Millar. 2013. *The Age of Migration*. 5th ed. London: Palgrave Macmillan.

Collyer, M. 2007. "In-Between Places: Trans-Saharan Transit Migrants in Morocco and the Fragmented Journey to Europe." *Antipode* 39 (4): 668–690.

Conlon, D. 2011. "Waiting: Feminist Perspectives on the Spacings/Timings of Migrant (Im)Mobility." *Gender, Place and Culture* 18 (3): 353–360.

Cranston, S. 2016. "Producing Migrant Encounter: Learning to be a British Expatriate in Singapore Through the Global Mobility Industry." *Environment and Planning D: Society and Space* 34 (4): 655–671.

Cranston, S. 2018. "Calculating the Migration Industries: Knowing the Successful Expatriate in the Global Mobility Industry." *Journal of Ethnic and Migration Studies* 44 (4): 626–643. doi:10.1080/1369183X.2017.1315517.

Cresswell, T. 2006. *On the Move: Mobility in the Western World*. London: Taylor & Francis.

Cresswell, T. 2010. "Towards a Politics of Mobility." *Environment and Planning D; Society and Space* 28 (1): 17–31.

Ernste, H., K. Martens, and J. Schapendonk. 2012. "The Design, Experience and Justice of Mobility." *Tijdschrift voor economische en sociale geografie* 103: 509–515.

Faist, T. 2014. "Brokerage in Cross-Border Mobility: Social Mechanisms and the (Re)Production of Social Inequalities." *Social Inclusion* 2 (4): 38–52.

Faulconbridge, J., J. Beaverstock, S. Hall, and A. Hewitson. 2009. "The 'War for Talent': The Gatekeeper Role of Executive Search Firms in Elite Labour Markets." *Geoforum* 40 (5): 800–808.

Findlay, A., and L. Garrick. 1990. "Scottish Emigration in the 1980s: A Migration Channels Approach to the Study of Skilled International Migration." *Transactions, Institute of British Geographers* 15: 177–192.

Findlay, A., and F. Li. 1998. "A Migration Channels Approach to the Study of Professionals Moving to and from Hong Kong." *The International Migration Review* 32 (3): 682–703.

Findlay, A., and D. McCollum. 2013. "Recruitment and Employment Regimes: Migrant Labour Channels in the UK's Rural Agribusiness Sector, from Accession to Recession." *Journal of Rural Studies* 30: 10–19.

Findlay, A., D. McCollum, S. Shubin, E. Apsite, and Z. Krisjane. 2013. "The Role of Recruitment Agencies in Imagining and Producing the 'Good' Migrant." *Social and Cultural Geography* 14 (2): 145–167.

Gammeltoft-Hansen, T. 2013. "The Rise of the Private Border Guard: Accountability and the Responsibility in the Migration Control Industry." In *The Migration Industry and the Commercialization of International Migration*, edited by T. Gammeltoft-Hansen and N. Nyberg Sorenson, 128–151. Abingdon: Routledge.

Gammeltoft-Hansen, T., and N. Nyberg-Sørensen. 2013. *The Migration Industry and the Commercialization of International Migration*. New York: Routledge.

Garapich, M. 2008. "The Migration Industry and Civil Society: Polish Immigrants in the United Kingdom Before and After EU Enlargement." *Journal of Ethnic and Migration Studies* 34 (5): 735–752.

Glick-Schiller, N. C. A. 2009. "Towards a Comparative Theory of Locality in Migration Studies: Migrant Incorporation and City Scale." *Journal of Ethnic and Migration Studies* 35 (2): 177–202.

Glick-Schiller, N., and N. Salazar. 2013. "Regimes of Mobility Across the Globe." *Journal of Ethnic and Migraton Studies* 39 (2): 183–200.

Goss, J., and B. Lindquist. 1995. "Conceptualising International Labour Migration: A Structuration Perspective." *International Migration Review* 29 (2): 317–351.

Groutsis, D., D. van den Broek, and W. Harvey. 2015. "Transformations in Network Governance: The Case of Migration Intermediaries." *Journal of Ethnic and Migration Studies* 41 (10): 1558–1576.

Harney, R. 1977. "Frozen Wastes: The State of Italian Canadian Studies, Immigration and Ethnicity." Proceedings of the Symposium held at Casa Italiana, Columbia University, New York. New York: Centre for Migration Studies.

Harvey, W. S., D. Groutsis, and D. van den Broek. 2018. "Intermediaries and Destination Reputations: Explaining Flows of Skilled Migration." *Journal of Ethnic and Migration Studies* 44 (4): 644–662. doi:10.1080/1369183X.2017.1315518.

Hernández León, R. 2008. *Metropolitan Migrants: The Migration of Urban Mexicans to the United States*. Berkeley, CA: University of California Press.

Hernández León, R. 2013. "Conceptualizing the Migration Industry." In *The Migration Industry and the Commercialization of International Migration*, edited by T. Gammeltoft-Hansen and N. Nyberg Sorenson, 24–44. Oxford: Routledge.

Hugo, G. 1996. "Environmental Concerns and International Migration." *International Migration Review* 30 (1): 105–131.

Hui, A. 2016. "The Boundaries of Interdisciplinary Fields: Temporalities Shaping the Past and Future of Dialogue Between Migration and Mobilities Research." *Mobilities* 11 (1): 66–82.

Khosravi, S. 2011. *'Illegal' Traveller: An Auto-Ethnography of Borders*. New York City: Springer.

King, R. 2015. "Migration Comes of Age." *Ethnic and Racial Studies* 38 (13): 2366–2372.

Koh, S. Y., and B. Wissink. 2018. "Enabling, Structuring and Creating Elite Transnational Lifestyles: Intermediaries of the Super-Rich and the Elite Mobilities Industry." *Journal of Ethnic and Migration Studies* 44 (4): 592–609. doi:10.1080/1369183X.2017.1315509.

Krissman, F. 2005. "Sin Coyote Ni Patrón: Why the 'Migrant Network' Fails to Explain International Migration." *International Migration Review* 39 (1): 4–44.

Kyle, D., and R. Koslowski. 2001. *Global Human Smuggling: Comparative Perspectives*. Baltimore, MD: Johns Hopkins University Press.

Laczko, F., and D. Thompson. 2000. *Migrant Trafficking and Human Smuggling in Europe: A Review of the Evidence with Case Studies from Hungary, Poland and Ukraine*. Geneva: IOM, International Organization for Migration.

Lemberg-Pedersen, M. 2013. "Private Security Companies and the European Borderscapes." In *The Migration Industry and the Commercialization of International Migration*, 152–172. Abingdon: Routledge.

Ley, D., and A. Kobayashi. 2005. "Back to Hong Kong: Return Migration or Transnational Sojourn?" *Global Networks* 5 (2): 111–127.

Lin, N. 1999. "Building a Network Theory of Social Capital." *Connections* 22 (1): 28–51.

Lin, N. 2001. *Social Capital: A Theory of Social Structure and Action*. Cambridge: Cambridge University Press.

Lindquist, J. 2010. "Labour Recruitment, Circuits of Capital and Gendered Mobility: Reconceptualizing the Indonesian Migration Industry." *Pacifica Affairs* 83 (1): 115–132.

Lindquist, J., B. Xiang, and B. Yeoh. 2012. "Opening the Black Box of Migration, Brokers, the Organization of Transnational Mobility and the Changing Political Economy in Asia." *Pacific Affairs* 85 (1): 7–19.

Lomnitz, L. 1977. "Migration and Network in Latin America." In *Current Perspectives in Latin American Urban Research*, edited by A. Portes and H. Browning, 133–150. Austin: University of Texas, Institute of Latin American Studies.

MacDonald, J., and L. MacDonald. 1974. "Chain Migration, Ethnic Neighbourhood Formation and Social Networks." In *An Urban World*, edited by C. Tilly, 226–236. Boston, MA: Little Brown.

Mainwaring, C., and N. Brigden. 2016. "Beyond the Border: Clandestine Migration Journeys." *Geopolitics* 21 (2): 243–262.

Massey, D., R. Alarcon, J. Durand, and H. Gonzalez. 1987. *Return to Aztlan: The Social Process of International Migration from Western Mexico*. Los Angeles: University of California Press.

McCollum, D., and A. Findlay. 2015. "'Flexible' Workers for 'Flexible' Jobs? The Labour Market Function of A8 Migrant Labout in the UK." *Work, Employment and Society* 29 (3): 427–443.

McCollum, D., and A. Findlay. 2018. "Oiling the Wheels? Flexible Labour Markets and the Migration Industry." *Journal of Ethnic and Migration Studies* 44 (4): 558–574. doi:10.1080/1369183X.2017.1315505.

Menz, G. 2013. "The Neoliberalized State and the Growth of the Migration Industry." In *The Migration Industry and the Commercialization of International Migration*, edited by T. Gammeltoft-Hansen and N. Nyberg-Sorenson, 108–127. Abingdon: Routledge.

Nyberg-Sørensen, N. 2012. "Revisiting the Migration–Development Nexus: From Social Networks and Remittances to Markets for Migration Control." *International Migration* 50 (3): 61–76.

Nyberg-Sørensen, N., and T. Gammeltoft-Hansen. 2013. "Introduction." In *The Migration Industry and the Commercialization of International Migration*, edited by N. Nyberg-Sørensen and T. Gammeltoft-Hansen, 1–24. London: Routledge.

Peck, J., N. Theodore, and K. Ward. 2005. "Constructing Markets for Temporary Labour: Employment Liberlization and the Internationalization of the Staffing Industry." *Global Networks* 5 (1): 3–26.

Poli, R. 2010. "Understanding Globalization Through Football: The New International Division of Labour, Migratory Channels and Transnational Trade Circuits." *International Review for the Sociology of Sport* 45 (4): 491–506.

Roberts, S. 2014. "Development Capital: USAID and the Rise of Development Contractors." *Annals of the Association of American Geographers* 104 (5): 1030–1051.

Ryan, L., R. Sales, M. Tilki, and B. Siara. 2008. "Social Networks, Social Support and Social Capital: The Experiences of Recent Polish Migrants in London." *Sociology* 42 (4): 672–690.

Salt, J., and J. Stein. 1997. "Migration as a Business: The Case of Trafficking." *International Migration* 35 (4): 467–494.

Schapendonk, J. 2018. "Navigating the Migration Industry: Migrants Moving Through an African-European Web of Facilitation/Control." *Journal of Ethnic and Migration Studies* 44 (4): 663–679. doi:10.1080/1369183X.2017.1315522.

Schapendonk, J., and G. Steel. 2014. "Following Migrant Trajectories: The Im/Mobility of Sub-Saharan Africans en Route to the European Union." *Annals of the Association of American Geographers* 104 (2): 262–270.

Schrooten, M., N. B. Salazar, and G. Dias. 2016. "Living in Mobility: Trajectories of Brazilians in Belgium and the UK." *Journal of Ethnic and Migration Studies* 42 (7): 1199–1215.

Sheller, M., and J. Urry. 2006. "The New Mobilities Paradigm." *Environment and Planning A* 38: 207–226.

Shubin, S., A. Findlay, and D. McCollum. 2014. "Imaginaries of the Ideal Migrant Worker: A Lacanian Interpretation." *Environment and Planning D: Society and Space* 32: 466–483.

Sinatti, G., and C. Horst. 2014. "Migrants as Agents of Development: Diaspora Engagement Discourse and Practice in Europe." *Ethnicities* 15 (1): 134–152.

Spaan, E. 1994. "Taikongs and Calos: The Role of Middlemen and Brokers in Javanese International Migration." *International Migration Review* 28 (1): 93–113.

Spaan, E. 1999. *Labour Circulation and Socioeconomic Transformation: The Case of East Java, Indonesia.* The Hague: Netherlands Interdisciplinary Demographic Institute.

Spaan, E., and F. Hillmann. 2013. "Migration Trajectories and the Migration Industry: Theoretical Reflections and Empirical Examples from Asia." In *The Migration Industry and the Commercialization of International Migration*, edited by T. Gammeltoft-Hansen and N. Nyberg Sorensen, 64–86. Abingdon: Routledge.

Spaan, E., and T. Van Naerssen. 2018. "Migration Decision-making and Migration Industry in the Indonesia-Malaysia Corridor." *Journal of Ethnic and Migration Studies* 44 (4): 680–695. doi:10. 1080/1369183X.2017.1315523.

Spener, D. 2004. "Mexican Migrant-Smuggling: A Cross-Border Cottage Industry." *Journal of International Migration and Integration* 5 (3): 295–320.

Spener, D. 2009. "Some Critical Reflections on the Migration Industry Concept." Accessed March 1, 2016. http://www.trinity.edu/dspener/clandestinecrossings/related%20articles/migration%20 industry.pdf.

Van der Velde, M., and T. Van Naerssen. 2015. *Mobility and Migration Choices: Thresholds to Crossing Borders.* Farnham: Ashgate.

Van Liempt, I. 2011. "'And Then One Day They All Moved to Leicester': The Relocation of Somalis From the Netherlands to the UK Explained." *Population, Space and Place* 17 (3): 254–266.

Walters, W. 2015. "Migration, Vehicles, and Politics Three Theses on Viapolitics." *European Journal of Social Theory* 18 (4): 469–488.

Wimmer, A., and N. Glick-Schiller. 2002. "Methodological Nationalism and Beyond: Nation-State Building, Migration and the Social Sciences." *Global Networks* 2 (4): 301–334.

Xiang, B., and J. Lindquist. 2014. "Migration Infrastructure." *International Migration Review* 48 (S1): S122–S148.

Žabko, O., A. Aasland, and S. B. Endresen. 2018. "Facilitating Labour Migration From Latvia: Strategies of Various Categories of Intermediaries." *Journal of Ethnic and Migration Studies* 44 (4): 575–591. doi:10.1080/1369183X.2017.1315508.

# Oiling the wheels? Flexible labour markets and the migration industry

David McCollum and Allan Findlay

**ABSTRACT**
The growing commercialisation of migration, often through a multiplicity of labour market intermediaries, is an issue of increasing academic interest. We seek to contribute to an emerging research agenda on the migration industries by exploring how one of the key actors that constitutes it, recruitment agencies, sits at the nexus between flexible labour market structures and migrant labour. Interviews with U.K. labour providers and low-wage employers form the evidence base for an analysis of the strategies developed by recruiters to derive commercial gain from connecting the so-called 'supply' and 'demand' sides of the flexible international labour market. We seek to contribute to understandings of the analytical categories within migration systems by illustrating how the migration industry interacts with other key stakeholders to structure international migration.

## Introduction

In the 'age of migration' (Castles, de Haas, and Miller 2013) an array of explanations have been formulated within the social sciences to try and explain the movement of people between places (Brettell and Hollifield 2015). A common but often overlooked aspect of population mobility is that most international migrants draw on some form of intermediary to help them migrate to and find employment and/or accommodation in another country (Salt and Stein 1997; McCollum et al. 2013; Van den Broek, Harvey, and Groutsis 2016). As noted by Lindquist, Xiang, and Yeoh (2012), the drivers behind individuals seeking to migrate, and what happens to them after they move are relatively well understood, but less is known about the 'black box' between these stages. Thus whilst the internal workings of intermediaries such as recruitment agencies, political and ethnic groupings and people smugglers have received some attention (Findlay 1990; Soysal 1994; Findlay and Li 1998; Friebel and Guriev 2006), understanding of their role in international migration remains underdeveloped in theoretical terms (Coe, Jones, and Ward 2010; Hernandez-Leon 2013; Cranston 2016). Building on research on migration intermediaries, the concept of the migration 'industry' has recently emerged to loosely encompass those individuals and organisations involved in enabling migration, such as money lenders, recruiters, transportation providers, travel agents, smugglers and lawyers, whose primary motive is profit (Sorensen and Gammeltoft-Hansen 2013; Cranston, Scha-pendonk, and Spaan 2018). The migration industry has thus been defined as 'the ensemble of entrepreneurs who, motivated by the pursuit of financial gain, provide a variety of ser-vices facilitating human mobility across international borders' (Hernandez-Leon 2008, 154). With some exceptions (Garapich 2008; Hennebry 2008), this still evolving concept has usually been equated with systems designed to facilitate irregular and quasi-legal migration across international borders (Kyle and Koslowski 2001; Bilger, Hofmann, and Jandl 2006; Lindquist 2010; Koser 2011). In practice the migration industry is much more engaged in legal migration flows, yet this dimension of the industry remains somewhat neglected.

Using the empirical lens of the unprecedented inflows of labour migrants to the U.K. from East-Central Europe over the period 2004–2010 (so-called 'A8' migrants), this research hopes to contribute to the developing research agenda on the migration indus-tries through a focus on how the labour provider industry operates to meet the preferences and needs of low-wage employers, and how in the process they are an important part of a migration system that produces 'flexible' workers for 'flexible' jobs. Specifically the analysis concentrates on the strategies used by recruiters to derive profit from the process of matching migrants seeking employment opportunities with employers seeking 'good' (migrant) workers.

## The migration industry: conceptual contributions

This research has been spurred by a desire to engage with what Hernandez-Leon has described as 'the gaping theoretical hole concerning the position, contribution and relations of profit-driven actors in the social organisation of international migration' (2013, 24). Whilst it is certainly the case that much remains to be conceptualised concern-ing the 'black box' between individuals wishing to engage in mobility and their arrival in a new country (Lindquist, Xiang, and Yeoh 2012), it would be foolhardy to take the view that the role of profit-orientated intermediaries in facilitating international migration is devoid of an evidence base. Migrants have long relied on others not only to help cross inter-national borders but also to adjust to life after moving. This has been achieved not just as a result of transnationalism from below, in terms of migrants' links to transnational communities (Vertovec 2009), but also as a result of transnational business connections and the structuring influence of corporate capital to engage external assistance to facilitate the mobility of expertise (Salt and Wood 2011; Hedberg, Hermelin, and Westermark 2014).

This in turn has resulted in a global migration industry that is concerned on the one hand with the technicalities associated with supporting international transfers and on the other hand with the very business of producing how migrants experience migration (Cranston 2016; Cranston, Schapendonk, and Spaan 2018). In the context of recent East-Central European labour migration to the U.K., researchers with a particular interest in recruitment practices have shown how dynamic the migration industries have been not only in adapting to changing economic circumstances but also to tailoring their role rela-tive to shifting cultural norms about 'the good migrant' (McDowell, Batnitzky, and Dyer 2008; Pemberton and Stevens 2010; Findlay and McCollum 2013; Sporton 2013; Jones 2014). Understandings of 'the good migrant' are central to discussions surrounding the migration industry, since they reflect prevalent normative understandings of what is understood to be the 'ideal' worker. These knowledge practices are of interest and importance because they shape recruitment and employment practices, and thus labour migration flows, by influencing who is recruited, from where and for what purposes (Findlay et al. 2013).

Whilst 'labour providers' (this term is used to indicate that international recruitment agencies and other profit-orientated individuals and organisations are engaged in much more than organising the spatial relocation of workers) have long been acknowledged as shaping patterns and processes of international migration, surprisingly little effort has gone into theorising the collective activities of these actors in commercialising the migration system. Building on the initial ideas of Harney (1977) and Salt and Stein (1997), the range of profit-orientated actors that are involved in facilitating mobility for commercial gain is increasingly being termed the migration 'industry'. Castles and Miller (2003), while doing little work on the topic themselves, coined the term, describing diverse actors such as international recruitment organisations, lawyers, agents, smugglers and other intermediaries as a migration industry. This operates as a 'meso-structure' between the micro and macro structures, as outlined earlier in the work of Findlay (1990) in terms of a migration channels framework. Initially the term 'migration industry' was used only sporadically as shorthand for the mixture of individuals and organisations that profit from facilitating migration. As a consequence it lacked theoretical depth and was critiqued for lacking coherence as an analytical contribution (Hernández-León 2005).

Whilst still a comparatively novel and evolving concept, research on migration industries can be loosely characterised as either focusing on how actors in relatively wealthy countries derive profit from reinforcing borders or on how individuals and organisations in less wealthy countries try and subvert them for commercial gain. The research discussed in this article is interpreted through the lens of segmented labour market theory and seeks to offer an alternative interpretation of migration industries. Recognising that segmented western labour markets have an inherent structural demand for migrant labour (Piore 1979; Anderson and Ruhs 2010; Friberg 2012; McCollum and Findlay 2015), the analysis explores the role of labour providers in 'oiling the wheels' of these processes. Earlier work mapped the role of recruitment agencies in structuring East-Central European migration to the U.K. This scholarship illustrated, first, how and why recruitment agencies recruited from this labour source (Findlay and McCollum 2013; Jones 2014), second, how these actors embedded themselves within transnational connections (Sporton 2013) and third, how these processes produced an increasingly globalised labour force (McDowell, Batnitzky, and Dyer 2008). However the workings of these intermediaries have rarely been explicitly considered within a migration industry analytical framework. Positioning these quantitatively significant actors as central to conceptualisations of the migration industry is the main theoretical contribution offered by this analysis.

An interesting exception to most research on the migration industry is Garapich's (2008) use of this concept to illustrate how profit-driven institutions have sought to stimulate recent Polish migration to Britain. His analysis contends that the migration industry has been especially responsive to the needs of migrants for information and access to host-society institutions. Thus international recruiters partially replaced traditional agents of civil society in stimulating mobility and easing adaptation. Garapich

(2008) calls for an analytical approach that does not view the practices carried out by actors that are driven by market forces as inherently distinct from those undertaken by organisations that are not profit driven, such as voluntary organisations and advocacy networks. This perspective challenges the conceptualisation found in the earlier literature which represented market forces as fundamentally opposed to civil society: the so-called 'liberal paradox' whereby political factors were seen as instinctively pro-migration control whereas market forces were presumed to be inherently pro-open borders (Hollifield 2004).

Taking inspiration from Garapich's (2008) deconstruction of the conventional analytical divisions between (a) the state as the principle regulator responsible for migration control, (b) labour providers as agents driven by primarily by profit and (c) migrant social networks as altruistic stakeholders, this approach encourages interrogation of the ways in which recruiter's link to other key actors in the migration system. In turn it recognises how their actions can 'blur the lines' between the roles served by organisations within the migration industry. Garapich's (2008) approach, and the perspective taken in this research, represents a positive response to Sorensen and Gammeltoft-Hansen's (2013) plea for research that links the migration industry to the outcomes observed in the wider migration system, as opposed to conventional perspectives which have tended to look at specific types of actors in isolation.

In addition to questioning the core definitions and analytical boundaries of the migration industries concept, the research reported in this paper seeks to make a number of other theoretical contributions. Much of the research literature relating to the migration industry views migration through the lens of the aspirations, experiences and outcomes of migrants, and/or the intermediaries that are engaged in facilitating their mobility (Sorensen and Gammeltoft-Hansen 2013). These approaches have tended to privilege individual micro and meso level perspectives over the wider macro structures that ultimately shape the context within which mobility occurs. This analysis is careful to not only pay attention to the perceptions and practices of important actors within the migration system, but also to the broader political and economic structures that shape these processes. In particular the investigation highlights the dynamism and resilience of migration industries in response to external challenges.

Related to this, there is a need for scholarship on the migration industries to focus on the nature of the connections between the various actors that constitute the migration system. In this paper we examine the perceptions and practices of labour providers, not in isolation, but in terms of their functions as intermediaries connecting the so-called 'demand' and 'supply' sides of the labour market at specific points in time and space. This entails consideration of how recruiters engage with both employers and migrants in the pursuit of profit, demonstrating the mutual dependencies that exist between providers and users of migrant labour as well as the strategies used by labour providers to recruit through migrant social networks. Finally, the analysis deepens understanding of the migration industries by illustrating how the act of facilitating migration is only one of many ways through which labour providers are able to generate commercial gain from acting as labour market intermediaries in the migration system.

Based on these approaches, the following overarching research objective has been formulated:

What strategies do labour providers develop to extract financial gain from their interactions with employers and migrant workers, and how do the practices that flow from these strategies help deepen understandings of the migration industry?

## Methodological perspective

Research on labour providers in migration studies, including within the migration industries paradigm, often focuses on migrants and their motives and experiences of using labour market intermediaries and the outcomes of these processes for individual movers (Lindquist 2010). The focus of research on this paper, by contrast, emphasises the important role that employers play in not only creating a (structural) demand for migrant labour but also sustaining the migration industry itself through the use of recruitment agencies to connect with this source of labour. Conceptually this shifts attention from the individual migrant towards the wider economic and political structures that shape the migration industry.

The analysis draws on in-depth interviews with providers (recruitment agencies) and users (employers) of migrant labour. The interviews were carried out across four U.K. case study sites as part of a larger research programme (2010–2012) investigating the demographic impacts on the U.K. of migration from East and Central Europe since 2004 (Travena, McGhee, and Heath 2013). The research concentrated on the food production and processing and hospitality sectors, which were judged to be key parts of the labour market associated with East-Central European workers (McCollum 2013). The case study sites included rural and urban areas of England and Scotland (West Sussex/Hampshire, Southampton, Angus/Fife and Glasgow). Recruiters were questioned on their experiences and strategies with regards to engaging with employers (clients) and migrant workers (candidates). Employers were asked about their motivations for and experiences of using recruitment agencies to source migrant labour. The logic behind these methodological choices was to examine the factors that create and sustain the demand for a migration industry to service the flexible labour market from the perspective of recruiters and their 'clients'.

East-Central European migration to the U.K. since the 2004 A8 accession to the EU is an appropriate empirical lens for a study of the migration industry for a number of reasons. First is that it has been remarkable due to the sheer volume of arrivals over a relatively short space of time and the geographically dispersed pattern of immigration (Burrell 2009). From a labour market perspective, the existing body of research has pointed to employers having positive perceptions of East-Central Europeans (Scott 2013a) and of these workers disproportionately occupying low paid and temporary forms of employment (Migration Advisory Committee 2014). East-Central European workers are often portrayed by employers as having a superior 'work ethic' to local workers (MacKenzie and Forde 2009). This represents a form of direct and indirect discrimination in recruitment practices whereby employers recruit based on national stereotyping, with the suitability of workers for particular roles being determined categorically rather than on individual merit (Lucas and Mansfield 2010). This leads to ethnically ordered hiring queues whereby employers devise an implicit hierarchy of nationalities according to their desirability as employees (Scott 2013a). These processes may be thought of as a form of cumulative causation whereby the ample supply of flexible migrant labour, and high employer demand for it, become mutually reinforcing and institutionalised over time (Ciupijus 2011). Existing research has identified the strategies used by low-wage employers to specifically target A8 migrants in their recruitment processes. These tactics include: direct recruitment from East-Central Europe, recruitment through migrant social networks and the use of recruitment agencies associated with A8 migrant labour (Findlay and McCollum 2013; McCollum et al. 2013). In turn migrant workers have been shown to respond to employer expectations by 'performing' in ways which meet the stereotypes associated with their ethnicity or region of origin (Waldinger and Lichter 2003).

Labour providers have been recognised as a key driver of the significant migration of East-Central European migrant labour into the U.K. labour market since 2004 (Garapich 2008; Sporton 2013). Accurate data on the means through which migrants find employment are scarce, but it can be reasonably assumed that around half of new arrivals from the Accession 8 countries (Poland, Czech Republic, Latvia, Lithuania, Slovakia, Slovenia, Hungary and Estonia) over the period 2004–2011 initially found work in the U.K. through recruitment agencies (McCollum 2013). The research involved 61 in-depth interviews. The labour providers interviewed all had at least one site in the case study areas and ranged from individuals who ran their own recruitment businesses to large nationwide and multinational recruitment agencies. The position held by most of the interviewees was overall director of the firm, or local/regional managers in the case of larger organisations. The labour users who were interviewed ranged from large multinational organisations to smaller employers. Most of the hospitality employers were hotel or restaurant chains and most interviewees were general or personnel managers. The food production and processing interviews focused on farms and vegetable and meat processing companies. Most of the interviewees held the job title of operations or human resource managers within their firm. Overall 26% of the organisations that were contacted agreed to take part in the research. Only 12% explicitly refused to participate in the study, the remaining 62% could not be contacted in a follow up round of telephone calls. Pseudonyms have been used in the quotations which follow to protect respondents' anonymity.

## The migration industry's strategies to serve the labour 'needs' of the low-wage economy

A criticism of the research literature on the migration industry is that there has been too little investigation of how the industry structures migration through the commercial interactions between labour providers and employers. In this section we identify (a) the practices that labour providers perceive to be central to making them attractive to employers and (b) the importance given by recruitment firms to their relationships with employers. In the next section we present evidence of how labour providers adapt to the restructuring of migration flows as a result of changing economic circumstances by sourcing migrants in different ways.

The recruitment industry is often thought of simplistically as actors seeking to derive profit from the process of matching employers 'seeking labour' with workers 'seeking work'. Early research represented recruiters as filters in the selection of workers to be channelled to given migration destinations (Findlay 1990). Later research (Rogaly 2008) revealed how in relation to low-wage labour much of the value extracted from migrants comes from the regulation of the workplace and the terms of employment. In this context, intermediaries such as international labour providers accrue surplus from organising the commodity (labour) so that it is provided in an appropriately packaged fashion that is attractive to the employer. In the context of recent East-Central European migration to the U.K., labour providers have taken particular advantage of sitting at the nexus between flexible migrant labour and flexible labour market structures (McCollum and Findlay 2015). In what follows we focus on those activities that reveal how value is extracted by labour providers. In particular, the way recruiters elect to engage with potential pools of migrant labour is crucial to their 'business interests' since their commercial success rests on the perennial provision of a supply of 'good' workers to employers. Furthermore, recruiters must simultaneously foster and maintain positive relationships with 'clients' (employers) in order to sustain a market for their 'product' (migrant labour).

### *Labour provider services to employers*

It is perhaps not surprising that recruitment agencies flourish in low-wage sectors since it is in this context that they are able to offer employers the greatest 'flexibility' in terms of how they use labour (Sporton 2013; McCollum and Findlay 2015). A major attraction is the ability of recruitment agencies to provide employers with a 'secondary' workforce to 'top up' their core staff. This is especially attractive in instances where employers are faced with frequent fluctuations in demand for their goods and services and thus demand for labour. The role of recruiters in this process is in facilitating the operation of segmented labour markets (Piore 1979; Waldinger and Lichter 2003), whereby particular functions become associated with specific pools of labour, in this case recent East-Central European migrants as a contingent labour force. Norma (an HR officer) offers us insight into how many of the firms we interviewed reported their perceptions of the role of recruitment agents:

> We don't even know what production is going to be like next week because we are so dependent on the weather and customer orders so the number of people we need changes constantly. So we have about 500 permanent people and we use an agency to top-up our numbers whenever we need them during the high production spells ... we contact the agency and they get the people in at very short notice and then they take them away again when production slows and that's better for us than hiring then making people redundant all the time. (Norma, HR officer, food processing plant, rural England)

Norma's coding of the value of recruitment agencies for a low-wage employer is that they 'get' and 'take away' labour, an employment service that is of value because it avoids the 'costs' of 'redundancy' in an uncertain labour market. Labour providers are presented as enablers providing labour as a commodity in a fashion akin to a tap which can be turned on and off easily and frequently.

Another key attraction of labour providers for employers was that they operated as a 'one stop shop' for staff recruitment and management, allowing effective outsourcing of human resources functions. Barry, a labour provider describes his self-perception of how recruiters provide a valuable role to low-wage employers by sourcing flexible labour, whilst simultaneously relieving them of the legal responsibilities associated with recruiting and employing staff directly themselves.

> Using someone like us gives them flexibility ... they might not have the facilities or be able to manage the hassle of taking staff on themselves because then they've got to go out and buy

them work wear and put them through health and safety training and they have got to do the interviewing for them. Whereas with us it is just one stop, we will give you that man and we'll pay them what we want and that is it, so there is no hassle. (Barry, managing director, labour provider firm, urban Scotland)

### *Labour provider relations with employers*

The examples above illustrate two ways in which recruitment agencies facilitate the operation of the flexible labour market. Whilst this has already been the focus of empirical research (Anderson and Ruhs 2010; Scott 2013b), much less is known about how recruiters establish and cultivate relationships with employers in order to try and extract profit from the provision of a flexible workforce. This focus builds on Sorensen and Gammeltoft-Hansen's (2013) call for research into the actual linkages between the migration industry and other actors in the migration system. It is already well established that employers rely on the migration industry to help them engage with flexible (migrant) labour (Jones 2014), meaning that the recruitment industry and low-wage employers are often mutually dependent on each other for commercial success within the highly competitive marketplaces that they each operate within.

> I mean it is absolutely cut throat in this industry, even with the farm market there are so many agencies getting into it now that you're finding that it is more difficult to survive … and guys [employers] are seeing how I'm working and then getting the people [workers] themselves, or are going through my agencies in Eastern Europe directly, so I'm gradually getting pushed out of the picture. (Ethan, managing director, labour provider firm, rural Scotland)

In the context of such a competitive industry, recruiters often emphasised the strategic importance of cultivating a positive business reputation and fostering strong interpersonal relationships to attracting and retaining clients.

> We deal with a number of key clients, supporting them with flexible staff and permanent solutions so in essence we can be a one stop shop for them … but there is a perception that clients can just turn the tap on and off again when they want: they think we've got people stacked up in a cupboard that we just open the door and they fall out. But that is not what happens and this is where we work closely with clients and trust is key so I am fully transparent with clients. I show them the pay rate, the holiday pay, national insurance, our profit, and the total charge rate. To have that long-term sustainable relationship you have to be open. (Ben, senior partner, labour provider firm, urban Scotland)

As the quotation from Ben suggests, interviewees noted the importance of positive relationships with employers to the sustainability of profitable longer term business dealings with them. This analytical emphasis on the functions served by recruiters in providing employers with a flexible labour supply, and the strategies used by them to develop relationships with clients has implications for understandings of migration industries in the context of a legislative environment whereby a large part of the function of labour market intermediaries does not involve subverting or negotiating the crossing of borders, but rather they involve providing a particular 'employment regime'. The actions of recruiters in this context are orientated towards offering services to employers that enable them to make use of flexible migrant labour, whether it be directly sourced from abroad or already in the host country. In this sense the role of labour providers in the migration industry is only partially about helping workers find employment overseas. Other commonplace recruitment and employment services offered by labour providers include language translation, staff training and onsite HR management (Findlay and McCollum 2013). Equally important to their commercial viability is developing and maintaining business relationships with the users of migrant labour. This distinction is important because the analytic focus on labour providers in migration research is often mostly or exclusively on how they help migrants move to and find employment in another country.

As discussed by Janine, the success or otherwise of recruiters is dependent upon their ability to satisfy both their clients and their candidates simultaneously. This intermediary role represents a significant challenge given that the aims of each group are mutually opposing: employers wish to extract as much value as possible from labour, whereas the aim of workers is to maximise the returns on their labour.

> For us it is not all about money and I think that comes across to our clients and we tend to retain our clients and I think that is because I regularly contact them and our account manager contacts them. The branch manager contacts them too. But as well as the client-facing part of my role I also try and find out how the candidates are experiencing our service. It is good to hear the story from both the client and the candidates' perspectives because it is 50/50: you can't do the job properly if you just service one side of that equation. (Janine, labour provider, urban England)

## Changing approaches to sourcing migrant workers

The attraction to employers of using migration industry intermediaries to source cheap flexible labour while at the same time outsourcing their legal obligations to migrant workers by asking the migration industry to provide this service is now evidenced by an increasing body of research (McDowell, Batnitzky, and Dyer 2008; Pemberton and Stevens 2010; Findlay et al. 2013; Sporton 2013; Jones 2014). What is less apparent and has been the subject of only a small number of studies is the strategy adopted by recruitment agencies to meet employers' expectations of constantly being able to supply flexible workers at short notice (discussed above by Norma). It is accepted that migrants' 'dual frame of reference' makes them tolerant of relatively poor employment conditions (Piore 1979). This could potentially explain the ability of recruiters to perpetually source and supply flexible migrant workers. However such an explanation fails to account for how migrants' willingness to accept unfavourable employment conditions erodes over time as they become attuned to norms surrounding earning expectations in their host society. This phenomenon was brought up by many interviewees, who bemoaned a perceived erosion of the 'work-ethic' of migrants with time spent in Britain.

> Their standards are starting to drop off now and they are beginning to go native a bit and display a lot of the characteristics of our own [UK] workforce … unfortunately they are adapting some of our cultures in terms of attitude to work. (Jack, food processing firm, rural Scotland)

The migration industry has once again seen this eroding 'work culture' effect as an opportunity to extend their services to employers through undermining the position of more established migrant workers. The quotation from Iris (below) shows how this operates through what neo-Marxian researchers would see as the periodic tapping of new reserve armies of labour. This interpretation is of interest as it theorises the expansion of potential pools of migrant labour as a novel spatial fix to the perennial problem of crises of over-accumulation within the capitalist system (Anderson and Shuttleworth 2004). The role of the enlargement of the EU eastwards in facilitating the control of capital over labour is an issue that merits much more attention than it has received to date.

> It is a cycle, the A8 countries joined the EU in 2004 and now we are a good few years into the process, so the honeymoon period is sort of over. So I always think: when are we going to have new countries coming in [to the EU], because we will always need them because you have those five to ten year periods where people are happy to do anything but as their economies pick up they will be gone and if they are not gone then they want better jobs. So it needs to be a cycle and we need to always bring new countries on board. (Iris, manager, labour provider firm, urban England)

In terms of labour supply, recruiters can be thought of as facing two significant challenges with respect to the business of migration. As discussed by Iris, the first is the ability to source and have 'on tap' a ready new supply of migrant workers who are tolerant of poor pay and employment conditions. This is difficult because migrant workers often become less accepting of undesirable jobs as the time spent in their host country increases. A second challenge faced by recruiters is that the extent to which employers and migrants rely on labour market intermediaries decreases as a migration system evolves (Hernandez-Leon 2013). In the case of East-Central European migration to the U.K., the field research confirmed that the use of labour providers diminished somewhat over time as migrant social networks came to play a bigger role in the recruitment practices of employers. For employers this approach had the attraction of subverting the charges made by recruitment agencies through enrolling their own migrant staff as recruiters of 'good workers', thus getting them to exercise social power over newly recruited staff. The discourse encouraged by employers is therefore that 'good' workers are likely to recommend other 'good' workers (McCollum and Apsite-Berina 2015). The field research revealed the strategies that labour providers use to manage these challenges in relation to their goals of recruiting and retaining a large flexible workforce supplied to employers at short notice.

### Challenge A: the perennial supply of 'good workers'

Many labour providers noted that their ability to meet the demands of employers for cheap labour was contingent upon external political and economic circumstances making it possible to source 'fresh' supplies of migrant labour. Interviewees alluded to three distinct phases between the accession of new countries to the EU in 2004 and the global recession that was to follow a few years later. The period following the 2004 accession represented a boom for the U.K. migration industry: employers were keen to engage with migrant labour but were unsure of how to go about doing so, and the novel nature of the new migration stream meant that migrants needed labour market intermediaries to help them move and find work in the U.K.

> If you went back to 2007 you'd find about 90 per cent of all the Eastern Europeans were in temporary jobs through agencies. And in the early days we did a lot of interviewing in the countries and brought people over and we set them up with banks, doctors, dentists and we even actually rented flats and sub-leased them to the EU folks and we had an existing group of English speaking Czechs and Hungarians employees who really integrated them. (Wallace, managing director, labour provider firm, urban Scotland)

The migration industry faced a number of challenges in the second phase, the period immediately preceding the recession. It became harder to recruit directly from East-Central Europe as the labour markets of these countries improved and the booming British labour market meant that migrants already in the U.K. were aiming for and achieving 'better' jobs than those offered by employers in low-wage sectors.

> Certainly 2007 and 2008 were awful years for making sure farms got enough people. You could have people earning £500 a week and they weren't happy. We had people walking into our recruitment offices in Latvia and saying I want a job at £12 an hour. And farms weren't happy because they didn't have enough people so a lot of fruit was left in the fields … that was good in one way because it made farms wake up to the fact that Eastern Europe is not a bottomless pit of labour. That you can't just send a bus to Warsaw and fill it up with strawberry pickers. (Josh, regional manager, labour provider firm, rural England)

The onset of the recession (the third phase) was described as something of a 'blessing in disguise' for the migration industry. It generated a resurgence in demand for their services from a new wave of 'crisis' migrants from Eastern and Central Europe, who were accepting of poor pay and conditions owing to the severity of the recession in their home countries. Migrants that were already in the U.K. were forced to turn to recruiters to seek employment opportunities and had lowered demands regarding pay and employment conditions.

> At the moment we don't need to do much searching for candidates, but before the recession the job was more about candidates than it was clients because the clients were desperate and candidates were all in work so you really had to search. Whereas now the clients aren't desperate and the candidates are so it has just switched the other way. But yeah the migrants have made a difference because they've come here to work, and the benefits just keep the local guys at home and stops them wanting to work. (Richard, recruitment consultant, labour provider firm, rural Scotland)

The three phases discussed above underline the shifting and sometimes insecure business environment within which individual actors in the migration industries operate. This dynamism relates not only to the influence of labour market metrics such as wage levels, but also to the role of perceptions and social practices of all actors involved in the process. This includes national and supra-national scale policies, employers and transnational communities both in the source and sending countries.

### Challenge B: migrant social networks

A second challenge faced by labour providers is that recruitment through informal migrant networks have become an increasingly popular channel through which low-wage employers source labour. Such an approach was interpreted as enabling the recruitment of 'good' workers, whilst exerting little or no financial cost on employers. Firms encouraged recommendations from 'good' staff members of potential future employees with appropriate traits and abilities. This application of the 'homophily principle' (Lin 1999), which refers to members of a network sharing similar attributes, implies that networks of 'good' workers' can reproduce and maintain a 'good' workforce through further migrant recruitment (McCollum and Apsite-Berina 2015). Aiden illustrates the principle in action:

> I actually set up a scheme where if somebody recommended a person to come and work with us and that person then stayed with us then I would give them £100. And that was a strategy

that worked because that way there was more pressure to make sure that the people that they were recommending were good and going to last. So that works really well. If they are prepared to vouch for somebody then I am prepared to give them a go. So there is absolutely no need for paying any agencies because it is all done through word of mouth. (Aiden, manager, restaurant, urban Scotland)

Recognising the futility of trying to compete with migrant social networks, one response of recruiters was to embed themselves within transnational networks and exploit them as potential suppliers of 'good' workers to the migration industry. These tactics often involve recruitment agencies employing migrants, usually former candidates, as consultants in order to use their networks to tap into potential pools of labour.

Word of mouth in the Eastern European communities is very important so they always share information about jobs and that is great for us because my guys [consultants] are all Eastern European so they have got their own networks too. So all the advertising for people is done predominantly through them and their word of mouth. So they can pick up the phone and get 20 people instantly because they have their own contacts and know so many people. (Samantha, director, labour provider, rural England)

The emphasis placed on enlisting migrants as recruitment agents in order to tap into their networks leads to a blurring of the conceptual lines between the migration industry and migrant social networks. The former is usually thought of as comprising those whose primary motivation in facilitating migration is commercial gain, whereas the motivations of the latter are conventionally thought of as being altruistic. Instead what seems to occur in this instance is a combination of both of these drivers: recruiters 'helping' their co-ethnics find jobs, but also contributing to the commercial success of organisations in the migration industry through these practices. The lesson from these findings is that the components of the migration industry, as defined purely by the profit motive, are analytically difficult to separate from the myriad of other individuals and organisations that are engaged in facilitating migration. Just as migration is multi causal, the drivers behind the practices that motivate individuals to enable it are also complex and overlapping. As such it would be inadvisable for researchers to try and set overly strict and mutually exclusive analytical categories and boundaries between the various actors that facilitate mobility in the migration system (Garapich 2008). The implications of these issues for conceptualisations of the migration industry are considered in the concluding section.

## Conclusions

A longstanding feature of international migration is the use by migrants of intermediaries to help cross international borders and find employment in another country. This investigation has focused on the internal workings of a quantitatively significant type of migration intermediary: recruitment agencies engaged in matching low-wage employers seeking 'flexible' workers with recent East-Central European labour migrants seeking employment in the U.K. It is hoped that this perspective contributes to the emerging literature on the migration industries, a concept that has been loosely and sporadically applied to the various individuals and organisations that seek to derive profit from the process of facilitating migration (Sorensen and Gammeltoft-Hansen 2013). In particular the analysis sought to offer useful insights into the strategies used by recruiters to engage with and sustain business links with employers, and the tactics used in the supply of a valued product: 'flexible' workers. This perspective is useful since positive relationships with clients (employers) and candidates (migrants) are both essential if recruiters are to successfully derive financial gain from the business of international migration. As opposed to the conventional focus on migrants and their motives for and experiences of using labour providers, this analysis has explored the migration industry from the perspective of the relationships and interactions between recruiters and the employers that utilise them to engage with migrant labour.

In terms of the focus of this special issue on theorising the migration industry (Cranston, Schapendonk, and Spaan 2018), the research has shed some light on the 'black box' between migrants wishing to engage in mobility and the outcomes of these moves (Lindquist, Xiang, and Yeoh 2012). Whilst wary of concurring with the notion of a 'gaping theoretical hole concerning the position, contribution and relations of profit-driven actors in the social organisation of international migration' (Hernandez-Leon 2013, 24), the authors share Garapich's (2008) interest in extending understanding of the ways in which recruiters link with other key actors in the migration system, and how these actions can 'blur the lines' between the roles served by individuals and organisations within the migration industry. Such a stance represents a positive response to Sorensen and Gammeltoft-Hansen's (2013) call for research that links together various components of the migration industry and migration system, as opposed to perspectives that look at specific types of actors within it in isolation.

Using the empirical lens of recent East-Central European migration to the U.K., the analysis emphasised how the strategies used by recruiters to engage with and satisfy both employers and migrant workers is essential to their ultimate goal of deriving commercial gain from migration. However this also illustrates the difficulty, and perhaps futility, of trying to define the migration industry as a strictly separate analytical category in migration studies. Much of the existing literature relating to this concept focuses on how profit-driven actors seek commercial gain from facilitating or controlling migration, when engaged by migrants and governments respectively. However this analysis indicates that enabling the act of migration is often only a minor part of the business activities of labour providers, actors who would be thought of as constituting a major cog in the migration industry. Theorisation of the migration industry therefore needs to go beyond just conceptualisation of how actors motivated by profit facilitate migration. These perspectives also need to focus on the other core activities of these actors and the aggregate effect of these actions on migration systems more generally.

Just as the strategies of labour providers extend beyond the facilitation of the act of migration, thus loosening the definition of the migration industry, the research also problematises some of the analytical categories within this conceptual framework. As with Garapich (2008), the findings question the analytical distinctions in the migration system between recruiters as driven by profit, and migrant social networks, whose actions are usually portrayed as being more altruistic. In the case of the recruitment of migrants by labour providers, strategies have developed which represent a combination of both of these drivers: recruitment consultants 'helping' individuals within their social networks gain employment opportunities, whilst also contributing to the commercial success of organisations in the migration industry through these practices. The lesson from these findings for understandings of the migration industry is that scholars need to pay careful attention to the links and analytical boundaries between the actors involved in the business of migration and the range of other individuals and actors that are involved in facilitating mobility.

Furthermore, the framing of the migration industry as a 'meso-structure' in migration systems, emphasises the significance of profit-motivated actors in shaping patterns and processes of international migration. It also highlights the resilience but also limited agency of the individual components of this industry. As discussed above, the recruitment agency sector is highly competitive and both clients (employers) and candidates (migrants) can have alternative means of connecting with each other beyond this 'industry'. As illustrated by the findings showing the shifting prominence of labour providers in structuring recent East-Central European migration to the U.K., the positioning of these profit-driven actors in the migration system (and thus of the migration industry itself) is contingent upon favourable external political and economic circumstances.

To conclude, this investigation has contributed to an already established body of evidence in relation to labour providers, East-Central European migrant labour and flexible labour market structures (Sporton 2013; Jones 2014; McCollum and Findlay 2015). But how does the concept of the migration industry fit into these understandings? The migration industry framework has only been applied in a loose and sporadic fashion by migration scholars and as such has lacked coherence as a longer term analytical concept (Hernández-León 2005). As such it has thus far made only a limited contribution to deepening understandings of migration. A challenge in this respect is the wide breadth of the stated defining features of the migration industry: the profit motive and the facilitation of migration. This research has highlighted complications with both aspects of this classification criteria. Of those who profit from being engaged in facilitating migration, and who are therefore a component of the migration industry, the actual process of promoting mobility can constitute only a minor part of their operations, as is the case with many of the labour providers interviewed as part of this research. Similarly, commercial gain is only one of many motivating factors amongst some of those who fall into the migration industry category, such as migrants working as recruitment consultants whilst assisting those within their social networks to find employment opportunities. Moving forward, greater attention to the links and analytical boundaries between profit-motivated individuals and organisations and other actors in the migration system, and the macro structural spatio-temporal context within which these relations play out, can help to advance this approach as a cohesive theoretical framework in migration studies.

## Disclosure statement

No potential conflict of interest was reported by the authors.

## Funding

This research was conducted by researchers in the Centre for Population Centre, funded by the Economic and Social Research Council (ESRC) [grant number RES-625-28-0001].

## References

Anderson, B., and M. Ruhs. 2010. "Migrant Workers: Who Needs Them?" In *Who Needs Migrant Workers?* edited by M. Ruhs, and B. Anderson, 15–52. Oxford: Oxford University Press.

Anderson, J., and I. Shuttleworth. 2004. "Theorising State Borders in Capitalism: Spatial Fixes Old and New." Centre for International Borders Research. Electronic Working Papers Series, Queens University Belfast.

Bilger, V., M. Hofmann, and M. Jandl. 2006. "Human Smuggling as a Transnational Service Industry: Evidence from Austria." *International Migration* 44 (4): 59–93.

Brettell, C., and J. Hollifield, eds. 2015. *Migration Theory, Talking Across Disciplines*. 3rd ed. London: Routledge.

Burrell, K. 2009. "Introduction." In *Polish Migration to the UK in the 'New' European Union*, edited by K. Burrell, 1–22. Farnham: Ashgate.

Castles, S., H. de Haas, and M. Miller. 2013. *The Age of Migration*. 5th ed. Basingstoke: Macmillan.

Castles, S., and M. Miller. 2003. *The Age of Migration*. 3rd ed. New York: Guilford Press.

Ciupijus, Z. 2011. "Mobile Central Eastern Europeans in Britain." *Work, Employment and Society* 25 (3): 540–550.

Coe, N., J. Jones, and K. Ward. 2010. "The Business of Temporary Staffing: A Developing Research Agenda." *Geography Compass* 4 (8): 1055–1068.

Cranston, S. 2016. "Producing Migrant Encounter: Learning to be a British Expatriate in Singapore Through the Global Mobility Industry." *Environment and Planning D: Society and Space* 34 (4): 655–671.

Cranston, S., J. Schapendonk, and E. Spaan. 2018. "New Directions in Exploring the Migration Industries: Introduction to Special Issue." *Journal of Ethnic and Migration Studies* 44 (4): 543–557. doi:10.1080/1369183X.2017.1315504

Findlay, A. 1990. "A Migration Channels Approach to the Study of High Level Manpower Movements: A Theoretical Perspective." *International Migration* 28 (1): 15–23.

Findlay, A., and F. Li. 1998. "A Migration Channels Approach to the Study of Professionals Moving to and from Hong Kong." *International Migration Review* 32 (3): 682–703.

Findlay, A., and D. McCollum. 2013. "Who is Recruited and How? Migrant Labour Channels in the Agribusiness Sector, from Accession to Recession." *Journal of Rural Studies* 30: 10–19.

Findlay, A., D. McCollum, S. Shubin, E. Apsite, and Z. Krisjane. 2013. "The Role of Recruitment Agencies in Imagining and Producing the 'Good' Migrant." *Social and Cultural Geography* 14 (3): 145–167.

Friberg, J. 2012. "The Stages of Migration. From Going Abroad to Settling Down: Post-accession Polish Migrant Workers in Norway." *Journal of Ethnic and Migration Studies* 38 (10): 1589–1605.

Friebel, G., and S. Guriev. 2006. "Smuggling Humans: A Theory of Debt-Financed Migration." *Journal of the European Economic Association* 4 (6): 1085–1111.

Garapich, M. 2008. "The Migration Industry and Civil Society: Polish Immigrants in the United Kingdom Before and After EU Enlargement." *Journal of Ethnic and Migration Studies* 34 (5): 735–752.

Harney, R. F. 1977. "The Commerce of Migration." *Canadian Ethnic Studies/Etudes Ethniques du Canada* 9: 42–53.

Hedberg, C., B. Hermelin, and K. Westermark. 2014. "Transnational Spaces 'From Above' – The Role of Institutions in Promoting Highly Skilled Labour Migration from India to Sweden." *Tijdschrift Voor Economische en Sociale Geografie* 105 (5): 511–525.

Hennebry, J. 2008. "Bienvenidos a Canadá? Globalization and the Migration Industry Surrounding Temporary Agricultural Migration in Canada." *Canadian Studies in Population* 35 (2): 339–356.

Hernández-León, R. 2005. "The Migration Industry in the Mexico–U.S. Migratory System." Online Working Paper Series 049–05. Los Angeles: UCLA, California Center of Population Research.

Hernandez-Leon, R. 2008. *The Migration of Urban Mexicans to the United States*. Jackson, TN: University of California Press.

Hernandez-Leon, R. 2013. "Conceptualising the Migration Industry." In *The Migration Industry and the Commercialisation of International Migration*, edited by T. Gammeltoft-Hansen, and N. Sorenson, 24–44. London: Routledge.

Hollifield, J. F. 2004. "The Emerging Migration State." *International Migration Review* 38 (3): 885–912.

Jones, K. 2014. "It Was a Whirlwind. A Lot of People Made a Lot of Money." *Central and Eastern European Migration Review* 3 (2): 105–125.

Koser, K. 2011. "Why Take the Risk? Explaining Migrant Smuggling." In *Global Migration, Ethnicity and Britishness*, edited by T. Modood, and J. Salt, 65–83. Basingstoke: Palgrave Macmillan.

Kyle, D., and R. Koslowski, eds. 2001. *Global Human Smuggling: Comparative Perspectives.* Baltimore, MD: Johns Hopkins University Press.

Lin, N. 1999. "Social Networks and Status Attainment." *Annual Review of Sociology* 25: 467–487.

Lindquist, J. 2010. "Labour Recruitment, Circuits of Capital and Gendered Mobility: Reconceptualising the Indonesian Migration Industry." *Pacific Affairs* 83 (1): 115–132.

Lindquist, J., B. Xiang, and B. Yeoh. 2012. "Introduction: Opening the Black Box of Migration." *Asia Pacific Affairs* 85 (1): 7–19.

Lucas, R., and S. Mansfield. 2010. "The Use of Migrant Labour in the Hospitality Sector: Current and Future Implications." In *Who Needs Migrant Workers?* edited by M. Ruhs, and B. Anderson, 159–186. Oxford: Oxford University Press.

MacKenzie, R., and C. Forde. 2009. "The Rhetoric of the 'Good Worker' Versus the Realities of Employers' Use and the Experiences of Migrant Workers." *Work, Employment and Society* 23 (1): 142–159.

McCollum, D. 2013. "Investigating A8 Migration Using Data from the Worker Registration Scheme: Temporal, Spatial and Sectoral Trends." *Local Economy* 28 (1): 35–50.

McCollum, D., and E. Apsite-Berina. 2015. "Recruitment Through Migrant Social Networks from Latvia to the United Kingdom: Motivations, Processes and Developments." *Migration Letters* 12 (1): 50–66.

McCollum, D., and A. Findlay. 2015. "'Flexible' Workers for 'Flexible' Jobs?" *Work, Employment and Society* 29 (3): 427–443.

McCollum, D., S. Shubin, E. Apsite, and Z. Krisjane. 2013. "Rethinking Labour Migration Channels: The Experience of Latvia from EU Accession to Economic Recession." *Population, Space and Place* 19 (6): 688–702.

McDowell, L., A. Batnitzky, and S. Dyer. 2008. "Internationalization and the Spaces of Temporary Labour: The Global Assembly of a Local Workforce." *British Journal of Industrial Relations* 46 (4): 750–770.

Migration Advisory Committee. 2014. *Migrants in Low-Skilled Work.* London: MAC.

Pemberton, S., and C. Stevens. 2010. "The Recruitment and Retention of Central and Eastern European Migrant Workers in the United Kingdom: A Panacea or a Problem Under the New Policies of 'Managed Migration'?" *Regional Studies* 44 (9): 1289–1300.

Piore, M. J. 1979. *Birds of Passage.* Cambridge: Cambridge University Press.

Rogaly, B. 2008. "Intensification of Workplace Regimes in British Horticulture." *Population Space and Place* 14 (6): 497–510.

Salt, J., and J. Stein. 1997. "Migration as a Business: The Case of Trafficking." *International Migration* 35 (4): 467–494.

Salt, J., and P. Wood. 2011. "Acquisition and Mobility of Expertise in Global Corporate Labour Markets." In *Global Migration, Ethnicity and Britishness*, edited by T. Modood, and J. Salt, 84–107. Basingstoke: Palgrave Macmillan.

Scott, S. 2013a. "Migrant-Local Hiring Queues in the UK Food Industry." *Population, Space and Place* 19 (5): 459–471.

Scott, S. 2013b. "Migration and the Employer Perspective." *Population Space and Place* 19 (6): 703–713.

Sorensen, N., and T. Gammeltoft-Hansen. 2013. "Introduction." In *The Migration Industry and the Commercialisation of International Migration*, edited by T. Gammeltoft-Hansen, and N. Sorenson, 1–23. London: Routledge.

Soysal, Y. 1994. *Limits of Citizenship.* Chicago, IL: University of Chicago Press.

Sporton, D. 2013. "'They Control My Life': The Role of Local Recruitment Agencies in East European Migration to the UK." *Population, Space and Place* 19 (5): 443–458.

Travena, P., D. McGhee, and S. Heath. 2013. "Location, Location?" *Population Space and Place* 19 (6): 671–687.

Van den Broek, D., W. Harvey, and D. Groutsis. 2016. "Commercial Migration Intermediaries and the Segmentation of Skilled Migrant Employment." *Work, Employment and Society* 30 (3): 523–534.

Vertovec, S. 2009. *Transnationalism*. London: Routledge.

Waldinger, R., and M. Lichter. 2003. *How the Other Half Works: Immigration and the Social Organization of Labour*. Berkeley, CA: University of California Press.

# Facilitating labour migration from Latvia: strategies of various categories of intermediaries

Oksana Žabko, Aadne Aasland and Sylvi Birgit Endresen

**ABSTRACT**

Within the broad category of migration industries, we focus on intermediaries between employers in Norway requiring migrant labour, and suppliers of Latvian workers willing to migrate. Mediation of labour power is a regulated domain in both countries, but regulations may change: regulations in Latvia have become more lenient, whereas in Norway, they have become stricter in response to increased migration. Intermediaries must be responsive to fluctuations in labour supply and demand, as well as to changing regulations. Today, destination countries are experiencing an overabundance of available migrant labour. This buyer's labour market represents a challenge for intermediaries, spurring adjustments and side-stepping of regulations. Formal temp agencies are supplemented by informal ones, challenging the conceptualisation of intermediaries. Also work migrants may become agents, shaping new forms of intermediation and expanding the concept of 'migration industry' to encompass facilitation of labour migration through social networks. In this article, we construct typologies inductively, establishing categories meaningful in the complex context of labour migration from Latvia to Norway. We distinguish between mediation through formal versus informal agencies, establish characteristics of agencies versus individual social network-based mediation and discuss mediation through the posting of workers by companies.

## Introduction: overview of migration industry in Norway and Latvia

In the last two decades, Norway has experienced a significant increase in the share of the workforce with immigrant backgrounds, especially following the 2004 European Union (EU) expansion which extended the free movement of workers to the citizens of the new member states. While not an EU member, Norway is part of the European Economic Area (EEA) and the European Free Trade Association (EFTA). Through EEA, Norway has adopted a vast number of EU rules, and is part of the internal market based on the free movement of labour, services, goods and capital. In recent years, Norway has been second only to Switzerland in work-migrant inflows as a share of the population (OECD 2014). Workers from the Central and East European EU member states, especially from Poland and the Baltic countries, comprise nearly one quarter of migrants in Norway, and their share has increased rapidly over the past decade (SSB 2016a). Excluding circular and non-registered migrants, there are now close to 11,000 Latvian immigrants, including their children born in Norway (SSB 2016b). Norway has become the sixth most common destination country for Latvian migrants, and the top one among the Nordic countries.

Recent studies have seen employment and recruitment agencies as powerful agents facilitating labour migration (McDowell, Batnitzky, and Dyer 2008; Fiałkowska and Napierała 2013; McCollum et al. 2013). Their competitive strategies (Jones 2014) now encompass linking potential labour markets to recruitment agencies in sending as well as receiving countries. However, perspectives of the sending country are underrepresented in these studies.

Since joining the EU in 2004, Latvia as a sending country of work migrants has experienced two major periods of labour emigration: immediately after joining, and later due to the 2009/2010 recession. Latvian scholars have focused on general patterns of migration (Hazans 2011; Apsīte-Beriņa 2013; Lulle 2014); the loss of human capital and the socio-demographic profiles of migrants (Hazans 2011, 2015). Several studies (Hazans 2011; Apsīte-Beriņa 2013; Lulle 2014) argue that, for Latvians, probably the most important labour migration channel is migrant social networks (family, friends, even strangers via the social media, sharing information and advice about job opportunities abroad). However, drawing on a self-recruited internet survey of Latvian work migrants, Tabuns (2015) argues that the role of employment agencies in finding a first job abroad differs among countries of destination. For example, Latvian work migrants in the UK have relied heavily on such agencies, whereas few Latvians in Norway found their first job through an employment agency (Tabuns 2015). Researchers need to be more sensitive to the varied approaches used by labour migrants in finding work abroad, and to the functions of agencies as they evolve over time and space (McCollum et al. 2013; Žabko 2015).

Therefore, perspectives of sending countries in the debate on the migration industry should be strengthened for two reasons. First, types of actors involved in channelling migrant workers and their common or distinguishable strategies should be studied. McDowell, Batnitzky, and Dyer (2008) find that, unlike post-colonial migrants in the UK, East European work migrants have had no intentions of staying long in low-paid jobs: they plan to move into better-paying work as soon as possible. Awareness of these intentions may influence the strategies of employment agencies, perhaps making them different from other migration channels linking EU employers and work migrants from non-EU countries. Thus, the migration industry may treat migrant labour from various sending countries differently.

Second, experiences of the migrants themselves may shed light on the performance of intermediaries. Empirical data collected in Latvia as country sending migrant labour to Norway definitely add complexity to the debate on the migration industry. Here we aim to 'map' different types of intermediaries that facilitate labour migration from Latvia to Norway, and demonstrate how their strategies as migration industries are responses to changes in the regulatory environments in both countries as well as to fluctuations in demand in Norway.

We begin by examining typologies of intermediaries presented in earlier studies; then discuss the regulatory environments of Latvia and Norway; and conclude by presenting the results of our empirical investigation of the types of intermediaries and their strategies.

## Reference points for typologies of intermediaries and their strategies

Nyberg Sorensen and Gammeltoft-Hansen (2013) divide all actors in the migration industry into five overlapping sets according to their degree of organisation and formalisation. Two sets of actors refer to different kinds of intermediaries that facilitate labour migration. The first are various agencies and companies that facilitate access to legal migration, often offering a package deal (job contacts, housing, legal paperwork and transportation). The second are individuals or smaller enterprises, typically set up by migrants themselves, who apply their transnational knowledge and networks to providing commercial services to prospective migrants. These actors may offer the same services as the first type, but also more specific services like advice on how to 'navigate' pre- and post-migration: meeting formal requirements, finding work, settling down. The term 'labour migration intermediaries' covers these actors.

When adding more to the rich literature review presented by Cranston, Schapendonk, and Spaan (2018), it should be noticed that scholars have studied the rise and operation (and sometimes decline) of agencies' industry around the world; however, they have generally focused on the strategies of legally operating companies that facilitate labour migration, such as employment and temporary employment agencies (Peck, Theodore, and Ward 2005; McDowell, Batnitzky, and Dyer 2008; Fiałkowska and Napierała 2013; Jones 2014). After the deregulation of labour markets, temporary agencies have received particular attention. Peck, Theodore, and Ward (2005) have developed a macro-level typology by distinguishing between emerging and mature markets in the temporary jobs sector. Emerging markets are characterised by minimal resistance to agencies when they enter newly liberalised segments of labour markets: the focus is on low-skilled, low-wage, readily substitutable labour. By contrast, mature markets build on a platform of high-volume business, constructing value-adding strategies designed to penetrate higher and less price-sensitive segments of the labour market.

At the meso-level, a typology developed by Forde and MacKenzie (2009) offers insights into 'new' kinds of agents that have become important in mediating relations between migrants and employers as result of dissatisfaction with traditional agents. They indicate three new types – gangmasters, 'firms-as-intermediates' and social enterprise employment agencies. The first are labour suppliers in sectors regulated by the Gangmasters' Licensing Authority (GLA) in the UK. The specific feature of this group is the acknowledged need to develop 'infrastructure' to secure compliance with GLA regulations and to facilitate the use of temporary migrant labour. In the second group are entrepreneurs that provide outsourced workers for the assembly lines of other companies. Enterprises in the third group focus on job placement activities that can move migrants into higher-skilled jobs. Digging more deeply, McCollum and Findlay (2012) base their micro-level typology of recruitment agencies on the degree of engagement of the *employer* in recruitment and management of migrant work, identifying five types of employment/management regimes in Britain's agribusiness sector.

The above approaches illustrate the range of typologies of labour-migrant intermediaries, all developed from the perspective of the individual receiving country. Although these approaches contribute valuable insights on the intermediary market, the enormous variety indicates an unexplored space in the migration industry that calls for discussion of demarcation indicators. There is a need to go beyond previously constructed typologies. In this study of intermediaries, we maintain a sending-country perspective, but go beyond the perception of intermediaries as single-country phenomena, thereby underlining the international nature of the migration industry. Further, we engage with internal processes of intermediaries in interaction with regulations, labour demand and migrants.

## Research design

This article builds on data collected within the project 'The impact of temporary work agencies on the politics of work', funded by the Research Council of Norway, project no. 227021. One objective of this research was to describe how Latvian labour migrants get to Norway, and investigate the working conditions of Latvian labour migrants compared to Norwegians. Our investigation encompasses recent policy changes and the 'mapping' of intermediaries. The term 'intermediaries' is broadly defined to include all agents that link the foreign (Norwegian) employer and migrant (Latvian) workers, regardless of how the link is established (written or verbal agreement, legal entity or individual). Specific types of intermediaries found are described and termed accordingly. The study is qualitative, based on 11 in-depth interviews with Latvian intermediaries with real (or attempted) cooperation experience with Norway, and 10 expert interviews with policy-makers and social partners like ministries and their agency representatives, trade unions and industry representatives. In addition, we employ cursory data from 10 in-depth interviews conducted with Latvian labour migrants with experience from working in Norway. The latter information allows cross-verification of types of intermediaries identified in the study, as well as analysis of workers' responses to the adaptation strategies of intermediaries. Interviews were conducted between October 2014 and June 2015.

Informants were recruited by (i) consulting the registers of companies with operating licences issued by the Latvian State Employment Agency (the supervisory body, SEA); (ii) reviewing discussions in social media on job-seeking in Norway; (iii) using information provided by social partners; and (iv) using data on companies with business relations with Norway.

The first source was used as the official and most visible information channel. Latvian regulations require licences for firms offering job placement services; SEA issues licences, supervises the industry and maintains a register of licenced companies. All employment agencies selected for our interviews were licensed for cooperation with Norwegian enterprises. The register listed 103 licenced job placement service providers as of 20 November 2014 (SEA 2014), of which 55 companies had received licenses for job placement abroad. With 10 licences, Norway is the third most frequently served country by Latvian agencies. Seven of our 11 interviews with Latvian intermediaries were conducted with representatives of these companies.

The second source, social media, was used for identifying other kinds of intermediaries (informal, circumventing registration and licensing). The Latvian social media channel *draugiem.lv* has a discussion page for those seeking work in Norway. Here information on vacancies, companies or individuals providing intermediary services is shared. We reviewed discussions posted between 2009 and 2014. Our third source, social partners, provided additional information on informal intermediaries; the fourth source was companies that regularly sent employees to work in Norway as 'posted workers'. Four interviews were conducted with other kinds of Latvian intermediaries.

## The employment agency environment in Latvia

Joining the EU in 2004 opened the labour markets of the UK, Ireland and Sweden to Latvian citizens. One year later, the Latvian government introduced the first regulations on private job placement, as a reaction to cases of fraud in migration intermediary services. Several amendments followed, responding to changes like the opening of the labour markets in other EU and EEA countries in 2006 and 2007. Regulations from 2007 apply to enterprises that provide any intermediary services between employer (local or foreign) and Latvian job-seekers. The regulations concern licensing, determining relationships between agency and clients, and monitor the performance of agencies. Irregularities may result in cancellation of a licence (Cabinet of Ministers 2007). Acquiring licence for operating in a country does not mean that actual cooperating will be established. We found that employment agencies acquire licences for job placement in some countries (like Norway) only because of high demand from job-seekers, without offering any jobs.

SEA wants to reduce the number of what are considered misleading licences by introducing more inspections and cancelling licences for 'non-served' countries. However, employment agency representatives argue that their strategy aims at flexibility, readiness in case of demand from new countries. The procedure for obtaining licences for each country is time-consuming. One agency representative explained that they had to compete with other new EU member states for a supply of cheaper labour migrants in the shortest period of time under the high demand of work abroad. The representative added that the migrants' nationality (whether Latvian, Lithuanian or Polish) is not considered important by the receiving country. What matters most is how quickly the required workforce can be supplied.

Regulations require the agencies to provide SEA with all information on foreign partners (including copies of contracts) and any amendments. That serves as an incentive for Latvian employment agencies to establish long-term cooperation with partners in receiving countries, and also spurs cooperation with other sending countries where intermediary services may be less regulated (e.g. Lithuania). This way, the time- and effort-intensive reporting to SEA can be minimised.

Some principles can be sacrificed on the altar of international competitiveness. Representatives of Latvian policy-makers and social partners emphasise that it is allowed to charge job-seekers for 'arrangement of documents' – which is not allowed in other Baltic states. Policy-makers say that such charges should be normally collected from the employer, as the more stable and powerful player. This 'compromise' follows from policy-makers' acceptance of the Latvian agencies' need to be more attractive to receiving countries. The tension between international practice to charge employer and local practice was evident in our discussions with representatives of employment agencies. They admitted that the practice of charging the employee is common – adding, however, that no double-charging takes place.

## The employment agency environment in Norway

The large supply of available labour from countries with lower wages, combined with willingness to work under harsher conditions than Norwegian workers normally do, has had major impacts on Norway's labour regulations and labour market, tilting power towards the employer side of labour relations. Employers have the choice of hiring workers from abroad through ordinary recruitment, or using employment services from agencies offering posted workers. In Norway, the latter practice has increased substantially in sectors requiring low qualifications, limited training requirements and low trade union membership – like construction, industry and the hospitality industry (Friberg 2016), and where knowing the language is often less important.

Wages of manual workers have decreased in relative terms compared to other types of work in Norway. In fact, foreign workers often have qualifications and education far higher than they make use of in their jobs abroad. Moreover, studies have described how the staffing industry deliberately recruits foreign workers and facilitates their use as a flexible work force, even when the employers' needs are permanent (Friberg 2016). In construction and the fishing industry, for instance, agencies typically offer 'zero-hour' contracts, whereby no wages are paid between work assignments. This means inferior working conditions as compared to permanent full-time employees.

The Norwegian labour market has been well regulated, with social partnership and compromise as the preferred model of industrial relations. In recent years, however, the country has experienced a selected and contested process of deregulation (Jordhus-Lier, Coe, and Bråten 2015). While hiring out of labour with certain exemptions was prohibited from 1971 to 2000, significant steps have been taken towards liberalisation since then, culminating with the incorporation of EU Directive 2008/104/EC on Temporary Agency Work into Norwegian law on 1 January 2013.

This Directive caused intense debate, with resistance from, *inter alia,* large segments of the trade union movement (Bergene and Ewing 2015). In Latvia, interviews with policy-makers showed that the signing of the Directive was widely considered as a positive development for worker protection, supported also by the trade unions. By contrast, in Norway there were widespread fears, voiced by the Confederation of Trade Unions (LO), that it would spur the use of temporary workers, in turn reducing the scope for employee influence on wages and working conditions and complicating Norway's well-established triangular work relations.

There can be little doubt that the increased inflow of foreign workers and deregulation of the labour market have contributed to expand the scope for speculative behaviour among employers. Evidence of social dumping, with dismal pay and working conditions, abounds in the Norwegian labour market. In addition to unregistered workers, who are probably the most vulnerable to exploitation, also posted workers are at risk. The regulations concerning posted workers apply when a Norwegian company enters into agreement with a foreign company (e.g. subcontracting) and staff from the foreign company are posted to fulfil the agreement; when the Norwegian company hires in temporary staff from a foreign recruitment agency; when an employee of a foreign company is posted to a Norwegian company that is part of the same enterprise; and when a Norwegian private citizen buys services from a foreign company. Studies of labour migrants show that posted workers receive the lowest pay, while those hired through 'temping' agencies report the poorest working conditions among workers in Norway (Friberg 2016, 23).

Although minimum rates have been introduced in certain sectors, there is no universal minimum wage in Norway. Unless they are covered by a general wage agreement, posted workers may be put to work at the wage level that is common in their home country, in this case Latvia. However, several measures have been taken in order to reduce the scope of exploitation of migrant workers. One such measure is the general application of collective agreements: agreements on wages and working conditions that apply to *all* working in that sector, regardless of whether they are party to the agreement. This has led to major controversies, with the trade unions usually in favour and the employers' organisations opposed. However, company managers in the sectors subject to these general agreements are generally positive (Lindahl 2011). To date, eight sectors, including construction, agriculture, cleaning and fish processing, are included in such agreements. The role of the Norwegian Labour Inspection Authority in checking on the wages and working conditions of foreign workers has also been strengthened.

## Types of intermediaries

Our research on Latvian intermediaries supplying the Norwegian labour market resulted in the typologies presented in Figure 1. We categorise according to the type of intermediary in Latvia; the country where activities take place (Latvia, Norway or both); and type of partner in Norway. Our results may apply more widely: according to our interviews with intermediaries, policy-makers and social partners, the patterns observed may be valid for labour export to EU countries as well.

Three broad categories of intermediaries can be distinguished in Latvia (see Figure 1): (i) formal agencies (employment agencies that work according the regulations for intermediaries; they are licensed and registered and have service contracts with the job-seeker); (ii) informal intermediaries (including legal entities and individuals that provide the same services as formal agencies, but avoid SEA registration and supervision; and (iii) posting enterprises (companies located in Latvia that post workers abroad, with employment agreements with these workers; they are not licensed or supervised by SEA).

As will be shown, formal agencies and informal intermediaries are quite similar, in terms of how they operate and in the effects of their operations. Posting enterprises are different. Expanding their business abroad, they produce a flow of posted workers.

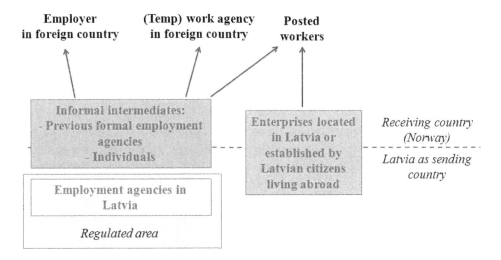

**Figure 1.** Types of intermediaries and flow of labour migrants from Latvia to Norway.

Operation of intermediaries is also linked to location. Formal agencies located in Latvia operate as classical service providers: they have foreign partners and they source labour only within the territory of Latvia. Informal intermediaries might work at both ends – in the sending as well as the receiving country. Enterprises that send posted workers to Norway may be registered and owned in Latvia or in Norway (or elsewhere) and thus operate in many locations.

The regulations on formal agencies require agencies to state what kind of service they provide, within the following categories: (i) work offers in international au pair programmes, educational and employment programmes, (ii) job-search assistance (service for job-seekers), (iii) services for employers regarding recruitment of potential employees and (iv) temporary work services (Cabinet of Ministers 2007). However, in interviews, agency representatives explained that they try to find workers who fit the needs of their clients (employers or foreign agencies) regardless of the above licence formalities. Their services are oriented towards employers, not towards job-seekers. Therefore, a distinction should be made between activities based on service agreements (i, ii and iii), and work contracts (iv). In contrast to other countries, Latvia's Labour Law requires temporary work agencies registered in Latvia to sign work contracts, making agency workers 'employees' with formal employment rights.

As Ruhs and Anderson (2010) have pointed out, control over the period of employment is an important factor which facilitates the usage of agency workers, at least in the UK. Our interview data show that, due to this 'unfavourable' regulation in Latvia, there are tensions between policy-makers and the temporary agency industry. This regulation may be one reason why the temporary agency business is weak in the Latvian internal market, but has had some success in providing labour for foreign employers. However, the recent adoption of the EU Directive on Temporary Agency Work has negatively influenced the temping agency market in Latvia.

Opening labour markets in Western EU countries was the first facilitating factor for the emergence of various types of intermediaries in addition to the traditional employment agencies (see Lulle 2014). In some countries, including Norway, coherent local migrant communities have developed, establishing networks that facilitate the formation of informal intermediaries. These might later on develop into formal agencies, if some basic conditions are favourable. Our interviews with stakeholders indicate three main factors which facilitate the growth of the market for labour migration intermediaries: (i) increased demand of labour migrants in receiving countries, (ii) rising unemployment in sending countries and the wish for better pay, (iii) changes in regulations in receiving and sending countries.

Having emerged, these types of intermediaries continue to exist in the market. Interviews with stakeholders show that SEA does not have resources to control the spread of informal players. Interviews with representatives of employment agencies show that, despite the formation of coherent migrant communities abroad, there is still a place for formal agencies as conditions in receiving countries change. One formal agent elaborated on 'rotation', the inconsistency which may describe migrants' relations with intermediaries:

> Most of those who come here are from recommendations – friend to friend, acquaintance to acquaintance, relative to relative. Some have gone six, seven years ago, picked strawberries somewhere, and after that got a need again.

Sometimes our clients come for the second or third time. One time he was in Greece, then in England, after that in Holland and after that somewhere else. Our experience shows that they come, they get a job with our help and not help from someone else. [..] They go for [work abroad] half a year, then return back here, to Latvia. Three months pass, they look for something here, maybe cannot find anything or do not like the wages, so they come to us again, and go back abroad.

## Distinguishing features of intermediaries

### The 'formal vs. the informal' dimension

When we examine the three groups of intermediaries, the first important distinguishing feature is SEA registration and application of the regulations as to agency performance. This is a reason for distinguishing between formal and informal types of intermediaries. Regulations refer only to formal employment agencies. Informal intermediaries emerge in various ways. For instance, if an employment agency fails in its operations, it might decide to turn to the 'grey' sector. Also, informal intermediation might be provided by the legal entity providing linked services (like language training). Speaking Norwegian is a powerful resource which boosts a job-seeker's chances. Language trainers may charge a fee for information, based on verbal agreement. Furthermore, informal intermediaries may form if an individual has the will and knowledge to work as intermediaries. These may be individuals providing only intermediary services and charging for them, or people who periodically go for work abroad and bring others with them, making teams, recruiting a certain number of workers for their employer. They may or may not charge for this service. If they do not charge, there are other benefits, like ensuring that they will have a good team that can be relied upon. This form of intermediation is widespread in construction and seasonal work in agriculture and hospitality.

When analysing labour migration from Latvia, researchers tend to see all individuals working as informal intermediaries as 'social networks'. However, our data show that the definition should be narrowed to apply only to individuals who are not engaged in employment relations with the same employer and do not get any benefit for their services. If they work regularly and benefit from their activities, they act as informal agencies. Thus, answering the question raised by Cranston, Schapendonk, and Spaan (2018), we claim that they are part of the migration industry.

There has been a decrease in demand for the services of Latvian formal agencies in recent years. This is allegedly due to improvements in Norwegian labour regulations, such as equal wages for foreign and native workers. Our interview data show that temporary agencies that are branches of Norwegian agencies may find themselves in a more stable situation. However, the range of their activities may be reduced. With the stricter regulations in Norway, it is no longer necessary to sign contracts in Latvia that allow paying less; contracting is gradually transferred to Norway and duties of local branches are reduced to the recruitment and preparation of migrant workers.

### The 'posted workers' dimension

The practices of formal agencies and posting companies are similar. Our interviews with agency representatives show that, before Norway adopted the EU Directive on Temporary

Agency Work, the common practice of Latvian temporary agencies was to have contracts signed in Latvia, thus applying local labour legislation, and then posting agency workers to Norway. With the adoption of the EU Directive, the demand for agency workers from Latvia has fallen, and some agencies have closed.

Workers posted in Norway thus deserve attention. A posted Latvian worker is sent to Norway to perform specific duties within given time-periods; there is a work contract, permanent or temporary, signed by the worker and a Latvian company or temporary work agency, or a parent company/agency in Norway. Our interviews show that workers are posted by two kinds of intermediaries: one is registered at SEA, but the other does not follow regulations and does not register as an employment agency. When posting companies are registered as formal agencies, they are subject to SEA supervision – one reason why they are reluctant to register. The business sector to which a company belongs is important in this respect. IT, construction and logistics companies do not consider themselves as temporary work agencies even though contracts between company and employee may be the same as those that formal agencies have with their workers. There are, according to our interviews with social partners and SEA, pressures on them to register as temporary work agency. Companies that post workers surface if there is a disagreement between a posted worker and the employer, and the employee contacts a trade union or SEA. As trade union membership in Latvia is comparatively low and member rates vary among sectors, there are many business sectors where disputes remain unresolved. The company sending posted workers sees registration as the last option for dealing with the problem. Registration may be chosen if the company has long-term goals in Latvia or operates in transparent sectors (e.g. health personnel recruitment). In other cases, the company may apply avoidance strategies, like clearing accounts and establishing another legal entity.

Although demand for the services of Latvian temporary agencies has declined, posting of workers has increased recently. Our interviews with various kinds of intermediaries show that flows of posted workers increase due to the activities of companies that export their business activities to Norway and also because Latvian migrants in Norway develop their business and recruit in Latvia. These companies try to avoid the status of intermediary: they have permanent contracts with their workers. The operations of these companies are closely linked to the next topic – the circularity dimension.

### The 'circularity' dimension

Circular migration is a feature that characterises some Latvian temporary work agencies as well as posting companies. Migrants maintain a home in Latvia and work in Norway for several weeks or months. Periods of work and rest are usually set by the contracting authority – the employer of the posted worker or an agency. The length of such periods depends on the *type of industry* to which a company belongs. According to our interviews, the most typical form of employment is two to four weeks' intensive work in Norway and a similar period of rest in Latvia. More regular employment with shorter periods of work and rest is found in healthcare and social services and logistics. Irregular employment with longer periods of work in Norway is typical of the construction industry.

Working conditions vary according to industry, but also within industries, as work regimes may differ among companies. Some companies require migrant workers to take a rest; no side jobs are permitted. Other companies allow side jobs during the stay in Latvia, in which case the worker gets no rest after an intensive work period. Circular migration organised in this way allows *work intensification* as compared to a normal labour regime. Having extensive work hours abroad in combination with *formally* no working hours at home corresponds to 'normal' full-time work, and *in practice* means applying normal work regulations to more intensive work.

According to our informants, circularity ensures flexibility during economic fluctuations. Rapid adjustments can be made when there are changes in labour demand in sending or receiving countries. Our findings also indicate that circularity as a competitive strategy develops when regulation becomes stricter. As wage dumping has been inherent to migrant labour, Norwegian authorities and social partners have worked to achieve the application of Norwegian wage standards to posted workers. This is seen as decreasing the competitiveness of Latvian labour migrants in Norway; therefore, a balancing of wages through the use of work and rest regimes is achieved. The 'equal pay' requirement is seen as diminishing competitiveness in Latvia as well, as Norwegian wages are considered unrealistically high. Thus, the balancing strategy entails paying wages according to Norwegian requirements and balancing this with no-wage or low-wage periods of 'rest' in Latvia.

According to stakeholder interviews, reduction of expenditures is the main reason for circular migration on the part of the company. However, other economic and political effects are found by Latvian companies, Norwegian temping agencies and client companies. Circular migrants do not formally live in Norway: thus, the flow of permanent labour migrants decreases while the flow of non-permanent migrants increases. Having experience with circular migration in one company, labour migrants might transfer this practice to other enterprises in Norway. One labour migrant said that agreement with the employer had been reached: by working more intensively and thereby squeezing the number of working days in Norway, migrants can be with their families the remaining days. As such arrangements are initiated by the labour migrants themselves, the length of work and rest regimes depends on their own abilities to do their jobs faster, saving working days. Circular migration may also be an option for migrants who remain poorly integrated into Norwegian society, despite lengthy stays. Distribution and wider acceptance of circularity by companies allows them to change the status from permanent migrant in Norway to circular migrant and re-consider re-migration options, like resettlement in Latvia while keeping the job in Norway.

## Latvian labour intermediaries: strategies for establishing partnerships

In the above, we have shed some light on how and why intermediates operate. This theme Cranston, Schapendonk, and Spaan (2018) consider an under-researched area. When continuing our examination, we turn to the question of which resources intermediaries draw upon and which are crucial to their performance. Firstly, we address to opportunities of Latvian formal and informal agencies to find foreign partners.

Explaining why they started the business, representatives of employment agencies acknowledge that it was in response to the demand from labour migrants facilitated by foreign employers or employment agencies:

> I left [Latvia] [..] to earn money for an apartment and went to Great Britain. There I got opportunity to earn enough in eight months for an apartment in Riga. When I was leaving [back to Latvia], the employer asked me to help him find more Latvians. I thought – relatives, friends, no problem. But when my phone bill reached 100 lats a month, I understood that I cannot help like this, it will have to be a business.

> It all began when one of our partners, he's in the fish trade, [..] offered to begin such a business here, because he was working with that kind of companies and knew that they needed workers. [..] Companies that take our employees are [his trade] partners.

Companies may start posting when they expand their business abroad, an option many Latvian companies explored after the 2009 decline. This caused increased flows of posted workers and circular migration, as one interviewee explained:

> In 2009, [the company] has searched partners in Scandinavia and has found them, the cooperation has gradually formed both in Sweden and in Norway. The principle is that we work with big [..] companies, who know [us], good reputation goes ahead of us. The other form is that we participate in public tenders in Norway. If we get them, we sign contracts directly with municipalities or some state institutions.

In recruiting informants, we found that only about half of the 10 employment agencies that have been granted licences for job placement services with Norway have actually engaged in cooperation with Norwegian partners. Our interviews indicate that some agencies rely on previously established contacts, and others try to expand them. The opportunities for attracting partners depend on the size of the company and the business contact networks of the company owners. All formal employment agencies and their informal counterparts are micro-size companies, but the size of posting companies varies from small to large ones.

Latvian agencies report that finding new foreign cooperation partners is costly, requiring significant investments in time and human resources on both sides, as reported by one interviewee:

> There are some where it takes half a year of negotiations to start work. They fly to us, we fly to them. They observe, observe our history, observe what has been in media.

Latvian formal agencies claim that they can distinguish 'disadvantageous' foreign job offers, where the actual work to be done may not correspond with the offer. They seek to avoid the risk of negative references in the media and the SEA, which may be followed by sanctions, even license cancellation. Latvian employment agencies say they may refuse job offers where they consider the work to be very intensive, where high rotation of employees is observed, and where local (i.e. non-Latvian) staff in management positions discriminate against foreigners. Job offers in Great Britain require careful examination; Norway is seen as safer and more attractive.

Some agency representatives claim that the abundance of migrant labour in Norway makes it difficult to establish contacts. Lately, Latvians have begun travelling to Norway to look for work through Norwegian agencies or by visiting companies on their own, in which case Latvian intermediaries are not needed.

Formal agencies have the broadest range of partnerships. Our research showed three types (i) similar foreign agencies which ensure intermediary services, (ii) the parent company of a temporary work agency to which the employees are posted, and (iii) foreign employers who provide workforce recruitment according to certain criteria. The first two options are used by Latvian formal employment agencies more frequently than the third one. These findings describe cooperation patterns not only in Norway, but also in EU countries. As regards cooperation, we have limited information on the partners of informal agencies. However, they certainly work directly with foreign employers and, in some cases, have cooperation with some foreign employment agencies.

We find that Latvian agencies tend to cooperate more with foreign agencies than directly with foreign employers, for several reasons. First, foreign employment agencies hold pools of foreign employers, whereas smaller employers may have few vacancies; and that makes them short-term and less advantageous partners. Agency representatives acknowledge that they have found themselves in this situation:

> Those employers also have their limits. [..] The cleaning business was one for which we pro-vided services. But there is nothing to do there anymore, because those ladies that we placed in work, they clean offices in Oslo at night, private houses during the day, also other objects. They do not change [i.e. look for other work].

Second, cooperating with an agency on a longer-term basis is easier, due to the Latvian regulations that require a SEA permit to establish cooperation with a new partner. Also, representatives of Latvian agencies find that cooperation with foreign employment agencies may give access to several employers, saving resources. In addition, Latvian employment agencies have encountered difficulties when establishing direct contacts with foreign employers. Other studies show that foreign employers opt to cooperate with their country's local employment agencies because it seems less risky (McCollum et al. 2013). As a result, Latvian labour migrants may go through 'double intermediaries' on their way to getting a job abroad – a Latvian and also a foreign agency. Our findings on the cooperation strategies used by Latvian employment agencies are similar to result from Poland: Fiałkowska and Napierała (2013) found that most employment agencies are involved only in job brokerage and collaborate with sister agencies from abroad, for whom they recruit workers, who will then probably be hired as temp workers.

## Demand and supply: adaptation strategies

Our interviews with intermediaries show that they adapt to changes in demand and supply of labour migrants. Latvian agencies are dependent on the demand from foreign partners. In response, formal agencies and posting companies show their willingness to be attractive cooperation partners in the destination countries of their workers.

Representatives of Latvian agencies say there are no important differences between demand for Latvian workers and migrants from other East European countries. They also consider the industries that require workers to be similar. In Norway, these are (i) sectors that offer low-qualified, low-paid jobs (construction, fishery, farming, hospitality and catering, provision of postal services, etc., including lower-qualification work for nurses in social care), (ii) some high-qualification professions found around the world (IT, engineering, healthcare, maritime) and (iii) workforce for specific Norwegian regions (usually peripheral regions in the North). In fact, many migrants consider the work environment in Northern Norway to be better than in the Oslo region, where high competition may lead to social dumping and short-term contracts.

Most agencies interviewed provide workers for companies in sectors (i) and (iii) above. Recognising the Norwegian labour market as highly competitive, Latvian agency representatives explain that they sometimes set criteria additional to those established by the potential employer, to ensure the best possible candidates among job-seekers.

Our interview data show that few jobs demand skills acquired through formal education or training, although these are required for 'classified' types of jobs within healthcare, maritime and a few other sectors. However, all intermediaries emphasise the high demand for 'soft skills' like certain physical and psychological capacities (including appearance, general health condition, adaptation skills, no addiction problems), family status and lifestyle preferences. This demonstrates that what Ruhs and Anderson (2010) call 'the fuzziness of "skill"'. The most important 'soft skill' is productivity. It is deemed crucial especially by Latvian posting companies when selecting staff for work abroad. Informants also explain that some foreign partners try to protect themselves against 'undesirable' personality traits that Latvians may not consider inherent in local work ethics:

> [The consultant] was telling us all the time about [..] how to evaluate 'work non-attendance', whether a person has missed work and I could not understand why she kept talking about that all the time. Something which for us is not urgent at all is a huge problem for them. When Norwegians ask for references [..] they all have the same questions: how much did she miss work, how much sick leave has she taken. That is a main problem for them, but is not something caused by our nurses.

In most cases, it is expected that Latvians looking for work abroad will know some English, at least at the level of everyday speaking. Knowledge of the Norwegian language increases the opportunities of finding a job in Norway. In some professions where Latvian workers are demanded (for example, nurses), workers are required to have Norwegian language skills before they take up their jobs. In these cases, the agency or its foreign partner provides the necessary language training. However, they will need to protect this investment, since other companies try to capture well-trained personnel. Norwegian employers have also come to Latvia to participate in agency interviews with job-seekers and assist in selection.

Underpinning the strategies described above, agencies argue that, in today's highly competitive market, they need to have good references from clients which enhances the opportunity to maintain good cooperation. Thus, they demonstrate features which Peck, Theodore, and Ward (2005) have described as an emerging market of temporary work business, a point also explored by McCollum and Findlay (2018).

What strategies do intermediaries use for adapting to changes in the supply of labour migrants? According to agency representatives we interviewed, the need to adapt has arisen in two situations. First, between 2009 and 2010 Latvian unemployment levels were high, and there was a very high demand for finding jobs abroad. This facilitated the growth of formal agencies and informal intermediaries. Second, when they experienced a shortage of workers willing to go abroad, agencies needed to develop survival strategies. One such strategy has been to expand abroad and seek market potentials also in other East European countries:

> We have an office in Tartu [Estonia] and in Bucharest, Romania. Now there is a lack of unskilled workers in Latvia, there is a great seasonal need for them. We can get workers from Bucharest, we go there, present ourselves in various places. [..] Now it's become hard

for us to get someone to leave Latvia, but Romanians go, they do not reject [offers] – especially if they live near the border to Moldova, where minimum wage is €107 a month, they will go there and do any kind of work. At some point we Latvians also would go like that, but not anymore.

In a Norwegian fish-industry town, this practice was confirmed by an informant who explained that the local industry had previously recruited workers from Poland, but moved on to workers from the three Baltic States, who accepted lower pay. After Romania joined the EU, the local labour market during the peak winter season has become dominated by Romanian circular migrants who are said to be willing to work under poorer conditions than the Baltic workers.

## Concluding remarks

The sending-country perspective applied in this research has disclosed a range of forms of mediation between buyers and suppliers of labour power involving cross-border migration. Latvian intermediaries supplying labour to Norway show features similar to those of other emerging markets described by Peck, Theodore, and Ward (2005). The Latvian market is small, and intermediaries work in a highly competitive East European market. To survive, they have introduced some additional strategies. Closely resembling the 'new' kinds of intermediaries described by Forde and MacKenzie (2009), important players in the Latvian intermediary market are 'firms-as-intermediates': posting companies that introduce specific work and rest regimes, thereby facilitating circular migration. In contrast to Forde and MacKenzie (2009), a stimulus for the emergence of these new forms has come from restrictions imposed by regulations and limitations of the market that facilitate long-term relationships with the same labour migrants, thereby ensuring the survival of the intermediary. These adaptations reflect labour migration intermediaries that seek a future in a highly changing and competitive environment where flexibility is a constant requirement.

Like Harvey, Groutsis, and van den Broek (2018), we hold that typologies of intermediaries need to encompass them as migration industries. Our study of the performance of intermediaries shows that the quality of services received by labour migrants depends on a set of characteristics: level of formalisation, range of services provided, acceptance or avoidance of regulations in sending and receiving country. Possible discrepancies between formal and actual performance need to be examined, underlining the need for further empirical research. A pertinent angle for future research could be the number of intermediaries between worker and job, indicating the power of the migration industry in specific cases. With Latvian work migrants to Norway, this varies from *no* intermediaries (Norwegian companies establish contact with workers directly) to *two* intermediaries. Spatial location of intermediaries determines which regulation must be navigated. Labour migration intermediaries develop a whole range of structures and international industrial networks for maintaining their position, reflecting the changing political and social environments in sending and receiving countries.

A major finding, and one which underlines the need for further research, concerns the concept of *social network*. Scholars have tended to see successful informal mediation between labour buyer and seller as 'the power of social networks'. However, we hold that many of these intermediaries share the characteristics of formal actors and should therefore be studied as part of the migration industry. The concept of 'social network' needs to be refined to cover relations that entail labour market agency.

## Disclosure statement

No potential conflict of interest was reported by the authors.

## Funding

This work was supported by the Norges Forskningsråd [grant number 227021].

## References

Apsīte-Beriņa, E. 2013. "International Migration in the European Union: Emigration from Latvia to the United Kingdom." Summary of Doctoral Thesis, Riga: University of Latvia.

Bergene, A. C., and K. D. Ewing. 2015. "Vikarbyrådirektivet: liberalisering eller likebehandling?" *Søkelys på arbeidslivet* 31 (01/02): 137–157.

Cabinet of Ministers of the Republic of Latvia. (2007). *Regulations of the Cabinet of Ministers No. 458 'Procedures for Licensing and Supervision of Merchants – Providers of Job Placement Services.* Riga: Cabinet of Ministers.

Cranston, S., J. Schapendonk, and E. Spaan. 2018. "New Directions in Exploring the Migration Industries: Introduction to Special Issue." *Journal of Ethnic and Migration Studies* 44 (4): 543–557. doi:10.1080/1369183X.2017.1315504.

Fiałkowska, K., and J. Napierała. 2013. "Mapping the Market for Employment Agencies in Poland." In: *Labour Migrants from Central and Eastern Europe in the Nordic Countries. Patterns of Migration, Working Conditions and Recruitment Practices*, edited by J. H. Friberg and L. Eldring, 59–64. Copenhagen: Nordic Council of Ministers.

Forde, C., and R. MacKenzie. 2009. "Migrant Workers, Agencies and the 'New' Intermediaries." Presentation at ESRC Seminar Series "The Impact of Migrant Workers on the Functioning of Labour Markets and Industrial Relations", Keele University, 11 November.

Friberg, J. H. 2016. *Arbeidsmigrasjon. Hva vet vi om konsekvensene for norsk arbeidsliv, samfunn og økonomi?* Oslo: Fafo.

Harvey, W. S., D. Groutsis, and D. van den Broek. 2018. "Intermediaries and Destination Reputations: Explaining Flows of Skilled Migration." *Journal of Ethnic and Migration Studies* 44 (4): 644–662. doi:10.1080/1369183X.2017.1315518.

Hazans, M. 2011. "The Changing Face of Latvian Emigration, 2000–2010." In: *Latvia. Human Development Report 2010/2011. National Identity, Mobility and Capability*, edited by B. Zepa and E. Kļave, 77–101. Riga: Advanced Social and Political Research Institute, University of Latvia.

Hazans, M. 2015. "Latvijas emigranti Eiropas darba tirgos." In: *Latvijas emigrantu kopienas: cerību diaspora*, edited by I. Mieriņa, 66–74. Rīga: Latvijas Universitātes Filozofijas un socioloģijas institūts.

Jones, K. 2014. "'It Was a Whirlwind. A Lot of People Made a Lot of Money': The role of Agencies in Facilitating Migration from Poland into the UK between 2004 and 2008." *Central and Eastern European Migration Review* 3 (2): 105–125.

Jordhus-Lier, D., N. M. Coe, and S. T. Bråten. 2015. "Contested Growth: the Development of Norway's Temporary Staffing Industry." *Geografiska Annaler: Series B, Human Geography* 97 (1): 113–130.

Lindahl, B. 2011. "Staffing Agencies Challenging the Nordic Model." *Nordic Labour Journal*, April 7, 2011. Accessed March 30, 2016. http://www.nordiclabourjournal.org/i-fokus/in-focus-2011/temporary-workers/article.2011-04-06.9358917797.

Lulle, A. 2014. "Time-space of Possibilities: Translocal Geographies of Latvians in Guernsey." Summary of Doctoral Thesis. Riga: University of Latvia.

McCollum, D., and A. Findlay. 2012. "East-Central European Migration to the UK: Policy Issues and Employment Circumstances from the Perspective of Employers and Recruitment Agencies." ESRC Centre for Population Change Working Paper No. 20. Edinburgh: The ESRC Centre for Population Change.

McCollum, D., and A. Findlay. 2018. "Oiling the Wheels? Flexible Labour Markets and the Migration Industry." *Journal of Ethnic and Migration Studies* 44 (4): 558–574. doi:10.1080/1369183X.2017.1315505.

McCollum, D., S. Shubin, E. Apsite, and Z. Krisjane. 2013. "Re-thinking Labour Migration Channels: The Experience of Latvia from EU Accession to Economic Recession." *Population, Space and Place* 19: 688–702.

McDowell L., A. Batnitzky, and S. Dyer. 2008. "Internationalization and the Spaces of Temporary Labour: The Global Assembly of a Temporary Workforce." *British Journal of International Relations* 46 (4): 750–770.

Nyberg Sorensen, N., and T. Gammeltoft-Hansen. 2013. "Introduction." In: *The Migration Industry and the Commercialization of International Migration*, edited by T. Gammeltoft-Hansen and N. Nyberg Sorensen, 1–23. London: Routledge.

OECD. 2014. *Recruiting Immigrant Workers: Norway 2014*. Paris: OECD.

Peck, J., N. Theodore, and K. Ward. 2005. "Constructing Markets for Temporary Labour: Employment Liberalization and the Internationalization of the Staffing Industry." *Global Networks* 5 (1): 3–26.

Ruhs, M., and B. Anderson, eds. 2010. *Who Needs Migrant Workers? Labour Shortages, Immigration and Public Policy*. Oxford: Oxford University Press.

SEA – State Employment Agency (Latvia). 2014. *Merchants That Have Received a License at the SEA for Provision of Job Placement Services*. Riga: State Employment Agency. http://www.nva.gov.lv/index.php?cid=446&mid=75.

SSB – Statistics Norway. 2016a. *Key Figures for Immigration and Immigrants. Figure 1: Immigrants and Norwegian-born to Immigrant Parents, by Country of Origin from 1 January, 2016*. Oslo: Statistics Norway. Accessed July 4, 2016. https://www.ssb.no/en/innvandring-og-innvandrere/nokkeltall.

SSB – Statistics Norway. 2016b. *Immigrants and Norwegian-born to Immigrant Parents. Table: 09817: Immigrants and Norwegian-born to Immigrant Parents, by Immigration Category, Country Background and Percentages of the Population*. Oslo: Statistics Norway. Accessed July 4, 2016. https://www.ssb.no/statistikkbanken/selectvarval/saveselections.asp.

Tabuns, A. 2015. "Privāto darbā iekārtošanas aģentūru pakalpojumu tiesiskā regulācija, izmantošana un to darbības vērtējums." In: *Latvijas emigrantu kopienas: cerību diaspora*, edited by I. Mieriņa, 75–84. Rīga: Latvijas Universitātes Filozofijas un socioloģijas institūts.

Žabko, O. 2015. "Darbiekārtošanās pakalpojumu sniedzēji kā aģenti migrācijai uz Norvēģiju." Latvijas Universitātes raksti/Acta Universitatas Latviensis, Vol. 808, Socioloģija/Sociology: 18–31.

# Enabling, structuring and creating elite transnational lifestyles: intermediaries of the super-rich and the elite mobilities industry

Sin Yee Koh ⓘ and Bart Wissink ⓘ

**ABSTRACT**
This article considers how the migration industries lens can be usefully employed in understanding how professional intermediaries enable, structure, and create transnational migration lifestyles of the super-rich. In particular, we examine how intermediaries and their services (1) enable the continued sustenance of transnational migration lifestyles for this group of elites; and (2) structure and create elite transnational lifestyles. This article primarily draws on interviews with professional intermediaries who service the super-rich, and content analysis of their websites and brochures. Inspired by insights from the new mobilities paradigm (and in particular the politics of mobility), we argue for an expanded conceptualisation of the migration industries beyond the literature's current focus on labour recruitment and migration management. Specifically, we suggest thinking of the migration industries as a collection of actors and services that enable, structure, and create different types of 'migrants', their spaces and their highly uneven transnational mobilities – including that of the super-rich and their elite transnational lifestyles. We conclude with suggestions for a research agenda that may help to better understand the role of intermediaries in the creation of differentiated mobilities.

## 1. Introduction

The existing literature on migration industries[1] and the closely related literature on migration infrastructure (Xiang and Lindquist 2014) have thus far focused on certain types of migrants (e.g. expatriates, refugees and irregular migrants, domestic workers, marriage migrants, student migrants) and their brokers (Collins 2012; Gammeltoft-Hansen and Sørensen 2013; Lindquist 2010; Lindquist, Xiang, and Yeoh 2012; Xiang 2012). As also discussed in the introduction to the special issue, this literature has highlighted the role of the migration industries in structuring migration by facilitating, governing, and controlling migration flows in specific migration corridors (e.g. Hernández-León's 2008 study of urban Mexican migration from Monterrey to Houston). Indeed, Sørensen and Gammeltoft-Hansen (2013, 2) note that the increasing commercialisation of international migration has opened up opportunities for migration industries to capitalise on the desires of migrants to move, as well as on the struggles by governments to manage migration flows.

With its focus on intermediaries and their relationship to migrants, this literature has contributed towards a nuanced understanding that the migration industries are made up not only of official actors such as state agencies and professional brokers, but also of informal actors such as members of the social networks of migrants (Fernandez 2013; Lindquist 2010; Lindquist, Xiang, and Yeoh 2012; Rahman and Kabir 2012). These 'systematically interlinked technologies, institutions, and actors … facilitate and condition mobility' (Xiang and Lindquist 2014, S124).

However, the existing literature has mostly focused on traditional forms of relatively permanent labour migration. Consequently, more flexible forms of mobility are often excluded from these debates (see Collins 2012, for an exception). As a result, there is a missed potential in investigating how the migration industries engage with 'lifestyle mobilities' (Cohen, Duncan, and Thulemark 2013) and migration as a privileged way of living transnationally.[2] A further related issue is how the migration industries actively structure and create transnational migration desires (Cranston 2016). These observations are especially relevant for the super-rich (i.e. economic elites and high net worth individuals)[3] and their 'elite mobilities' (Birtchnell and Caletrío 2014).

Following these observations, in this article we argue that the migration industries lens can be usefully employed in understanding how professional intermediaries enable, structure, and create transnational migration lifestyles of the super-rich. In particular, we address the following research question: What are the roles of intermediaries in enabling, structuring, and creating elite transnational lifestyles of the super-rich? We draw upon material from a larger comparative project on the super-rich and their transnational real estate investments in Hong Kong and London, specifically interviews with professional intermediaries who service the super-rich (e.g. concierge services, private travel, real estate, wealth management), and from content analysis of their marketing collaterals. By focusing on the super-rich and their mobilities industry (see also Cranston, this issue), we enhance our understanding of migration and mobility-related services, therefore contributing to a more differentiated picture of how segments of the migration industries work.

It is productive to bring together the literatures on the migration industries and the super-rich for a number of reasons. Firstly, this enables an expanded conceptualisation of the migration industries beyond the literature's current focus on services which cater to certain types of migrants and on narrowly defined stages of the migration process. This allows us to interrogate services catering to alternative 'migrants' that would otherwise remain invisible. Secondly, this also accords a more critical and nuanced perspective in understanding what migration truly means in this 'age of migration' (Castles, de Haas, and Miller 2014). Migration, after all, is no longer *only* about permanent movements from one place to another. It is increasingly about being 'permanently on the move and … liv[ing] in transit' (Featherstone 2014, 25). This article thus offers an analysis of the super-rich as a case of *elite* transnational lifestyles.

## 2. The migration industries and migration infrastructure literature

Many scholars credit Salt and Stein's (1997) article on 'migration as business' for the introduction of the migration industry concept (e.g. Spener 2009).[4] In the years that followed, others started writing about similar and related concepts, such as migration networks (Hernández-León 2005), 'fixers and brokers' (Cohen 2008, 163), and 'agents of transnationalism' (Sauer 2012). This migration industry literature has a common focus on actors providing a range of legal and illegal services that encourage and facilitate migration. Typical services include labour recruitment and brokerage, transportation and travel, trafficking, communication, remittances, legal and tax advice, banking, interpretation, and housing (e.g. Hernández-León 2005; Salt and Stein 1997). Scholars have also noted that migration industries develop out of migration networks and that intermediary agents 'have an interest in the continuation of migration' (Castles 2004, 859). Indeed, Hernández-León (2008, 24) notes that migration industry actors are involved in

> stimulating, initiating, facilitating, and sustaining human mobility, opening and institutionalizing new destinations for migration, mediating newcomers' incorporation into host societies, and, in the current regime of heightened restrictions to international migration, bypassing border controls and internal inspections aimed at detecting clandestine entrants and residents.

Recently, contributions to the edited volume *Migration Industry and the Commercialisation of International Migration* (Gammeltoft-Hansen and Sørensen 2013) focus especially on the rapidly expanding range of commercial migration management services, including border security control, detention centres, and human trafficking. In such a conceptualisation, the migration industry has come to be understood as a collection of intermediaries linking migrants to sending and receiving states. In the context of state policies, the migration industries are predominantly understood as services focusing on the border-crossing concerns of both migrants and states.

However, in response to this shift in the migration industries literature towards technologies of border control, Xiang and Lindquist (2014, S142) argue that the concept of migration industry is too narrowly focused on migration as a form of business, and thus misses out on the opportunity to examine migration as a 'multi-faceted space of mediation' where certain migration related systems and technologies come into existence. They suggest thinking of the migration infrastructure as encompassing five dimensions: 'the commercial (recruitment intermediaries), the regulatory (state apparatus and procedures for documentation, licensing, training, and other purposes), the technological (communication and transport), the humanitarian (NGOs and international organisations), and the social (migrant networks)' (S124). The migration infrastructure thus consists of agents with different functions, motivations, and 'logics of operation' (S124, original italics).

What is clear from this brief overview is that scholars have understood the migration industries and migration infrastructure as a broad array of actors 'greasing' (Harney 1977) the migration process. While the migration industries literature has placed particular emphasis on actors and services that move and settle (labour) migrants,[5] the migration infrastructure literature has focused much more on a collection of actors and technologies that mediate and produce migration mobilities (see Lin, Lindquist, Xiang, and Yeoh 2017). In this article, we attempt to refine and expand the migration industries conceptually by borrowing from the material insights that the migration infrastructure literature highlights.

Above all, we would like to highlight Spener's (2009, 33) suggestion to use the term 'migration industry' as a figure of speech, and to include services offered by a range of actors who operate on a 'social logic of mutual interest' (e.g. in-kind services offered by members of migrants' personal social networks) that facilitate, and more importantly, *sustain* the transnational mobilities of migrants. This expands the conceptual boundaries of the migration industries to include 'second tier' services that support migrants' 'quality of life abroad' (Light 2013, 272). In the context of this article, this means including services related to the maintenance of transnational migration lifestyles, in addition to the more conventional services of labour recruitment, cross-border transportation, and migrant integration.

## 3. The super-rich and the elite mobilities industry

Until recently, the social sciences paid little attention to the rich and super-rich, as they were not perceived as a problem (Koh, Wissink, and Forrest 2016). With the recent attention for the problematic nature of growing inequalities this has changed (e.g. Forrest, Koh, and Wissink 2017a; Hay 2013; Hay and Beaverstock 2016). Research on the super-rich adds an interesting dimension to the migration industries literature. In the former literature, the super-rich are generally depicted as powerful agents determining their own worlds (e.g. Lundberg 1968). However, this misrecognises the crucial roles played by intermediaries to produce super-rich mobilities, as they create greater opportunities and capabilities for the super-rich to fulfil transnational lifestyles compared to other groups. Therefore, we have argued for a structural analysis of the super-rich and related inequalities (Koh, Wissink, and Forrest 2016; Wissink, Koh, and Forrest 2017). Such attention can build on the migration industries literature, as well as on research into the role of intermediaries in structuring super-rich agency (Merrifield 2013; Davies 2014; Forrest, Koh, and Wissink 2017c; Forrest and Wissink 2016). In line with this suggestion, we aim to focus attention on services that help to enable, structure, and create elite transnational lifestyles, in addition to the more conventional services of labour recruitment, cross-border mobilities, and migrant integration.

Attention to the super-rich can also help to develop the purview of the migrant industries literature. For some super-rich – especially from countries like Russia and China – travel results in a permanent departure from the home country (Short 2015). Many others, however, are more constantly on the move between their main residence and multiple other destinations, resulting in transnationality as a permanent way of life. This world of flux contrasts sharply with dominant perspectives in the social sciences that for long focused on durability and stasis (Cresswell and Merriman 2010; Sheller and Urry 2006; Urry 2007). Recently, the emergence of transit as a more permanent character of social life has resulted in growing attention within the social sciences for the daily movement of people, goods, and ideas, resulting in a plethora of publications on *mobilities*. As Sheller and Urry (2006, 210) put it,

> the new paradigm attempts to account for not only the quickening of liquidity within some realms but also the concomitant patterns of concentration that create zones of connectivity, centrality, and empowerment in some cases, and of disconnection, social exclusion, and inaudibility in other cases.

The new mobilities paradigm has by now produced a considerable literature, including work on the uneven mobilities of the poor (e.g. Jaffe, Klaufus, and Colombijn 2012), middle-class and upper middle-class groups (e.g. Brooks and Waters 2013; Nowicka 2012; Smith and Favell 2006) and the super-rich (e.g. Birtchnell and Caletrío 2014; Elliott and Urry 2010). This politics of mobility literature suggests that the opportunities and capabilities to fulfil mobility and activity needs are increasingly unequal, resulting in 'mobility related social exclusion' (Church, Frost, and Sullivan 2000; Cresswell 2010; Ernste, Martens, and Schapendonk 2012; Lucas 2012; Preston and Rajé 2007). Furthermore, while there are different types of elites with different mobilities (Forrest, Koh, and Wissink 2017b), at least a part of the super-rich are perceived as very mobile (Birtchnell and Caletrío 2014; Elliott and Urry 2010). A recent report by the Economic Intelligence Unit and RBC Wealth Management (2012), for instance, describes a segment of the super-rich as 'internationally mobile wealthy individuals (IMWIs)'. In contrast, the mobility opportunities for other groups can be much more restricted. Mobility thus has a highly exclusionary *and* exclusive character. Exclusion and exclusiveness are, as we illustrate later, actively produced.

Super-rich mobilities and transnational lifestyles are distinctively elite in nature. Consequently, the corresponding intermediary services also cater towards this elite character. In addition to the personalised and specialised natures of these services, the assurance of hassle-free convenience, privacy, confidentiality, gatekeeping, safety, and security sets the intermediaries of the super-rich apart as an elite service industry. As Paris (2013, 106–107) puts it, '[t]he super-rich occupy and move through spaces that are inaccessible to the vast majority of global inhabitants, both due to the sheer cost of property and also the widespread privatization and securitization of space'.

However, how does the elite service industry link up to the maintenance of transnational lifestyles? Transnational migration is understood as cross-border mobilities that 'tak[e] place within fluid social spaces that are constantly reworked through migrants' simultaneous embeddedness in more than one [national] society' (Levitt and Jaworsky 2007, 131). While the super-rich clients of the elite service industry may not necessarily fit the classical understanding of the *migrant* (i.e. someone who has crossed an international border on a more-or-less permanent basis), they are living transnational lives and are simultaneously embedded in multiple geographies (Elliott and Urry 2010). Thus, the transnational lifestyles of the super-rich challenge existing understandings of transnationalism in two ways: first, their mobile lives go beyond the existing dual framework of immigration–emigration in either receiving or origin countries; and second, their multi-locational mobile lives challenge the existing transnational framework that understands life as operating mainly in two places.[6] Building on the migration industries literature, we argue that intermediaries of the super-rich constitute an elite mobilities industry that enable, structure, and create these highly uneven, multi-locational elite lifestyles.

## 4. Researching the elite mobilities industry

As Hannam, Sheller, and Urry (2006, 3) rightly point out, we cannot examine mobilities without also paying attention to 'the necessary spatial, infrastructural and institutional moorings that configure and enable mobilities'. Likewise, we cannot examine transnational migration lifestyles and mobile lives (Elliott and Urry 2010) without paying attention to the migration industries and the migration infrastructures that enable, structure, and create how transnational lives are actually lived out.

This article interrogates the linkages between the migration industries and super-rich transnational lifestyles, by drawing on a larger exploratory project on the super-rich and their transnational real estate investments in Hong Kong and London (Atkinson et al. 2017; Wissink, Koh, and Forrest 2017). Work on the Hong Kong part of the project took place between February 2014 and May 2015. As it proved difficult to gain access to super-rich individuals themselves, we mainly focused on intermediaries who service super-rich clients. In total, we interviewed one super-rich couple in finance and 23 intermediaries in concierge service, private travel, real estate investment, wealth management, legal and tax advice, art investment, and health insurance. The majority of our intermediaries-respondents (16 out of 23) are Asians from Hong Kong, China, and Singapore. The remaining seven are Anglo-Westerners from the U.S.A. and Europe. It is important to point out that the majority of our intermediaries-respondents are themselves globally mobile (with various Asian and Anglo-Western experiences), and have a 'global outlook' (Hay and Muller 2012, 179) – an essential characteristic for understanding and meeting their super-rich clients' expectations.

The empirical discussion below results from our analysis of these semi-structured interviews, as well as a content analysis of their marketing collaterals. We developed an interview guide, customised to each respondent, which covered the intermediary's (1) career history and company; (2) insights on recent trends; and (3) thoughts on statements about the super-rich. Most interviews were conducted face-to-face in the intermediary's office or in a café, with the exception of a couple of Skype and telephone interviews. On average, the interviews lasted for about an hour. We voice recorded the interviews with consent from our respondents. The recordings were then transcribed and analysed alongside our interview notes and any informative e-mail correspondences with the intermediaries before and after the interviews. The transcripts were supplemented with marketing materials from the intermediary's company website, brochures, and e-mail newsletters.

## 5. The workings of an elite migration industry

Unexpectedly stumbling into the expansive world of intermediary services for the super-rich, we soon came to realise the significance of this elite mobilities industry. Intermediaries may operate as individuals or as representatives of a company (or companies) and can be broadly categorised into five areas: *lifestyle services* (e.g. concierge services, luxury items, elite clubs, fine dining, catering and events planning, wedding planning, personal trainers, fine art, and health services); *homes and fixed assets services* (e.g. real estate management, architecture and interior design, insurance products, butlers, domestic helpers, and personal chefs); *private travel services* (e.g. chauffeurs and private cars, private jets, and private yachts); *investments and legal services* (e.g. wealth management, financial advice, legal advice, tax advice, and immigration advice; see Beaverstock 2012; Beaverstock, Hall, and Wainwright 2011, 2013); and *family and relationship services* (e.g. matchmakers, nannies, tutors, education and schooling consultants, and family offices;[7] see also Cranston 2016).

While some of the services offered to the super-rich are available in the mass market, we argue that the (financially and socially) exclusive nature and carefully guarded accessibility distinguish this as an elite mobilities industry. For example, travel planners, domestic helpers, lawyers, and financial advisors are readily available to middle-income clients. However, only the super-rich need, and can afford, intermediaries who offer unique and bespoke solutions. Think, for instance, of a luxury concierge that can organise a surprise party for a 100 handpicked guests[8] in a city across the globe at a moment's notice; a butler who knows the protocols and social etiquette such as 'manage a wine cave, book a limousine service and handle art works with care' (Balenieri 2012); a yacht captain who coordinates the necessary immigration and mooring paperwork and the logistics of sailing across international seas; or a dedicated family office that handles all wealth management issues of the household, including marriage, divorce, inheritance, mergers, and acquisitions.

In his conceptualisation of social transnationalism as 'lifeworlds of individuals' beyond nation-states, Mau (2010, 28) highlights that 'the increase of options and autonomy … means that social relationships and mobility depend more on personal preferences and lifestyles than on pre-given social conditions'. Indeed, in our conversations with intermediaries of the super-rich, the picture emerged that super-rich clients are living truly transnational lifestyles. These transnational lifestyles are in turn lived out in accordance to personal preferences and desires. Clients may have multiple homes and businesses spread across the world that require constant travel. They may prefer to spend time in different places during different seasons of the year. They are also likely to have lived in different locations previously, met elite 'transnationalites' like themselves, and therefore accumulated social networks that spread across the world. This transnational lifestyle is eloquently captured by our super-rich respondent (Anglo-Western, female, husband works in finance):

> People have lived and moved, especially in the finance world. In finance and law, you are living this strange rock star life, where you are travelling so much. … It's like this strange life, but it means that your worlds are very scattered at the end of the day. … The people that you've met will be all over the place. And so you own properties in different places so that you can continue to feel connected to the places that mean something to you and people that you are close to.

What, then, are the roles of intermediaries in relation to the transnational lifestyles of the super-rich? Although there is great diversity and range in the types of intermediary services for the super-rich, we find that intermediaries ultimately perform the paradoxical functions of enabling, structuring, and creating super-rich transnational lifestyles. On the one hand, the intermediaries are first and foremost service providers who *enable* the elite transnational migration lifestyles of their super-rich clients. On the other hand, by actively (re)creating services and products, intermediaries directly and indirectly *structure* and *create* the transnational migration lifestyles and aspirations of elites and non-elites as well. We elaborate on these functions below.

### 5.1. Enabling super-rich transnational lifestyles

As we alluded to above, super-rich transnational lifestyles come with assets and social relations scattered across multiple national borders; and consequently, the need for frequent international travel. It is here that intermediaries come into the picture: they enable the smooth functioning of super-rich transnational lifestyles by taking care of things on behalf of the physically absent super-rich, or by facilitating their super-rich clients' transnational mobilities.

One obvious intermediary service relates to the acquisition and management of real estate properties, including main residences, holiday homes and investment properties. Our interviews illustrate that some super-rich are highly involved personally in the acquisition of these properties – especially the ones for private use. However, others prefer to work through real estate companies. One such company targeting super-rich clients brands itself as being 'responsible for … the masterful care of clients purchasing property … internationally'. The firm offers a range of end-to-end services, including search and acquisition ('an efficient, cost effective and highly beneficial process to secure a residential property in the fast moving and daunting … property market'); investment and specialist advisory ('a strong network of professional relationships across the legal, surveying, accounting, and banking markets'); and home management (including mundane tasks like errand running and dry cleaning). Oftentimes, it is the maintenance of vacant homes that requires most work. As one real estate intermediary (Anglo-Western, female) explains:

> There's a lot of care that goes on after [the property is purchased]. It's a lot of manpower. … You've got to have people running around dropping keys off, … fixing the boiler. You know, all that type of stuff. … It's just very labour intensive.

This rather invisible intermediary service labour makes it possible for the super-rich to arrive to a comfortable, well-kept, and fully functioning home after an absence of weeks, months, or years. While existing research has highlighted feminised work as a form of invisible labour (e.g. Kim 2016; Teo 2016), we argue for a more expansive view of invisible labour that includes intermediaries facilitating and maintaining elite transnational lifestyles. This, we believe, will contribute towards a more nuanced understanding of the workings *and* expansive reach of the migration industries.

Private travel is another intermediary service enabling super-rich transnational lifestyles. An intermediary in the private jet industry (Asian, female) observes that 'wealthy people have a fixation on the ability to fly' because private aviation offers the ability to fly 'quickly and conveniently' to cities that are not on direct commercial routes. Private jets thus help to schedule time efficiently. As she explains:

> For example they go to Jeju [Island in South Korea] for a meeting at 7 o'clock in the morning, and then off to Taipei at 10 o'clock in the morning, and then off to Hong Kong at 2 o'clock in the afternoon. These are things that cannot be done if you are in a commercial airliner. You basically plan out your day accordingly if you have your own jet.

Private jets also offer the super-rich the flexibility 'to essentially go as [they] please', subject to authority permissions for departures, flight routes, and landings. Private jets are also expensive 'toys' that require specialised maintenance, certification, repairs, and storage in hangars – some with 'heated floor panels [and] air conditioned if it's hot'. This means that the ability of the super-rich to fly as they wish relies heavily on private jet services. Due to the high costs of owning, operating and maintaining private jets, these specialised intermediary services are only available to the top tier super-rich.

The frequency of transnational travels can reach such an extent that according to one intermediary (Anglo-Western, male, wealth management), some super-rich clients have 'exactly the same closets and the same clothes' in each of their homes across the globe.[9] This has been deliberately organised to minimise the hassle of physical travel ('you don't have to have a lot of suitcases'), so that they can arrive and immediately continue with their day – as if they have just walked into the walk-in closet from their bedroom, instead of having flown 5000 kilometres across the world. Another intermediary (Asian, female) runs an online business, offering a luxury wardrobe rental service that delivers customer outfits directly to homes or hotel rooms and collects them afterwards. According to this intermediary, the service is about 'solving other people's problems' – or more specifically, minimising the wardrobe hassles of transnational frequent travellers. As she explains:

> Say for example I go to Beijing and then I go to Indonesia. I don't have to prepare two sets of clothing. Beijing is extremely cold and Indonesia is extremely hot. Just preparing for my luggage is going to be a nightmare. So there are people [who] travel a lot ... and have events to go to. To pack something, even if you iron it perfectly when you were in New York, by the time you got to Hong Kong, it's going to be all wrinkly. And some of the stuff is hard to carry anyway if you want to look good in a city.

Super-rich transnational mobilities thus rely on a range of intermediaries. As the private jet services clearly illustrate, such '[m]obility is a resource that is differentially accessed' (Cresswell 2010, 21), even by the super-rich. The increasing ease of elite mobilities thus highlights a more fundamental question about the production of differentiated mobilities and the invisible labour that enables and sustains these uneven mobilities.

### 5.2. Structuring super-rich transnational lifestyles

As we listened to the stories of these intermediaries of the super-rich, we noticed that the expression 'educating them' comes up repeatedly. This is especially the case when intermediaries refer to 'new money' from Mainland China, which is obviously also attributed by the fact that we conducted this research in Hong Kong. One concierge service intermediary (Anglo-Western, female), for example, explains:

> They have a lot of new money in Mainland China ... and they don't necessarily know how to spend their money. So they look to us to basically advise them on lifestyle coordination, mainly looking at the global market. You know, international experiences, international investments.

For this reason, concierge service intermediaries who want to 'wow' their existing clientele partner with private bankers and with companies that have loyalty programmes (e.g. hotels and exclusive clubs). On the one hand, this helps private bankers and companies to 'strengthen the [client] relationship [by providing] a different element of service'. On the other hand, this enables the concierge service intermediary to grow its clientele and services once clients are 'hook[ed] in'. In addition to satisfying the desire of clients for 'the "talkability" factor and ... the unique experience factor', the firm also pushes content such as 'thought leadership' and 'advice on foundations, investment, [and] opportunities'. In these ways, the firm 'educates' its clients about the latest elite lifestyle trends. Over the past five years, this particular concierge service firm has seen an increase in the proportion of local, non-expatriate clients in Hong Kong and Mainland China. Our respondent thinks that this results from a cumulative education and socialisation process through which clients attain 'familiarity [with] what's being offered'.

We heard similar narratives of 'educating clients' when talking to fine art investment advisors. According to one intermediary (Anglo-Western, male) who works with super-rich clients based in Hong Kong and Mainland China, investing in contemporary art is a relatively new socio-cultural practice in this region. As such, the prime task of an art intermediary is to build and nurture a long-term relationship to 'educate' and expose the novice super-rich art collector to the do's and don'ts of fine art investment. In fact, this intermediary, representing a gallery based in the U.K., moved from a city in China to Hong Kong to be 'closer to [his] clients' as part of 'client development', which entails 'keep[ing] in touch with them … know[ing] what they are doing [and] what they are interested in'. He explains the difficulties of marketing 'a Western product' in 'a new market in a new area', where 'you can't be seen just to be exporting something'. Thus, the long process of relationship building entails many informal meetings, emails and phone chats, private viewings, accompanied visits to international art events and studios, as well as attending invitation-only social events before and after these events. Exhibitions and shows 'become a vehicle … to engage in conversations with people that [you are] cultivating'. Another art intermediary (Asian, male, representing an international blue-chip gallery) concurs:

> People just need to be repeatedly exposed to a certain kind of art, and then they begin to click. Once they click, then they can compare. … Once you are being exposed enough you can tell: 'Oh, this is something new, something fresh'. … It's the hardest thing to get the person to buy the first piece. They [i.e. super-rich clients who are novice art investors] really need to be initiated.

Interestingly, while performing the role of the *educator*, the art intermediary is also performing the role of the *gatekeeper* by controlling who gets to buy a specific piece of art, as these intermediaries may also be working with galleries that represent certain artists. In such cases, the sale of an art piece entails finding the right owner who will not jeopardise the career of the artist. Thus, the art intermediary needs to be assured that the super-rich collector is 'serious about building his collection', and not focused on making a quick profit by 'flipping' the artwork.

Art intermediaries thus actively structure super-rich transnational lifestyles by steering them towards certain artworks and artists. This not only protects the reputation and marketability of the artists; it also supports the sustainability of the fine art market, which our first art intermediary describes as 'a very sensitive and quite fragile market that functions on certain kinds of understandings', and a 'subtle kind of mechanism [that differs from] a simple supply and demand' market. As he puts it,

> If you've got very limited access to something very high in demand, you prioritise your good buyers, right? You don't just give it to anybody. You've got a waiting list. … It's actually a very, very subtle ecosystem that is dependent on all sorts of things falling into place.

This echoes Van den Broek, Harvey, and Groutsis (2016, 527) observation of the interventionist role of commercial labour migration intermediaries who 'explicitly channel migrants into certain occupations and areas of the labour market' – except that in this case, it is not jobs but lifestyle products associated to the social status and disposition of mobile elites (see also Cranston this issue).

Returning to the concierge service firm with which we started this section, our inter-mediary (Anglo-Western, female) informs us that the firm has a tiered membership system. Membership in the top tier, which could come with attendance at 'very high profile events such as … dining with the royal family at Buckingham Palace', is by invita-tion only. According to this intermediary:

> [The top tier members] have to be vetted by the founders. They have to meet the founders, and it is usually the founders who will recommend this person to join in. Because the access is so high profile, you want to make sure that this is the right profile of the person as well. … A lot of research goes into who [to] select to be part of that top tier. … [We conduct] trend fore-casting, demographic insight into which clients to choose.

Like the art intermediaries, this luxury concierge service firm is also actively structuring super-rich transnational lifestyles by determining who gets to be among the elite of an already exclusive club. By doing so, these intermediaries directly and indirectly influence and shape the uneven transnational mobilities and lifestyles of different groups of super-rich. This presents an interesting twist to Bourdieu's (1977, 1990) conceptualisation of habitus – instead of the reproduction of habitus and taste through familial and educational socialisation, it is the elite mobilities industry that transmits ideas of elite distinction *and* mediates the entry of individuals into layered elite sections.

### 5.3. Creating super-rich transnational lifestyles

Intermediaries do not only meet the needs and demands of the super-rich, they also actively create new products, services, and markets (see also Cranston this issue). An intermediary in healthcare insurance (Asian, male) informed us that his firm currently offers a concierge service which includes facilitating medical appointments, and accompanying patients for medical care in prime international locations where patients may need language interpreters. However, he thinks that there will increasingly be 'different tailor-made pro-ducts' where clients 'can pick and choose' the services they require and desire. As he puts it, 'healthcare … will become more specialised, targeting these really rich people'. In fact, his firm is introducing a new, 'really high end' service where clients can enjoy direct priority access to the best medical experts globally. With this service, clients will be able to jump the queue in accessing first and second opinions, and fast-track referrals to prime hospitals and clinics anywhere in the world.

Interestingly, the conceptualisation of this new healthcare service came about as the firm was attempting to break into the Mainland Chinese market for healthcare insurance. Similarly, an intermediary in the private jet industry (Asian, male) told us about efforts to expand on the relatively restricted Chinese private aviation market. In China, only about 30% of the airspace is open for commercial and private jets, compared to about 80% in the U.S.A., as a result of the Chinese national air force and safety regulations. China's private aviation market is further curtailed by the small number of airports where business jets can land and hangar. This intermediary explained that the private jet industry players in China are actively negotiating with relevant authorities and decision-makers to ease restrictions and limitations and unlock the industry's market potential. Intermediaries from other industries – like the private yachting industry – admitted to similar lobby activities.

These examples illustrate our preliminary observations that intermediaries are actively creating super-rich transnational lifestyles by opening up new markets and expanding existing markets. Success in creating new products and markets will likely produce new super-rich clients, while existing clients may find that they too, would like to enjoy and incorporate the new service into their transnational lifestyles. For example, if super-rich clients can enjoy prioritised medical care, then higher middle-class clients might aspire to higher levels of medical privilege as well. In these ways, intermediaries are creating *new* needs and aspirations that the super-rich (and others) may not require or desire in the first place. Intermediaries thus *create* elite transnational lifestyles and mobilities through a rapidly expanding elite 'mobilities market' (Ono 2015, 611).

## 6. Discussion and conclusion

Xiang and Lindquist (2014, S125) claim that

> [t]he development of migration infrastructure has turned migration into an object of inten-
> sive regulation, commodification and intervention, but has not necessarily enhanced people's
> migratory capability in terms of making independent decisions, exploring new paths, and
> cultivating transnational social relations.

This focus on migratory capability is in line with the politics of mobility perspective, which stresses the unevenness of mobilities between groups. This is supported by Skeggs (2004, 49) who argues that '[m]obility is a resource to which not everyone has an equal relation-ship', while Gössling and Nilsson (2010, 250) note that '[a]ir travel and highly mobile lifestyles [are] only for a small share of humanity'. In this paper, we have extended the migration industries lens to one segment of society that seems to be very capable of fulfilling its mobility and activity needs: the super-rich. We concluded that professional intermediaries actively enable, structure, and create elite transnational lifestyles. They thus help a larger share of – still elite – segments of society to enjoy transnational lifestyles. But our research also suggests that within this elite group, mobility is highly uneven as well.

We argue that intermediaries of the super-rich can be conceptualised as an elite *mobilities* industry, rather than a migration industry per se. Garapich (2008, 738) has suggested think-ing of the migration industry as 'a sector of service markets that uses human mobility, adap-tation in the host country and the sustenance of a transnational social field as its main resource'. Indeed, the concept of mobilities, which encompasses the act of moving and the sustenance of transnational mobile lives, more accurately captures the nature of services provided by intermediaries of the super-rich as well as the transnational lifestyles enjoyed by these super-rich. More importantly, we wish to highlight that the seemingly frictionless transnational mobilities of the super-rich actually depend on an invisible labour force of intermediaries that support a higher level of mobility for the super-rich than for other groups; and – as our analysis suggests – for some super-rich more than for others. Without the specialised knowledge, skills, technologies, and networks of these intermedi-aries, these elite transnational mobilities would not be possible.[10] Intermediaries thus play a crucial role in enabling, structuring, and creating the highly unequal opportunities and capabilities of groups to fulfil mobility and activity needs that the politics of mobilities literature draws attention to. Crucially, in contrast to the image of unskilled, undocumented, and precarious workers with which the term 'invisible' is often associated, this invisible labour force consists of skilled and affluent experts spread across the world.[11]

Building on these conclusions, we suggest four future research directions. A first direction is to investigate and identify other actors, complicit in enabling, structuring, and creating elite transnational lifestyles; for instance within the state apparatus and elite social networks. One possible starting point is to look at elite school networks, and to see how these evolve into 'migrant' networks (and thus a specific 'mobilities industry') later on. Studies on elite business schools (Hall 2011) have noted the importance of alumni networks in the transfer of social capital into graduate careers. Using the 'education-institutions-practice nexus' as a conceptual frame, Faulconbridge and Hall (2014) highlight the relationships between postgraduate education and the financial industry in the city of London. There is obviously a close link between educational institutions and the production of professional intermediaries in certain industries. A fuller examination of such links could shed light on the production of specific 'mobilities industries' through schools and alumni networks.

A second direction examines how professional intermediaries work internationally. Research could, for example, map out the networks and flows of professional intermediary services that operate beyond nation-state boundaries. Beaverstock (2012) has examined the global spread of private banking and wealth management services. Future research could build on this by following the operations of specific services, with a particular focus on transnational flows. Another possibility is to follow the careers and transnational mobilities of individual professionals within the same multinational company. This includes focusing on different forms of mobilities – including that of the brokers and intermediaries themselves – in order to understand the 'linkages' (McCollum and Findlay, this issue) that make up the migration industry.

A third direction would further explore the uneven mobilities of different groups of super-rich. Beaverstock and Faulconbridge (2014) suggest that wealth segmentation between the high net worth, very high net worth, and ultra high net worth correlates to different tiers of mobilities. Further research into super-rich mobilities and the related role of intermediaries could shed a light on such differentiations.

Finally, a fourth direction is to examine the geographies of professional intermediaries in relation to their markets and clients. Do professional intermediary services and their clients, for example, differ in Europe, U.S.A., and Asia? In their examination of the private wealth management industry in the U.K., Beaverstock, Hall, and Wainwright (2011) point out that the industry is segmented geographically as well as functionally. Future research could examine other industries and services (e.g. real estate investment and management) that constitute the mobilities industries of the super-rich.

Almost two decades ago, Tseng (1997, 277) observed that '[t]he involvement of brokers in facilitating the migration of the upper and upper middle class is rarely discussed'. In this article, we have sought to address this lacuna by bringing together recent debates in the literatures of the migration industries and the super-rich. In the context of rapidly rising inequalities and the corresponding expansion in pressures and opportunities that motivate mobilities, our article confirms that it is high time to cast a critical eye on these expanding intermediary services that enable, structure, and create different types of 'migrants', their spaces, and their highly uneven transnational mobilities.

## Notes

1. We use 'industries' in the plural as there is a diverse range of services for different kinds of migration mobilities.
2. This also implies an expanded understanding of 'migration', and may include an investigation of how the migration industry relates to return migration. This, however, is beyond the scope of this article.
3. High net worth individuals (HNWI) is a term used by the wealth management industry to designate clients whose investible assets exceed a given amount. These super-rich clients are typically categorised according to their net worth. For example, Capgemini and RBC Wealth Management (2013) use a three-tier category: 'millionaire next door' (US$1–US$5 million); 'mid-tier millionaire' (US$5–US$30 million); and 'ultra high net worth individual' (UHNWI) (more than US$30 million).
4. But see Sørensen and Gammeltoft-Hansen (2013, 5) who claim that the concept can be traced back to Harney's (1977) analysis of the 'commerce of migration'.
5. Especially focusing on the pre-departure stage of recruitment and transportation, and the settling-in stage when migrants seek assistance to maintain their lives and social relations in both origin and destination countries.
6. We thank the anonymous reviewer for highlighting this point.
7. Private family business institutions set up to manage a single, or multiple families' financial affairs (Maude 2006). Some family offices also manage clients' non-financial affairs (see Glucksberg 2014).
8. As an intermediary explains, the super-rich clients 'want to be at events where people are of the same calibre'.
9. This raises the question of home-making and local embeddedness for mobile elites (Andreotti, Le Gales, and Moreno-Fuentes 2015). However, this is beyond the scope of this article.
10. We thank the editors of this special issue for highlighting this.
11. This invisibility is also in part due to the high level of confidentiality surrounding their clients' business and private lives.

## Disclosure statement

No potential conflict of interest was reported by the authors.

## Funding

The work described in this article was supported by a grant from the ESRC/RGC Joint Research Scheme sponsored by the Research Grants Council of Hong Kong and the Economic and Social Research Council (Project reference no. ES/K010263/1).

## ORCID

*Sin Yee Koh* ⓘ http://orcid.org/0000-0001-9350-1119
*Bart Wissink* ⓘ http://orcid.org/0000-0001-7307-8528

## References

Andreotti, Alberta, Patrick Le Gales, and Francisco Javier Moreno-Fuentes. 2015. *Globalised Minds, Roots in the City: Urban Upper-Middle Classes in Europe*. Chichester: John Wiley & Sons.
Atkinson, Rowland, Roger Burrows, Luna Glucksberg, Hang Kei-Ho, Caroline Knowles, and David Rhodes. 2017. "Minimum City? The Deeper Impacts of the 'Super-rich' on Urban Life." In *Cities*

*and the Super-rich: Real Estate, Elite Practices, and Urban Political Economy*, edited by Ray Forrest, Sin Yee Koh, and Bart Wissink, 253–271. New York: Palgrave Macmillan.

Balenieri, Raphael. 2012. "Serve the (Rich) People: China's Butler Boom." *Aljazeera*, December 14. http://www.aljazeera.com/indepth/features/2012/12/2012121011245575630.html.

Beaverstock, Jonathan V. 2012. "The Privileged World City: Private Banking, Wealth Management and the Bespoke Servicing of the Global Super Rich." In *International Handbook of Globalization and World Cities*, edited by Ben Derudder, Michael Hoyler, Peter J. Taylor, and Frank Witlox, 378–389. Cheltenham: Edward Elgar.

Beaverstock, Jonathan V., and James R. Faulconbridge. 2014. "Wealth Segmentation and the Mobilities of the Super-rich: A Conceptual Framework." In *Elite Mobilities*, edited by Thomas Birtchnell and Javier Caletrío, 40–61. Abingdon: Routledge.

Beaverstock, Jonathan V., Sarah Hall, and Thomas Wainwright. 2011. "Servicing the Super-rich: New Financial Elites and the Rise of the Private Wealth Management Retail Ecology." *Regional Studies* 47 (6): 834–849. doi:10.1080/00343404.2011.587795.

Beaverstock, Jonathan V., Sarah Hall, and Thomas Wainwright. 2013. "Overseeing the Fortunes of the Global Super-rich: The Nature of Private Wealth Management in London's Financial District." In *Geographies of the Super-rich*, edited by Iain Hay, 43–60. Cheltenham: Edward Elgar.

Birtchnell, Thomas, and Javier Caletrío, eds. 2014. *Elite Mobilities*. Abingdon: Routledge.

Bourdieu, Pierre. 1977. *Outline of a Theory of Practice*. Cambridge: Cambridge University Press.

Bourdieu, Pierre. 1990. *The Logic of Practice*. Cambridge: Polity.

Brooks, Rachel, and Johanna Waters. 2013. *Student Mobilities, Migration and the Internationalisation of Higher Education*. Basingstoke: Palgrave Macmillan.

Capgemini, and RBC Wealth Management. 2013. "World Wealth Report 2013." http://www.capgemini.com/resource-fileaccess/resource/pdf/wwr_2013_0.pdf.

Castles, Stephen. 2004. "The Factors That Make and Unmake Migration Policies." *International Migration Review* 38 (3): 852–884. doi:10.1111/j.1747-7379.2004.tb00222.x.

Castles, Stephen, Hein de Haas, and Mark Miller. 2014. *The Age of Migration: International Population Movements in the Modern World*. 5th ed. Hampshire: Palgrave Macmillan.

Church, Andrew, Martin Frost, and Karen Sullivan. 2000. "Transport and Social Exclusion in London." *Transport Policy* 7 (3): 195–205. doi:10.1016/S0967-070X(00)00024-X.

Cohen, Robin. 2008. *Global Diasporas: An Introduction*. 2nd ed. London: Routledge.

Cohen, Scott A., Tara Duncan, and Maria Thulemark. 2013. "Lifestyle Mobilities: The Crossroads of Travel, Leisure and Migration." *Mobilities* 10 (1): 155–172. doi:10.1080/17450101.2013.826481.

Collins, Francis Leo. 2012. "Organizing Student Mobility: Education Agents and Student Migration to New Zealand." *Pacific Affairs* 85 (1): 137–160. doi:10.5509/2012851137.

Cranston, Sophie. 2016. "Producing Migrant Encounter: Learning to be a British Expatriate in Singapore Through the Global Mobility Industry." *Environment and Planning D: Society and Space* 34 (4): 655–671. doi:10.1177/0263775816630311.

Cresswell, Tim. 2010. "Towards a Politics of Mobility." *Environment and Planning D: Society and Space* 28 (1): 17–31. doi:10.1068/d11407.

Cresswell, Tim, and Peter Merriman. 2010. *Geographies of Mobilities: Practices, Spaces, Subjects*. Burlington, VT: Ashgate.

Davies, William. 2014. "The Tyranny of Intermediaries: Who Writes the Rules of Our Modern Capitalism?" *Institute of Public Policy*, February 17. http://www.ippr.org/juncture/171/11905/the-tyranny-of-intermediaries-who-writes-the-rules-of-our-modern-capitalism.

Economic Intelligence Unit (EIU), and RBC Wealth Management. 2012. "Wealth through the Prism of Culture and Mobility: An Economist Intelligence Unit Report on behalf of RBC Wealth Management." http://www.rbcwealthmanagement.com/_assets-custom/pdf/eiu/internationally-mobile-wealthy.pdf.

Elliott, Anthony, and John Urry. 2010. *Mobile Lives*. London: Routledge.

Ernste, Huib, Karel Martens, and Joris Schapendonk. 2012. "The Design, Experience and Justice of Mobility." *Tijdschrift voor economische en sociale geografie* 103 (5): 509–515. doi:10.1111/j.1467-9663.2012.00751.x.

Faulconbridge, James R., and Sarah Hall. 2014. "Reproducing the City of London's Institutional Landscape: The Role of Education and the Learning of Situated Practices by Early Career Elites." *Environment and Planning A* 46 (7): 1682–1698.

Featherstone, Mike. 2014. "The Rich and the Super-rich: Mobility, Consumption and Luxury Lifestyles." In *Consumer Culture, Modernity and Identity*, edited by Nita Mathur, 3–44. New Delhi: SAGE.

Fernandez, Bina. 2013. "Traffickers, Brokers, Employment Agents, and Social Networks: The Regulation of Intermediaries in the Migration of Ethiopian Domestic Workers to the Middle East." *International Migration Review* 47 (4): 814–843. doi:10.1111/imre.12049.

Forrest, Ray, Sin Yee Koh, and Bart Wissink. 2017a. *Cities and the Super-rich: Real Estate, Elite Practices, and Urban Political Economy*. New York: Palgrave Macmillan.

Forrest, Ray, Sin Yee Koh, and Bart Wissink. 2017b. "In Search of the Super-rich: Who Are They? Where Are They?" In *Cities and the Super-rich: Real Estate, Elite Practices, and Urban Political Economy*, edited by Ray Forrest, Sin Yee Koh, and Bart Wissink, 1–18. New York: Palgrave Macmillan.

Forrest, Ray, Sin Yee Koh, and Bart Wissink. 2017c. "Hyper-divided Cities and the 'Immoral' Super-rich: Five Parting Questions." In *Cities and the Super-rich: Real Estate, Elite Practices, and Urban Political Economy*, edited by Ray Forrest, Sin Yee Koh, and Bart Wissink, 273–287. New York: Palgrave Macmillan.

Forrest, Ray, and Bart Wissink. 2016. "Whose City Now? Urban Managerialism Reconsidered (Again)." *Sociological Review*. doi:10.1111/1467-954X.12415.

Gammeltoft-Hansen, Thomas, and Ninna Nyberg Sørensen. 2013. *The Migration Industry and the Commercialization of International Migration*. New York: Routledge.

Garapich, Michal P. 2008. "The Migration Industry and Civil Society: Polish Immigrants in the United Kingdom Before and After EU Enlargement." *Journal of Ethnic & Migration Studies* 34 (5): 735–752. doi:10.1080/13691830802105970.

Glucksberg, Luna. 2014. "On the Frontline: Family Offices and the Lives of the Super-rich." *Discover Society*, December 1. http://www.discoversociety.org/2014/12/01/on-the-frontline-family-offices-and-the-lives-of-the-super-rich/.

Gössling, Stefan, and Jan Henrik Nilsson. 2010. "Frequent Flyer Programmes and the Reproduction of Aeromobility." *Environment and Planning A* 42 (1): 241–252.

Hall, Sarah. 2011. "Educational Ties, Social Capital and the Translocal (Re)production of MBA Alumni Networks." *Global Networks* 11 (1): 118–138. doi:10.1111/j.1471-0374.2011.00310.x.

Hannam, Kevin, Mimi Sheller, and John Urry. 2006. "Editorial: Mobilities, Immobilities and Moorings." *Mobilities* 1 (1): 1–22. doi:10.1080/17450100500489189.

Harney, Robert Forrest. 1977. "The Commerce of Migration." *Canadian Ethnic Studies* 9: 42–53.

Hay, Iain. 2013. *Geographies of the Super-rich*. Cheltenham: Edward Elgar.

Hay, Iain, and Jonathan V. Beaverstock. 2016. *Handbook on Wealth and the Super-rich*. Cheltenham: Edward Elgar.

Hay, Iain, and Samantha Muller. 2012. "'That Tiny, Stratospheric Apex That Owns Most of the World' – Exploring Geographies of the Super-rich." *Geographical Research* 50 (1): 75–88. doi:10.1111/j.1745-5871.2011.00739.x.

Hernández-León, Rubén. 2005. "The Migration Industry in the Mexico-U.S. Migratory System." California Center for Population Research On-Line Working Paper Series (CCPR-049-05). http://papers.ccpr.ucla.edu/papers/PWP-CCPR-2005-049/PWP-CCPR-2005-049.pdf.

Hernández-León, Rubén. 2008. *Metropolitan Migrants: The Migration of Urban Mexicans to the United States*. Berkeley: University of California Press.

Jaffe, Rivke, Christien Klaufus, and Freek Colombijn. 2012. "Mobilities and Mobilizations of the Urban Poor." *International Journal of Urban and Regional Research* 36 (4): 643–654. doi:10.1111/j.1468-2427.2012.01119.x.

Kim, Youna. 2016. "Mobile Phone for Empowerment? Global Nannies in Paris." *Media, Culture & Society* 38 (4): 525–539. doi:10.1177/0163443715613638.

Koh, Sin Yee, Bart Wissink, and Ray Forrest. 2016. "Reconsidering the Super-rich: Variations, Structural Conditions and Urban Consequences." In *Handbook on Wealth and the Super-rich*, edited by Iain Hay and Jonathan Beaverstock, 18–40. Cheltenham: Edward Elgar.

Levitt, Peggy, and B. Nadya Jaworsky. 2007. "Transnational Migration Studies: Past Developments and Future Trends." *Annual Review of Sociology* 33 (1): 129–156. doi:10.1146/annurev.soc.33.040406.131816.

Light, Ivan. 2013. "The Migration Industry in the United States, 1882–1924." *Migration Studies* 1 (3): 258–275. doi:10.1093/migration/mnt021.

Lindquist, Johan. 2010. "Labour Recruitment, Circuits of Capital and Gendered Mobility: Reconceptualizing the Indonesian Migration Industry." *Pacific Affairs* 83 (1): 115–132.

Lindquist, Johan, Biao Xiang, and Brenda S. A. Yeoh. 2012. "Opening the Black box of Migration: Brokers, the Organization of Transnational Mobility and the Changing Political Economy in Asia." *Pacific Affairs* 85 (1): 7–19.

Lin, Weiqiang, Johan Lindquist, Biao Xiang, and Brenda S. A. Yeoh. 2017. "Migration Infrastructures and the Production of Migrant Mobilities." *Mobilities*, 1–8. doi:10.1080/17450101.2017.1292770.

Lucas, Karen. 2012. "Transport and Social Exclusion: Where Are We Now?" *Transport Policy* 20: 105–113. doi:10.1016/j.tranpol.2012.01.013.

Lundberg, Ferdinand. 1968. *The Rich and the Super-rich: A Study in the Power of Money Today*. New York: L. Stuart.

Mau, Steffen. 2010. *Social Transnationalism: Lifeworlds Beyond the Nation State, International Library of Sociology*. Abingdon: Routledge.

Maude, David. 2006. *Global Private Banking and Wealth Management: The New Realities, Wiley Finance*. Chichester: John Wiley & Sons.

Merrifield, Andy. 2013. "Intervention – Whose City? The Parasites, of Course … ". *Antipode Foundation*. http://antipodefoundation.org/2013/06/18/intervention-whose-city/.

Nowicka, Magdalena. 2012. "Cosmopolitanism, Spatial Mobility and the Alternative Geographies." *International Review of Social Research* 2 (3): 1–16. doi:10.1515/irsr-2012-0024.

Ono, Mayumi. 2015. "Commoditization of Lifestyle Migration: Japanese Retirees in Malaysia." *Mobilities* 10 (4): 609–627. doi:10.1080/17450101.2014.913868.

Paris, Chris. 2013. "The Homes of the Super-rich: Multiple Residences, Hyper-mobility and Decoupling of Prime Residential Housing in Global Cities." In *Geographies of the Super-rich*, edited by Iain Hay, 94–109. Cheltenham: Edward Elgar.

Preston, John, and Fiona Rajé. 2007. "Accessibility, Mobility and Transport-related Social Exclusion." *Journal of Transport Geography* 15 (3): 151–160. doi:10.1016/j.jtrangeo.2006.05.002.

Rahman, Md Mizanur, and M. A. Kabir. 2012. "Bangladeshi Migration to Italy: The Family Perspective." *Asia Europe Journal* 10 (4): 251–265. doi:10.1007/s10308-012-0333-3.

Salt, John, and Jeremy Stein. 1997. "Migration as a Business: The Case of Trafficking." *International Migration* 35 (4): 467–494. doi:10.1111/1468-2435.00023.

Sauer, Angelika. 2012. "agents of Transnationalism: German-Canadian Immigration Agents in the Second Half of the Nineteenth Century." In *Transnational Networks: German Migrants in the British Empire, 1670–1914*, edited by John R. Davis, Stefan Manz, and Margrit Schulte Beerbühl, 117–140. Leiden: Brill.

Sheller, Mimi, and John Urry. 2006. "The New Mobilities Paradigm." *Environment and Planning A* 38 (2): 207–226.

Short, John Rennie. 2015. "The Other Immigrants: How the Super-rich Skirt Quotas and Closed Borders." *The Conversation*, September 9. https://theconversation.com/the-other-immigrants-how-the-super-rich-skirt-quotas-and-closed-borders-47244.

Skeggs, Beverley. 2004. *Class, Self, Culture, Transformations*. London: Routledge.

Smith, Michael Peter, and Adrian Favell, eds. 2006. *The Human Face of Global Mobility: International Highly Skilled Migration in Europe, North America and the Asia Pacific*. New Brunswick, NJ: Transaction.

Spener, David. 2009. "Some Critical Reflections on the Migration Industry Concept." Migration in the Pacific Rim Workshop. http://www.trinity.edu/dspener/clandestinecrossings/related%20articles/migration%20industry.pdf.

Sørensen, Ninna Nyberg, and Thomas Gammeltoft-Hansen. 2013. "Introduction." In *The Migration Industry and the Commercialization of International Migration*, edited by Thomas Gammeltoft-Hansen and Ninna Nyberg Sørensen, 1–23. New York: Routledge.

Teo, Youyenn. 2016. "Not Everyone has 'Maids': Class Differentials in the Elusive Quest for Work-Life Balance." *Gender, Place & Culture* 23 (8): 1164–1178. doi:10.1080/0966369X.2015.1136810.

Tseng, Yen-Fen. 1997. "Immigration Consulting Firms in Taiwanese Business Immigration." *Asian and Pacific Migration Journal* 6 (3-4): 275–294. doi:10.1177/011719689700600302.

Urry, John. 2007. *Mobilities*. Cambridge: Polity.

Van den Broek, Di, William Harvey, and Dimitria Groutsis. 2016. "Commercial Migration Intermediaries and the Segmentation of Skilled Migrant Employment." *Work, Employment & Society* 30 (3): 523–534. doi:10.1177/0950017015594969.

Wissink, Bart, Sin Yee Koh, and Ray Forrest. 2017. "Tycoon City: Political Economy, Real Estate and the Super-rich in Hong Kong." In *Cities and the Super-rich: Real Estate, Elite Practices, and Urban Political Economy*, edited by Ray Forrest, Sin Yee Koh, and Bart Wissink, 229–252. New York: Palgrave Macmillan.

Xiang, Biao. 2012. "Predatory Princes and Princely Peddlers: The State and International Labour Migration Intermediaries in China." *Pacific Affairs* 85 (1): 47–68. doi:10.5509/201285147.

Xiang, Biao, and Johan Lindquist. 2014. "Migration Infrastructure." *International Migration Review* 48 (S1): S122–SS48. doi:10.1111/imre.12141.

# Adapting to change in the higher education system: international student mobility as a migration industry

Suzanne E. Beech

**ABSTRACT**

Of late there has been considerable interest in understanding international student mobility, and this has tended to focus on the perspective of the students who take part in this mobility. However, international students are part of a considerable migration industry comprised of international student recruitment teams, international education agents and other institutions selling an education overseas (such as the British Council in a UK context) and as yet there is little research which analyses these relationships. This paper investigates a series of interviews with international office staff to examine the methods they use to recruit international students, and in particular the relationship that they have with international education agents who work with them on a commission basis. It focuses on recent changes to the UK visa system which have led to a decline in the numbers of Indian students choosing to study towards a UK higher education. However, it also reveals that some universities have managed to avoid this trend. This paper investigates why this is the case, demonstrating that there is a need to think about the intersections between migration industries, visa regulations and international student mobility.

## Introduction

Over the last 15 years, there has been a profound shift in our understanding of how and why international students choose to study overseas. This research has tended to focus on the perspectives of the students themselves and the structural factors that lead to the pursuit of an overseas education with issues of demand outstripping supply often cited as one of the key influences for higher education mobility (Gribble 2008; Simpson, Sturges, and Weight 2010). Such work has also been attuned to other social, cultural and economic factors which may encourage a student to study abroad. The work of Brooks and Waters (2011), in particular, has identified how mobility often relates to a desire for greater social and cultural capital, which students believe will be almost immediately transferable to economic capital when they enter into the global job market. This has been reinforced by evidence that even when the higher education infrastructure improves in sending countries (such as those in South-East Asia), the desire to study overseas is maintained as an overseas qualification becomes a way of differentiating oneself from the local graduate market (Waters 2009; Findlay et al. 2012). There are other possible reasons for this as well, work by Collins (2008) and Beech (2015) discusses how students are influenced by their social networks in the decision to study overseas. These networks then normalise the process of choosing an international education, so that study abroad becomes an accepted stage in the life course.

Consequently, there is a steady stream of prospective international students who are eager to study abroad as a result of these structural and socio-economic factors. However, the work of those who recruit international students is a subject of very little systematic study, and yet it is these individuals who are ultimately responsible for creating and distributing information about their universities to prospective students. This information is critical because higher education is now a key export industry for many industrialised countries, in particular for the UK, USA, Canada, Australia and New Zealand (Pandit 2009; Brown, Edwards, and Hartwell 2010; Naidoo 2010; Zheng 2014) and has been since the neoliberalisation of their tertiary education systems in the 1980s and 1990s. It is therefore crucial that these dynamics are given far greater attention, as this neoliberalisation has enabled universities to actively seek out new sources of funding, including focusing on the recruitment of 'high value', full-fee paying students.

It is their high value of these students that has led to the development of a global migration industry in higher education has become established. This could be defined as the actors, entrepreneurs or systems of governance involved in facilitating student mobility and migration (Betts 2013; Hernández-León 2013; Cranston, Schapendonk, and Spaan 2018). Within a higher education context, these 'industries' operate in two ways. First, many UK higher education institutions (HEIs) can, in themselves, be considered migration entrepreneurs, they provide opportunities for mobility and often invest considerable financial capital in outreach activities to access these students. Second, as demand for overseas education has risen (both from the students seeking opportunities for study and the universities wishing to recruit these students), a network of international education agents has also become established. These agents are employed by private companies which have links and contacts at universities worldwide, and are paid a commission by the universities for every student recruited successfully to one of their programmes. It is important to note that agents will not necessarily have either studied abroad themselves, or even visited all, if any, of their university partners, nonetheless they can be useful and valuable middleman in international student recruitment as they have the same cultural and local understandings as the students. This can make it easier for them to gain the students' trust, benefitting the university. Furthermore, as higher education is also subject to governance and policy systems which provide or limit opportunities for international study, agents can also help students to negotiate these hurdles, or even encourage them to seek out alternative overseas education destinations. Over time and as a result of the benefits that they can bring, agents have become integral to international student recruitment, with both universities and students viewing agents as gatekeepers to international students and higher education opportunities, respectively. Thus, similar to the calculative practices discussed by Cranston (2018), this relationship does more than describe the economy, but also produces it.

With this in mind, this paper considers how the end of the UK Post-Study Work Visa in 2012 (which allowed international students to remain for two years on completion of their studies) has affected international student recruitment. This paper will analyse a series of interviews conducted with higher education recruitment officers working at a range of UK universities. It investigates the methods used by universities to recruit students and the measures taken to ensure that they remain competitive in a saturated market. This also details their response to these changing visa policies which have impacted upon the UK's 'desirability' as a destination for overseas study. In so doing it shows not only how government policy leads to the establishment of different migration industries (in particular the agent/university relationship), but also how policy reform affects the success of these industries and an analysis of the university response to maintain competitiveness despite these changes.

## Higher education and the 'migration industry'

Higher education in a UK context has expanded rapidly since the 1960s with student numbers quadrupling between then and the beginning of the twenty-first century (Blanden and Machin 2004). In particular, focus has often been upon the Further and Higher Education Act of 1992 which fundamentally changed the UK higher education system by removing the binary divide between universities and polytechnics (Mayhew, Deer, and Dua 2004). This was significant as institutions, which in the past had focused on vocational training, were now able to apply for university status and were often appealing to students because of their long-standing reputations and the applied nature of the degrees that they offered (HEFCE 2004). Consequently, by 2011, there were 140 university and university colleges in the UK (a rise from 33 universities in 1960) with a 42% participation rate in higher education at an undergraduate level for the relevant age cohort (Foskett 2011). The result of this is a 'highly differentiated HE [system]' (Tindal et al. 2015, 94), comprised of HEIs which have a variety of different histories and sociocultural understandings of what the universities can offer in terms of their research and education, and therefore also in terms of their reputations.

The neoliberal reforms which facilitated these changes also enabled universities to adopt free-market principles and generate some of their own funding with the aim of increasing efficiency through competition and streamlining (Deem 2001; Harvey 2005; Olssen and Peters 2005). As a result of this, alongside developments in internationalisation and globalisation which facilitate international travel, communication and relationships, universities now operate on a global scale and aim to exploit international opportunities for funding and growth. The investment into international student recruitment and the development of an international student migration industry within the UK is testament to this, as are the range of different strategies which universities use to exploit these alternative markets; such as distance learning, transnational higher education opportunities, collaboration with overseas partners (in both research and teaching), branch campuses overseas, and opportunities for student and staff mobility (Leung and Waters 2013; Gopinath 2015).

There are short-term financial benefits to these various strategies – universities are able to reach prospective students in new markets and recruit high value, internationally mobile students which may help to maintain healthy finances and support research and development (Zheng 2014). Lange (2013) noted that in the UK students from non-EU countries (who pay higher fees than both their domestic and EU counterparts[1]) contributed some £2.5 billion to higher education funding. Thus, in the short-term, it makes sense to put considerable effort into recruiting these 'international' students. Furthermore, the influence of social networks on student mobility could lead to opportunities for greater student recruitment in the future, as links between the sending and receiving countries, or even links to particular universities, become more established (Beech 2015).

With so much at stake, competition for these students is fierce, and in recent years (and partly as a response to this competition), we have witnessed increased use of third parties and international education agents to grow student enrolment numbers. Pioneered in Australia (Choudaha and Chang 2012), the agent model of recruitment is now widespread. They inform students on their higher education options, and may also offer a wide range of services including help with visas and travel, English language testing, accommodation and counselling (Collins 2012). This has led to the development of what is effectively a Global Mobility Industry facilitating the movement of these highly skilled migrants (Cranston 2016; 2018). Agents themselves are free to prospective students and are paid on a commission basis by the universities which they recruit to. For universities they therefore offer a 'one stop shop' for student recruitment in exchange for a fee, and this can often reap considerable reward as agents also tend to understand better the specific cultural context of where the international students are coming from – something which is often not the case for university recruitment officers.

In addition to this, international students can also reap longer term recruitment rewards should they choose to remain on graduation, with evidence suggesting that even on a temporary basis this can have advantages for sectors of the economy which rely on a university-educated workforce (Adnett 2010). Thus, immigration policies are often designed to encourage students to stay and fill particular skills shortages, such as those in the science and engineering sector, which may be less popular with home graduates (Gribble 2008; Madge, Raghuram, and Noxolo 2009; Lange 2013; Tang et al. 2014). It was with these aims that the Post-Study Work Visa was established in the UK, granting leave for international graduates to remain for two years without the need to establish a sponsor beforehand. However, swelling anti-immigration sentiment and fears over the abuse of the system led to changes to UK immigration policy and the Post-Study Work Visa ended in April 2012. Now, should international students wish to remain in the UK, they have to either qualify for a Tier 2 visa which requires a sponsor in advance and that the applicant is in receipt of an offer of employment with a salary of £20,800 or more, or a Tier 1 visa for aspiring entrepreneurs. Neither of these options were (or indeed are) as appealing as the Post-Study Work Visa. At the time Mavroudi and Warren (2013) suggested that these changes were likely to act as a deterrent for potential international students and impact upon their recruitment, at least on a temporary basis until the workings of the replacement visa system became clearer. This hypothesis seems to have been confirmed in a recent report by Universities UK (2014) which showed a marked decline in the numbers of international students from outside of the EU to the UK between 2010–2011 and 2012–2013 (the numbers of Indian student enrolments had almost halved in this time period). This was particularly notable when compared with the levels of growth experienced before 2010.

However, the report also drew attention to the fact that there are now a number of different options available to international students, reflecting on evidence that the top five study destinations had all experienced some decline in international student numbers since 2000 due to growing opportunities in destinations such as China, Malaysia,

Egypt, Saudi Arabia and the United Arab Emirates for both local and international students (Collins and Ho 2014; Ma 2014; Universities UK 2014). Thus, while reforms have occurred, the shape of the international student market is very different and established markets, like the UK, need to work harder to maintain their market position (Universities UK 2014). This makes policy and recruitment spaces (and practices) crucial to the future of the international student body on campus. Despite this, whilst we have a well-rounded understanding of what attracts them to study overseas, our knowledge and understanding of the geographies of this recruitment process are limited. We understand why universities want to recruit these students, and what enables them to do so, but we do not yet understand the processes that they employ and why, or how they have responded to these market changes.

## Methodology

This paper draws on findings from a study of recruitment practices in UK HEIs. In order to recruit from as many HEIs as possible, an email was sent out on a forum for professionals working in international higher education in early 2014. The only requirements were that participants had to be presently or very recently employed in international higher education recruitment in the UK. A total of 20 members of staff responded to the call for participants. However, primarily due to time constraints, only 10 decided to take up the offer of a semi-structured interview. To maintain their anonymity, all names used in this study have been changed for pseudonyms, and their universities have not been named directly.

The participants came from universities throughout England and Scotland, and could be considered representative of the diversity of the UK higher education system. This research captures the essence of this variety by including interviewees from a range of different HEIs. Two interviewees were from Russell Group institutions, a self-styled collective of the 24 most research intensive universities in the UK, and which often are ranked highly in both national and international ranking systems. Three were from post-1992 universities which were founded under the terms of the Further and Higher Education Act of 1992. One participant was from a Redbrick institution, a term which loosely refers to universities formed in the nineteenth and early twentieth centuries. One was from a New University formed after the post-1992 wave, but which was not a former polytechnic. The final three were from, what I have termed, specialist higher education providers such as arts colleges, music conservatoires or subject-specific HEIs. A number of participants had also worked at multiple universities or in private sector student recruitment and at least five had over 10 years' experience working in international student recruitment or admissions more generally. They were therefore well placed to offer their reflections on changing international student recruitment policies.

The universities were also diverse in terms of the proportion of international and EU (or overseas) students that they hosted. At one institution, over 50% of the registered students were classed as overseas or international according to the HESA statistics for 2014–2015, but at others there were significantly less. Two of the HEIs (a New University and a Specialist HEI) included in the sample had very small international student communities and in both cases less than 3% of their students were domiciled outside of the UK. On average, 21.16% of the students registered at the HEIs in the study were overseas or international and again, this is broadly comparable to the UK average of just over 19% (HESA 2016). It is also important to note that within the analysis of the interviews with the international office staff they refer to international students as those from outside of the EU unless they state explicitly to the contrary (Table 1).

All of the interviews were conducted via Skype or telephone between August 2014 and June 2015 and lasted between 30 minutes and an hour. Using Skype and telephone as an interview method offered greater flexibility and the proposed timings of the interviews could vary if the availability of the participants changed (see Deakin and Wakefield 2014 for further discussion of the benefits of Skype interviews). There were some issues with this method, however, with the internet connection failing on occasion which affected the flow of the interview, at least temporarily. Questions have also been raised regarding the ability to develop a rapport with interviewees when not meeting face-to-face, particularly given that the non-verbal cues that interviewers use to make their participants feel more relaxed are often lost (O'Connor et al. 2008) although this is less the case with Skype where it is possible to use both audio and video to communicate. However, a number of the participants mentioned that they either used Skype or telephone to talk to prospective international students on a regular basis and as such seemed comfortable with this arrangement.

## International student recruitment: policy and practice

As noted, a number of interviewees had extensive experience working in the international student recruitment sector. One of the participants, Luke, had been employed at his current Specialist HEI since 2012 and had worked at a post-1992 institution prior to that. He offered a vibrant picture of the 'industrialisation' of student migration and reflected that the emergence of the international student sector was almost organic. He discussed how, early in the 1990s, recruitment had been student driven and the university had no well-defined strategy for targeting these students.

> Luke: I became, whatever it was, Head of International around about ninety, well the late 90s and then the international office built up from one person … Now, think about that in terms of employment and development. A whole new industry developed from the early 90s through to the 2000s.

**Table 1.** Participants and their HEI type.

| Name | HEI type | % International and overseas students[a] | % International students[a] |
|---|---|---|---|
| Simon | Russell Group | 28.98 | 22.48 |
| Judith | Post-1992[b] | 20.62 | 11.71 |
| Lois | Red Brick | 26.88 | 20.98 |
| Rhoda | Post-1992[b] | 29.78 | 19.50 |
| David | New University[c] | 2.57 | 1.56 |
| Sarah | Specialist HEI | 13.99 | 10.72 |
| Nathan | Specialist HEI | 6.90 | 4.45 |
| Candace | Post-1992[b] | 12.85 | 10.17 |
| Luke | Specialist HEI | 2.56 | 1.28 |
| Joel | Russell Group | 66.51 | 48.54 |

[a]Adapted from HESA (2016).
[b]Former polytechnics.
[c]New University, formed after 1992, but not a former polytechnic.

The policies of Luke's former HEI were in stark contrast to his current employer. He stated that whereas in his prior appointment they perhaps had 30,000 students, the specialist institution in which he was now employed had fewer than 2000. He commented that in his current employment it was like 'going back in time'. He was, initially, 'the International Office of one' which offered an interesting case of *déjà vu* of his experience 15 years previously. In his new employment, he was dealing with issues and questions which he had dealt with long ago at his previous HEI. His experience offers interesting insights into the rapid development of the migration industry over a relatively short period of time and in response to growing student demand. Not only that, but it also demonstrates that internationalisation is now also a focus for smaller, specialist HEIs as well.

In response to these rapid changes the majority of universities had adopted a triad of recruitment methods. First, direct applicants who apply to the university with no, or limited external help. Second, by developing partnerships with universities overseas which may include exchange or other teaching and learning arrangements (such as a 'two-plus-two' programme where a student begins their degree in one location, but finishes it overseas, graduating with a degree from the host HEI). The third principle method was agent-led recruitment, whereby, as mentioned, the student comes to the university through a third party who is paid a commission for every student they recruit to the university (Matthews 2012). These would then be supplemented with a range of other activities such as academic visits or attendance at international student recruitment fairs which can be either based in the UK or within key markets globally. The two latter of these methods (and possibly the first) include a relationship of some description with 'migration entrepreneurs' (Hernández-León 2013) who facilitate the mobility of the students for financial gain – in these cases either the agents or the universities themselves.

In addition to these, two of the universities interviewed also mentioned how they were trying to encourage academics to use trips overseas (either for research or conferences) as opportunities to also engage with prospective international students, ensuring that they were making the most of their staff time abroad. Lois, who worked at a Redbrick institution in England, stated that this was a particularly good method for reaching out to potential postgraduate students:

> Lois: Often if we have academics that are travelling for conferences we will see if there are partner universities that … they can go and visit, so we can really sustain strong relationships with the universities that we already work with, even if it's giving a lecture in the department that the professor would be affiliated with … In the past we have seen a huge amount of success having an academic meet with faculty and also give one of these lectures and in return you see a lot of [postgraduate] interest.

This changing institutional policy could have interesting ramifications for the shape and size of international recruitment teams for the future. If there is a demand for this more specialised information, future trends may see a move away from large international teams towards greater reliance on academic faculty to drive the recruitment process, perhaps even at a departmental or subject group level.

Despite these potential changes, overwhelmingly universities cited direct and agent-led as the two key recruitment methods with some having substantial agent teams into which they invested considerable money and time. Simon, who worked at a Russell Group institution and had over 15 years experience of international student recruitment, stated that his university worked with between 240 and 250 education agents and every year they conducted a performance review of those agents. The use of migration entrepreneurs was therefore central to their recruitment strategy and they invested considerable efforts in monitoring the performance of these third parties. He described how there was an expectation that certain markets, such as India and China, agents would bring large numbers of students to their university annually and this was primarily because these markets were agent-led. Simon discussed how, among Indian and Chinese students, the agent model is now so entrenched that it was almost accepted that they would make their higher education choices with the help of a third party. If an agent failed to perform in these cases, the university would then consider severing their relationship with them. By contrast, in other countries there was a significantly smaller agent market. Judith and Candace, who were both employed at Post-1992 universities stated that in Nigeria very few students would come to a university through an agent. Judith explained this by saying that in Nigeria there is 'a real suspicion of the middle person' and therefore it was more normal to have very small numbers of students coming through an agent. As such universities make decisions on whether or not to continue relationships with agents not only on the basis of the number of incoming students but also their recruitment expectations with regard to the prevalence and centrality of agents in those markets.

The introduction of a third party into student recruitment can cause difficulties because it has the potential to dilute the universities' messages and advertising. Therefore, to use agents also leads to a need for greater safeguarding. Amongst the interviewees it was a standard procedure to monitor agents or to visit them regularly. Rhoda, who also worked at a post-1992 university, said that building a relationship with an agent or agency is important, and they also encouraged agents to assist at recruitment fairs so that they could monitor how they sold their university:

> Rhoda: we try not to have such a big network that we don't visit those agents or aren't in contact with those agents on a more or less regular basis ... [If] we do a British Council exhibition we would ask agents to come and help us on the stand ... that's a great training opportunity but also a good quality control, because then we can hear what they are saying to the students.

One university did reflect on the risks inherent to the agent relationship. Simon stated that they were 'essentially able to use [their] name, [their] brand, and if they are not very closely engaged with [the university] that could ... put [the university's] name at risk'. His university had received some negative publicity in the past on their use of agents and their recruitment methods. Consequently, they were now much more aware of how many agents their team could support and only established contracts if they were certain that they could observe the activities of those agents effectively.

Whilst agents were a key recruitment method for the majority of the universities that were interviewed, three of the universities stated that they did not have any agencies working for them at present. Two of these were small, specialist institutions. In her interview, Sarah said that at present there was no need for them to use agents because the markets in which they worked were relatively small and they were able to manage the applications on their own. They did not tend to work in the large, agent-led markets of India and China and, whilst they had experimented with agents some four years previously, the returns from these efforts had not been great enough to warrant continuing the contracts. Similarly, the markets that Nathan was working with were also relatively small, and there was a focus in their institution on recruiting a number of students from Australia, the South-East Asia (especially Singapore), Canada and the USA. However, in the USA context, the use of agents and third parties in recruitment is illegal, primarily due to the ethics of incentivised recruitment, although it should be noted that at present this does not extend to universities recruiting international students into the USA (ICEF Monitor 2012). To counter their lack of agents, Nathan's HEI instead relied on attendance at some university fairs, partnerships with other institutions and higher education counsellors who did not have the same commission-based relationship with the university, and also focused on recruiting international students already in the UK for secondary education study.

By contrast, the third university was a Russell Group institution that consistently performs well in league tables. Whilst operating on a much larger scale than Sarah and Nathan's HEIs, the interest from students, and the reputation was enough to ensure a steady stream of applicants. Joel went on to say that he was 'surprised that larger universities with brilliant reputations use them', he said:

> I can very much understand from a university that may not be high profile … I don't see why a university that it is in the top ten would need to do that really.

This represents a stark contrast to Simon (mentioned earlier) who noted that agents were central to their recruitment strategy, despite also being a member of the Russell Group. This suggests that 'excellence' among students is perhaps focused more closely on the top performers in league tables rather than on other indicators of esteem – like Russell Group membership. In addition, Joel felt that the ease of communications now was such that there was really no need to involve a third party in the recruitment process, although was keen to point out that as he had only worked in one institution and he did not know whether this was the same experience for every HEI. These three exceptions aside, agents did appear to be an accepted method of recruiting students to UK universities. However, even those who choose not to employ agents directly, are still involved directly in activities designed to facilitate international mobility whether that be staff visits overseas, attending international recruitment fairs or prioritising contact with the students themselves. Thus, all took part in the wider migration industries of higher working to recruit students to their universities.

From this it is apparent that there are complex power relationships involved in maintaining and recruiting agents. Universities, in some cases feel bound by the agent relationship and the access this gives them to wider student markets. This is evidenced by the scale of the agent networks at some institutions (upwards of 200 agent partners in some cases) and the scaffolding that goes into monitoring agent partners' performances and understanding of the universities. However, the power in this case tends to lie with the universities themselves who can sever relationships on the basis of performance (in terms of the number of students recruited) or if they have a high number of rejections amongst the students applying through them, which Rhoda suggested was indicative of a misunderstanding of the 'product' on offer at the university.

The means by which universities and agents establish relationships with one another was less clear. As mentioned, agents work for private companies and may have no prior relationship with a university. However, the British Council does provide a list of agents who have successfully passed their agent training programme and thus acts as one source of potential connections although none of the interviewees mentioned this directly. Rhoda, in her discussion of agent monitoring (of which tracking application success was a part), went into greater detail of their selection process which involved letters of reference from staff at other universities and relying on wider nationwide networks:

> there is a general email distribution list to all international staff across universities so quite often if there are issues cropping up with agents people send an email to their colleagues and say, "have you had this particular problem?" and then you can also see whether it's a specific counsellor that hasn't been trained properly or … whether it's an agency, whether it's just with us, or whether it's also spread across other institutions.

Her comment highlights that not only do these power structures operate on an institutional scale, but also on a wider national scale as well. Failure to perform or concerns regarding agent ethics will be shared more widely, potentially affecting multiple relationships which agents have with universities. In saying this, the powers of the agent should not be undervalued either. As the following section reveals agents can have significant sway in terms of where students choose to study, sending them elsewhere if market conditions change.

## The end of the post-study work visa: changing student demands

Migration entrepreneurs in the form of higher education agents are a major factor influencing student recruitment, and, as noted above, they are widely used in UK HEIs (Huang, Raimo, and Humfrey 2014). Furthermore, agents tend to have considerable power over where students from certain countries, like China and India, are likely to study given that they are paid on a commission basis and are therefore incentivised to send students to particular locations. However, as middlemen, they also have to take account of students' desires and wishes as it is only with their mobility that they will get remunerated. This is most noticeable given the recent changes in higher education policy in the UK which have influenced the numbers of incoming international students and the decisions that they make regarding their study destinations. One of the most influential of these changes has been the ending of the Post-Study Work Visa in 2012. As Mavroudi and Warren (2013) suspected, this change from allowing graduates to stay for work without an initial sponsor for two years, to one which requires either a sponsor for a graduate level job has had a profound effect on both the courses that international students are interested in taking, and the countries from which those students are coming from.

Three of the universities mentioned either changing or decreasing interest from students, or a reformation of their target markets. Judith worked at a post-1992 institution. She noted that they had experienced a 70% drop in students coming to her university from India. She acknowledged that this was a steep decline, but noted that it was 'actually in line with a number of universities and a drop in interest from India to the UK as a study destination' (this is particularly significant when you take account of the human capital and potential international students which the country provides (Gopinath 2015)). Universities UK (2014) stated that the sudden decline was in part due to the changing visa policy in the UK, but that these changes had coincided with a period of change in the higher education marketplace more generally, and there are now much greater opportunities for students to study overseas. David, who worked at a new university, also commented on this. He had joined his university about three years prior to the interview, and almost immediately decided to end their recruitment activities in India. This was in part because he felt that as a relatively small institution it would be very difficult for them to compete in such a large market, but that this had also been made worse by the changing perceptions of the UK as a higher education destination from an Indian perspective. He commented that increasingly the 'perception of coming to study and the welcome that they get in the UK has changed'.

There was speculation regarding why the Indian market in particular had been so affected by these reforms. David believed firmly that it was due to funding models that different countries subscribed to. He stated that students from India tend to take out a loan to study overseas for a masters, similar to students from the UK, and because of this they are interested in ensuring that they get a job quickly after graduation in order to pay off their debt. Whilst they aspire to graduate level employment, 'any job' would be welcome. Additionally, the ability to stay and work in the UK also meant access to employment with greater financial rewards than a job in their home country, thus they would be able to pay off their debts much more quickly. He contrasted this with the Chinese model of funding, a market which had been relatively unaffected by the changing visa policies:

> In China ... you get a lot of ... parents and relations who are paying for their nephews, nieces, sons and daughters to go and study in the UK and the reason is that they want them to come back and be the new finance manager for their small business.

For them the opportunity to remain in the UK would serve as further work experience prior to taking up a post at home or as a stepping stone to a better job when they did return home, rather than as a necessity as in the Indian case. Therefore, if Chinese students are not as bound by the opportunity to work on completion of their studies it is unlikely that the changed visa policy would be so critical.

These funding arrangements are also reflected in the fact that certain subject areas and universities appear to have, to a certain extent, buffered the downwards trend in student numbers. Judith and Candace, both of whom worked at Post-1992 universities which prided themselves in their vocational focus, noted that some subject areas were experiencing growing international student numbers, including from Indian student communities. Judith commented that whilst they did not notice a change in what students wanted initially, about a year after the reforms had come into being, students were increasingly more interested in the value of the degrees for which they were applying. They measured this by investigating more thoroughly their career prospects on graduation.

> Judith: they were interrogating us much more when they were visiting countries ... there was increasing [interest] to get the course right. Whereas before a masters in business, any type of business, that was enough, or something like international business which takes in a lot of different elements ... I think a lot of people thought that would give them more choice ... but after a few years the reality became obvious that companies ... for them to sponsor [someone] they really wanted to know that they were taking on somebody that knew their stuff and they wanted much more specific knowledge than perhaps a graduate with a masters that covered a wider base.

Candace noticed a similar trend. She commented that in many cases they had managed to buffer the downward trend in incoming international students from India. Instead it had continued to be one of their biggest markets and she commented that the recruitment officers for South Asia would spend around 70% of their time focusing on the India market. Like Judith, she reflected on the changing student demand, whereas before the changes in visa regulations students were very interested in MBA and masters in business programmes, now they were much more interested in more specialist degrees and even undergraduate options. She believed that this was due to a continued undersupply in India for these courses and increasing competition to study at public universities. It was, therefore, not so much a case of limited demand from India, but that the markets were changing, and universities had to respond quickly to capture that demand as in any other market.

Furthermore, Candace also commented on the importance of their international agents' conference to which they invite a number of delegates (perhaps as many as 50) every year. She felt that this was a crucial element of how they sold not only the university (including teaching styles) to their agent partners, who in turn sell it to the students, but also how they sell the city more widely and the student experience:

> we don't just put them in front of PowerPoint presentations but we actually allow them to engage with the style of lectures students might be taking or we show them the labs where they do practical based activities … we take them out for a meal … and we don't take them to a posh restaurant we take them to a restaurant … which is of a realistic budget for a student to go, so they can see the city through a student's eyes rather than through … a professional delegate's view because … we think that reinforces [the university] when they then talk to potential applicants in the future.

With so much effort going into the conference and the opportunities for agents to not only experience classes and nightlife, but also to meet students that they had recruited to the university was deemed to have an overall positive influence. Perhaps not surprising then that they had not suffered in the same way as other universities. All of this was at the expense of the university with the belief that showing them good hospitality and an excellent student experience would be reflected in future enrolments.

This research shows that it is possible to maintain or buffer the downward trend and this appeared to be easiest for universities which had a greater vocational focus, such as some of those which had formerly been polytechnics, or those who had adapted rapidly to the changing marketplace. The effects of the changing visa policy were also felt less keenly by universities at the top of the league tables who were perennially popular with international students and did not have to rely on agent-led recruitment because their reputations far exceeded this (note how this differs from the intermediaries involved in skilled migration who produce the reputation outcomes of certain locations (such as Harvey, Groutsis and van den Broek 2018)). In contrast to this, those that did not feature as highly on league tables, and nor were they renowned for their vocational focus, appeared to suffer more from the end of the post-study work visa. Agents and other similar migration entrepreneurs were therefore key to driving recruitment unless the university was at the top of the league tables, thus from this perspective the power relationship is reversed with universities reliant on agents to facilitate mobility.

## Conclusions and new directions

This is only one study, and it needs to be investigated in a variety of different education contexts in greater detail, it nevertheless has drawn critical attention to the role of higher education recruitment agents within international student mobility, moving the focus away from the role of the student in this process. Whilst these are important, the student perspective ignores how mobility involves multiple actors (such as international education agents) who work on a transnational basis to support migration (Spaan and Hillman 2013; Spaan and Von Naerssen 2017). Given the role that these individuals play in encouraging mobility and the complex power relationships that evolve between international education agents and universities, it is crucial that we recognise the role they play in student recruitment, especially in markets such as India and China.

International student recruitment is a key migration industry with UK HEIs competing for international students on a global scale. In the UK, universities routinely establish agent relationships to promote their higher education offering, and will pay them commission for every student that they recruit on their behalf (Matthews 2012; Huang, Raimo, and Humfrey 2014). Given the strength of the agent relationships in the Indian market, it therefore comes as little or no surprise that this market has suffered in particular from the end of the Post-Study Work Visa. An agent's role is to advise and guide students in their decision-making and respond to their particular needs and demands (Collins 2012). They are able to offer suggestions to students and promote individual universities. Furthermore, research shows that students tend to follow predetermined 'pathways' to their mobility, following in the footsteps of their social networks in terms of destination (Beech 2015; see also Harvey et al. 2018). With this in mind, and as more and more students choose alternative higher education destinations other than the UK, there could be significant longer term recruitment issues which develop.

However, this research shows that having the 'right' degree programme can help to overcome this downward trend. It is notable that the two universities which stated that they had maintained their Indian student recruitment were post-1992 universities which prided themselves in their vocational focus and also emphasised work placement opportunities during their degrees. It appears that Indian students view this positively, and believe that such experiences will lead to better career outcomes which, given how they fund their university education, makes them an appealing prospective when choosing where to study. It is important to note that neither of these universities were high achievers in league tables (either on a national or international scale), a common issue with many post-1992 HEIs and the bias which persists towards research intensive and longer established universities within these tables (Bowden 2000). This suggest that whilst league table performance at the highest level was one way of maintaining healthy student recruitment in spite of visa changes, it was by no means the only way of ensuring a healthy international student community. It should also be noted, of course, that expectation of what was a good performance in terms of international student recruitment did vary depending on past performances and the existing international student community. Nonetheless, universities could potentially learn from this and tailor their university degrees or highlight placement opportunities to appeal to these students.

Whilst there is continued debate on the influence of the end of the Post-Study Work Visa in the UK tertiary education system,[2] we should not underestimate the speed with which the expectation of an opportunity to stay in the UK for work took hold. Judith, who worked at a Post-1992 university, which had maintained international and Indian student communities articulated this when she discussed the sudden cultural shift in student expectations:

> I was based in the Indian subcontinent for a long time … there's a lot of people who came and studied in the UK 40 years ago, 30 years ago, 20 years ago, 10 years ago and … if you ask them about the Post Study Work Visa they laugh at you because it is such a foreign concept that you would automatically be given a right to [work] somewhere, but I suppose it's a real sign of the times. In a very short period of time people became accustomed and then accepted that you could stay after you had completed your studies.

Her reflections only serve to highlight that student mobility is now an industry driven by market forces of supply and demand. Students are interested in obtaining the best possible higher education qualifications available to them, but also in their longer term economic trajectories. Consequently, they have increasingly sought opportunities to study in destinations where they could pursue longer term migration opportunities such as Canada and Australia. Articulating opportunities to agents for vocational opportunities built into degree programmes may help to revive markets which have experienced recent decline as they pass these messages on to prospective international students, and facilitate their mobility to the UK.

## Notes

1. EU policy states that any incoming students from elsewhere in the EU must be treated as local students, so there is no opportunity for variable fees.
2. The devolved Scottish Parliament has debated at length the need to reinstate the policy, citing significant losses in international student numbers and therefore significant financial losses, not only to the sector but to the economy more generally (BBC 2016).

## Acknowledgements

I would like to thank Carl Griffin for his comments on earlier versions of this paper and the two anonymous reviewers for their insightful feedback. Thanks are also due to Sophie Cranston, Joris Schapendonk and Ernst Spaan, the editors of this special issue, for all their work in putting it together.

## Disclosure statement

No potential conflict of interest was reported by the author.

## References

Adnett, N. 2010. "The Growth of International Students and Economic Development: Friends or Foes?" *Journal of Education Policy* 25 (5): 625–637.
BBC. 2016. "MSPs Call on Government to Reinstate Post-Study Work Visa [Online]." Accessed March 11, 2016. http://www.bbc.co.uk/news/uk-scotland-scotland-politics-35561131.
Beech, S. E. 2015. "International Student Mobility: The Role of Social Networks." *Social and Cultural Geography* 16 (3): 332–350.

Betts, A. 2013. "The Migration Industry in Global Migration Governance." In *The Migration Industry and the Commercialization of International Migration*, edited by T. Gammeltoft-Hansen and N. N. Sørensen, 45–63. Abingdon: Routledge.

Blanden, J., and S. Machin. 2004. "Educational Inequality and the Expansion of UK Higher Education." *Scottish Journal of Political Economy* 51 (2): 230–249.

Bowden, R. 2000. "Fantasy High Education: University and College League Tables." *Quality in Higher Education* 6 (1): 41–60.

Brooks, R., and J. Waters. 2011. *Student Mobilities, Migration and the Internationalization of Higher Education*. Basingstoke: Palgrave Macmillan.

Brown, L., J. Edwards, and H. Hartwell. 2010. "A Taste of the Unfamiliar. Understanding Meanings Attached to Food by International Postgraduate Students in England." *Appetite* 54 (1): 202–207.

Choudaha, R., and L. Chang. 2012. *Trends in International Student Mobility*. New York: World Education Services.

Collins, F. L. 2008. "Bridges to Learning: International Student Mobilities, Education Agencies and Inter-Personal Networks." *Global Networks* 8 (4): 398–417.

Collins, F. L. 2012. "Organizing Student Mobility: Education Agents and Student Migration to New Zealand." *Pacific Affairs* 85 (5): 137–160.

Collins, F. L., and K. C. Ho. 2014. "Globalising Higher Education and Cities in Asia and the Pacific." *Asia and Pacific Viewpoint* 55 (2): 127–131.

Cranston, S. 2016. "Producing Migrant Encounter: Learning to be a British Expatriate in Singapore Through the Global Migration Industry." *Environment and Planning D: Society and Space* 34 (4): 655–671.

Cranston, S. 2018. "Calculating the Migration Industries: Knowing the Successful Expatriate in the Global Mobility Industry." *Journal of Ethnic and Migration Studies* 44 (4): 626–643. doi:10.1080/1369183X.2017.1315517.

Cranston, S., J. Schapendonk, and E. Spaan. 2018. "New Directions in Exploring the Migration Industries: Introduction to Special Issue." *Journal of Ethnic and Migration Studies* 44 (4): 543–557. doi:10.1080/1369183X.2017.1315504.

Deakin, H., and K. Wakefield. 2014. "Skype Interviewing: Reflections of Two PhD Researchers." *Qualitative Research* 14 (5): 603–616.

Deem, R. 2001. "Globalisation, New Managerialism, Academic Capitalism and Entrepreneurialism in Universities: Is the Local Dimension Still Important?" *Comparative Education* 37 (1): 7–20.

Findlay, A. M., R. King, F. M. Smith, A. Geddes, and R. Skeldon. 2012. "World Class? An Investigation of Globalisation, Difference and International Student Mobility." *Transactions of the Institute of British Geographers* 37 (1): 118–131.

Foskett, N. 2011. "Markets, Government, Funding and the Marketisation of UK Higher Education." In *The Marketisation of Higher Education and the Student as Consumer*, edited by M. Molesworth, R. Scullion, and E. Nixon, 25–38. London: Routledge.

Gopinath, D. 2015. "Characterizing Indian Students Pursuing Global Higher Education: A Conceptual Framework of Pathways to Internationalization." *Journal of Studies in International Education* 19 (3): 283–305.

Gribble, C. 2008. "Policy Options for Managing International Student Migration: The Sending Country's Perspective." *Journal of Higher Education Policy and Management* 30 (1): 25–39.

Harvey, D. 2005. *A Brief History of Neoliberalism*. Oxford: Oxford University Press.

Harvey, William S., Dimitria Groutsis, and Diane van den Broek. 2018. "Intermediaries and Destination Reputations: Explaining Flows of Skilled Migration." *Journal Of Ethnic And Migration Studies* 44 (4): 644–662. doi:10.1080/1369183X.2017.1315518.

HEFCE. 2004. *Higher Education in the United Kingdom*. Bristol: HEFCE.

Hernández-León, R. 2013. "Conceptualizing the Migration Industry." In *The Migration Industry and the Commercialization of International Migration*, edited by T. Gammeltoft-Hansen and N. N. Sørensen, 24–44. Abingdon: Routledge.

HESA. 2016. "Student, Qualifiers and Staff Data Tables [ Online]." Accessed March 11, 2016. https://www.hesa.ac.uk/content/view/1973/239/.

Huang, I. Y., V. Raimo, and C. Humfrey. 2014. "Power and Control: Managing Agents for International Student Recruitment in Higher Education." *Studies in Higher Education, Online Early Publication*. doi:10.1080/03075079.2014.968543.

ICEF Monitor. 2012. "NCAC Panel Continues the Debate on US Agent Usage [Online]. Accessed June 9, 2016. http://monitor.icef.com/2012/03/nacac-panel-continues-the-debate-on-us-agent-usage/.

Lange, R. 2013. "Return Migration of Foreign Students and Non-Resident Tuition Fees." *Journal of Population Economics* 26 (2): 703–718.

Leung, M. W. H., and J. L. Waters. 2013. "British Degrees Made in Hong Kong: An Enquiry into the Role of Space and Place in Transnational Education." *Asia Pacific Education Review* 14: 43–53.

Ma, A. S. 2014. "Social Networks, Cultural Capital and Attachment to the Host City: Comparing Overseas Chinese Students and Foreign Students in Taipei." *Asia Pacific Viewpoint* 55 (2): 226–241.

Madge, C., P. Raghuram, and P. Noxolo. 2009. "Engaged Pedagogy and Responsibility: A Postcolonial Analysis of International Students." *Geoforum* 40 (1): 34–45.

Matthews, D. 2012. "Grand Fee Paid for Each Foreign Student." *Times Higher Education*, July 2. Accessed March 7, 2016. https://www.timeshighereducation.com/news/grand-fee-paid-for-each-foreign-student/420468.article.

Mavroudi, E., and A. Warren. 2013. "Highly Skilled Migration and the Negotiation of Immigration Policy: Non-EEA Postgraduate Students and Academic Staff at English Universities." *Geoforum* 44: 261–270.

Mayhew, K., C. Deer, and M. Dua. 2004. "The Move to Mass Higher Education in the UK: Many Questions and Some Answers." *Oxford Review of Education* 30 (1): 65–82.

Naidoo, V. 2010. "From Ivory Towers to International Business: Are Universities Export Ready in Their Recruitment of International Students?" *Journal of Studies in International Education* 14 (1): 5–28.

O'Connor, H., C. Madge, R. Shaw, and J. Wellens. 2008. "Internet-Based Interviewing." In *The SAGE Handbook of Online Research Methods*, edited by N. Fielding, N. Lee, and G. Blank, 271–289. London: SAGE.

Olssen, M., and M. A. Peters. 2005. "Neoliberalism, Higher Education and the Knowledge Economy: From the Free Market to Knowledge Capitalism." *Journal of Education Policy* 20 (3): 313–345.

Pandit, K. 2009. "Leading Internationalization." *Annals of the Association of American Geographers*, 99 (4): 645–656.

Simpson, R., J. Sturges, and P. Weight. 2010. "Transient, Unsettling and Creative Space: Experiences of Liminality Through the Accounts of Chinese Students on a UK-Based MBA." *Management Learning* 41 (1): 53–70.

Spaan, E., and F. Hillman. 2013. "Migration Trajectories and the Migration Industry: Theoretical Reflections and Empirical Examples from Asia." In *The Migration Industry and the Commercialization of International Migration*, edited by T. Gammeltoft-Hansen and N. N. Sørensen, 64–86. Abingdon: Routledge.

Spaan, Ernst, and Ton Von Naerssen. 2018. "Migration Decision-making and Migration Industry in the Indonesia–Malaysia Corridor." *Journal Of Ethnic And Migration Studies* 44 (4): 680–695. doi:10.1080/1369183X.2017.1315523.

Tang, A. Z. R., F. Rowe, J. Corcoran, and T. Sigler. 2014. "Where are the Overseas Graduates Staying On? Overseas Graduate Migration and Rural Attachment in Australia." *Applied Geography* 53: 66–76.

Tindal, S., H. Packwood, A. Findlay, S. Leahy, and D. McCollum. 2015. "In What Sense 'Distinctive'? The Search for Distinction Amongst Cross-Border Student Migrants in the UK." *Geoforum* 64: 90–99.

Universities UK. 2014. *International Students in Higher Education: The UK and its Competition.* London: Universities UK.

Waters, J. L. 2009. "In Pursuit of Scarcity: Transnational Students, 'Employability', and the MBA." *Environment and Planning A* 41 (8): 1865–1883.

Zheng, P. 2014. "Antecedents to International Student Inflows to UK Higher Education: A Comparative Analysis." *Journal of Business Research* 67 (2): 136–143.

# Calculating the migration industries: knowing the successful expatriate in the Global Mobility Industry

Sophie Cranston ⓘD

**ABSTRACT**
This paper argues that we need to pay more theoretical attention to the ways in which migration industries come into being, how they produce a need for themselves within the management of migration processes. Using the example of the Global Mobility Industry (GMI), an industry that supports expatriate migration, the paper suggests that we can theorise migration industries as being part of the knowledge economy. It shows how the GMI is produced around the practices of knowing the successful expatriate which work to 'calculate' what expatriate migration should look like. In doing so, the paper shows the way in which the calculative practice of compartmentalisation, in producing knowledge about expatriate migration, produces a need for the GMI. This illustrates the importance of widening our understanding of the economy when researching the migration industries.

## Introduction

Research on the migration industries can be loosely characterised as that which is concerned with the infrastructures that facilitate mobility, what was until recently described as the 'black box' in our understanding of migration (Lindquist, Xiang, and Yeoh 2012). In contributing to our understanding of migration, this type of research has enabled a wider understanding of the hows and whys of migration by looking at the intersections between structure and agency, that 'migration is determined neither by autonomous markets, policy logic, nor according to individual migrant agency, but is rather constituted by a multitude of activities, practices, and technologies that must be considered in specific contexts' (Xiang and Lindquist 2014, s143; see also Cranston, Schapendonk, and Spaan, 2018). This means that it has re-imagined how migration is understood, looking at journeys and trajectories as opposed to origins and destinations (Schapendonk and Steel 2014). This reimagining of how migration is understood allows us to explore the intersections between migrant journeys and migration industries, the 'various public and private agencies and actors [that] provide for such information, products and services relating to migration, thereby promoting, facilitating and organizing the process of migration' (Spaan and Hillmann 2013, 64).

However, through this paper, I argue that while it is important for us to understand the ways in which migration industries facilitate and control mobility, there remains a need to investigate how these industries produce a market for themselves within migration processes. While existing research on the migration industries highlights the role that infrastructures play in facilitating and controlling migration, arguably a 'black box' remains in our understanding of the ways in which migration industries are themselves instituted. This reflects gaps in our understanding of the economy more widely, where 'the market remains a black box and is simply taken as a pre-given' (Berndt and Boeckler 2009, 540). When thinking about the economy, the market for a product or service is often assumed, as opposed to being seen as something that is actively produced. Addressing this gap means focusing our attention not on the intersections between migration industries and migration, but interrogating our understanding of 'industry'. Although what industry is has been the subject of some discussion within the migration industries literature (Gammeltoft-Hansen and Nyberg–Sørensen 2013), this debate centres on what the most appropriate lexicon is to cover the wide array of institutions that facilitate or control migration. My question in this paper then is not what industry is per se, but how do these industries produce a need for themselves within migration processes in the contemporary economy. We can see how this type of question has been addressed by scholars looking at the control functions of migration industries, through an exploration of the neoliberal retrenchment of the state and privatisation (Menz 2013; Andersson 2014) –what we can characterise as the political economy of migration industries. However, through this paper I argue that in order to understand the economy of migration industries, we need to expand our understanding of the economy. Specifically, I draw upon research within cultural economy that looks at the sociology of the economic, that markets are 'bundles of practices and material arrangements always in the making' (Berndt and Boeckler 2010, 565). That is, I argue that we need to explore the practices of migration industries themselves in order to understand their markets – that these do not only come from neoliberalised logics of state retrenchment.

Drawing upon a wider relational turn in understanding the economic (Jones 2014), the paper looks at how migration industries operate in practice, focusing on the case study of the Global Mobility Industry (hereafter GMI). Through this, I argue that we can understand migration industries as part of the knowledge economy, industries that utilise the production, circulation and reproduction of knowledge as an economic resource (Thrift 2005). This draws upon Spaan and Hillman's (2013, 64) observation that 'Information [about migration] has become a commodity that can be capitalized upon for profit'. In this paper, I argue that it is through knowledge, and knowing the migration process, that migration industries produce a need for themselves within migration processes. That is, in exploring how knowledge about migration processes is produced, we can advance our understanding of migration industries, and through this, migration itself. This means we reorient our questioning from how does the state or migration produce industry, to thinking about how does industry produce migration.

The paper looks at this question by exploring how 'successful expatriate' migration becomes known within the GMI. Expatriate, as a term, whilst multiple in definition, is commonly used within transnational organisations to describe an employee on an international assignment or secondment.[1] The expatriate in this paper is a temporary, highly skilled migrant who moves abroad for a period of time with the company that they work for, otherwise described as 'intra-company transferees' (Beaverstock 2004, 2012). As such it is a distinct form of highly skilled migration, in that it is both temporary and often led by the organisation as opposed to the individual moving. We can see it as a form of corporate mobility, one that is linked to processes of globalisation as Millar and Salt (2008, 27) highlight: 'managing the mobility of expertise has become a key element in corporate globalization'. It is also often seen as a form of privileged migration, for example, in terms of the lifestyles that these migrants are able to live (Fechter 2007; Leonard 2010). For example, Knowles and Harper (2009) illustrate the ways in which corporate expatriates in Hong Kong can be seen as the winners in the workings of the global economic system. However, less is understood about the (corporate) mechanisms through which expatriates move, including the industry that works to support this, and how understandings of privilege become entrenched within this (Cranston 2016a).

The move of corporate expatriates is facilitated by their employer organisation – usually involving some input from the human resource department, supported by the GMI who act as an outsourcer for International Human Resource Management (IHRM) processes. The GMI then works to assist with the relocation of the transnational corporation's employees, describing itself as helping with 'the movement of your workforce for which you need data, tools and advice' (Mercer 2010, 2). It provides services in immigration, tax compliance, relocation management, accommodation services, household goods removal and cross-cultural training (Cranston 2014). In assisting with the management of expatriates, its targeted audience is not necessarily the migrants themselves, but helping transnational organisations move their employees globally. It has an estimated worth of $500 billion (event advertising material, November 2011). The 'data, tools and advice' are the ways in which the GMI works to assist expatriate mobility, meaning we can clearly see it as a migration industry in that it works to facilitate this type of corporate migration (Nyberg–Sørensen and Gammeltoft-Hansen 2013). However, I argue that we can see the 'data, tools and advice' as calculative practices which work to make expatriate migration known. It is through exploring these calculative practices that we can understand how the GMI operates as part of the knowledge economy.

In this paper, I examine the calculative practices that both make the 'successful expatriate' known and produce a need for the GMI within expatriate management. The next section of the paper looks at how we can utilise theoretical insights from cultural economy to explore migration industries. Specifically, it looks at the way in which cultural economists draw upon science and technology studies to theorise and explore 'calculative practices' (Callon 1998). After a methods section, the paper will draw upon Callon's framework to explore the ways in which the GMI makes expatriate migration known. First, through a drawing of a list of world states as producing knowledge on how to manage expatriation. Second, the ranking of states as success and failure of expatriate management. Third, highlighting how their products and services are a part of achieving success – describing the actions to produce the steps. This will illustrate how calculative practices work to produce a need for migration industries within processes of mobility, showing the contribution of cultural economy approaches to understanding the operation of migration industries.

## Calculating the migration industries

As highlighted above, within research on the migration industries, there is a need to widen our understanding of their economy. Clearly, the ways in which the economy can be understood and researched is in itself a contested terrain, one that reflects different disciplinary and epistemological traditions. In this paper, I draw upon two interlinked arguments about how we understand the economic. The first of these is conceptual – looking at cultural economy readings of migration industries. The second is empirical – looking at the knowledge economy as part of a shift in how economic value is globally produced.

Cultural economy perspectives speak to a reconceptualization of the economic, where it is not seen as a measurable and distinct entity, but as 'varied impulses and articulations through which value is formed, added, and circulated' (Amin and Thrift 2003, xv). A central idea within this is an understanding of the performativity of the economic, where people, objects and ideas work to 'form', 'add' and 'circulate' value. This understanding of the performativity is often utilised to understand the knowledge economy, where economic markets are produced through the production and circulation of knowledge, in so far that knowledge acts as an economic resource in itself. The aspect of this that the paper focuses on is what Thrift (2005) describes as 'soft capitalism' – economies based on new ideas and thinking. Thrift argues that the knowledge economy has:

> chiefly been conjured into existence by the discursive apparatus of the cultural circuit of capital, which through the continuous production of propositional and prescriptive knowledge, has the power to make its theories and description of the world come alive in built forms, new machines and new bodies. (Thrift 2005, 11)

Within this, producing, circulating and reproducing knowledge become ways in which organisations create their market. Knowledge of the economic can be seen as performative, in that it works to produce itself as being a required part of the practices of the economy – it becomes part of the circuit. For the migration industries, a cultural economy approach involves a re-scaling of thinking about the economy, to looking at its micro-scale articulations. It is through this that I argue we should think about the practices of migration industries. The 'built forms, new machines and new bodies' are the everyday performances of people, objects, ideas and spaces in the economy that produce the economic, or what we can describe as being practices of knowing.

Although there are different ways in which we can theorise practice within accounts of the economic (Jones and Murphy 2011) this paper draws upon science and technology studies that see markets as being produced by apparatus, which in turn are produced by people, objects and knowledge: 'markets are performative effects of complex embodied and concrete socio-material arrangements' (Barnes 2008, 1436). For example, MacKenzie (2006) illustrates the ways in which people, the computer screen and financial models worked to produce financial markets. This shows that financial theory is not merely descriptive, that it works to produce what it purports to describe. One example he uses is the Black–Scholes model, which in modelling derivative investment, worked to legitimise and thus produce the options market. This practice of knowing is a calculative practice. Calculation is a way through which the social is made known, both quantitatively, for example through numbers and qualitatively, such as in processes like organising

(Crampton and Elden 2006). Hence, calculative practices are practices 'that make the economy visible and measurable qua economy' (Miller 2001, 379). Significantly, these practices do not just describe the economy, but act to produce it – what MacKenzie (2006) might describe as an engine not a camera. For example, Larner and Le Heron, in looking at benchmarking in New Zealand universities argue that 'rather than being neutral measuring tools providing information about "outputs" or "outcomes", calculative practices govern … The emerging processes have new content, influenced by new imaginings of outcomes, and new strategies for assembling people and resources to achieve new ends' (2005, 846). Or Miller (2001) illustrates that accounting, as a calculative practice, works to shape social and economic relations, for example, how we understand the nation's educational successes. This means that calculative practices, in making processes known, work to produce these processes in their image, they: 'do not merely record a reality independent from themselves; they contribute powerfully to shaping it, simply by measuring it, the reality that they measure' (Callon 1998, 23). In looking at the ways in which migration industries produce knowledge and information on migration then, we can see this as not merely describing migration, but producing migration in its image. Migration industries in working to make migration known, produce themselves as being part of the migration process – this is the performativity of this knowledge.

In this paper, I focus on one calculative practice of the GMI – compartmentalisation. This is a way through which migration becomes known through calculative practices of knowledge, the breaking down of the migration of the expatriate into smaller steps so that both expatriate migration, and each of these individual steps, become known. Callon argues that for calculated decisions to be taken, the agent must be able to: 'a) draw up a list of possible world states; b) hierarchize and rank these world states; c) identify and describe the actions required to produce each of the possible world states' (1998, 260). Hence, we can see how calculative practices are themselves produced through knowledge, as they work to make the 'incommensurable commensurable' (Larner and Le Heron 2002, 759). That is, calculative practices turn something unknown, like the process of migration, into something that is known and can be compared. The paper will show that compartmentalisation acts as a way through which expatriate migration is drawn up, compared and how to achieve success in expatriate management identified – an action that is seen as involving using the services offered by the GMI. Therefore, while the services that migration industries like the Global Mobility Industry offers help to facilitate migration, they are produced from practices associated with knowing the migration process that are in turn produced by the industry. The 'Knowing the successful expatriate' section will illustrate that this knowledge, rather than merely describing the migration process, plays an active role in shaping the migration process – this after all is its intention – working to shape migration processes in the image through which it purports to describe.

## Methods

The paper draws upon ethnographic methods carried out with the GMI and IHRM between 2011 and 2012 in the U.K. and Singapore. The focus of this research was to look at the production, dissemination and reproduction of knowledge about the expatriate, the ways in which this type of migration was organised 'unfolds and is enacted'

(Schwartzman 1993, 36). This involved utilising three methods: texts, observation and interviews. First, I analysed texts that looked at expatriate management more widely both as an academic discipline through textbooks and journal articles, and as a practice in terms of surveys, management reports and policy documents which were provided to me by organisations that I carried out research with, or were referred to by participants in my research. Second, I carried out participant observation in two ways: at nine global mobility conferences and events (see Cranston 2014) and through participation in activities within the GMI, working both at events and helping a group compile surveys for their annual report. Third, I carried out 15 interviews with global mobility service providers and 8 interviews with individuals who work in international human resource departments of transnational organisations. The data from these methods were analysed through a close discursive reading, looking at the similarities and differences between practices of managing the expatriate as a 'patchwork of thoughts, words, objects, events, actions, and interactions in discourses' (Gee 1999 in Dittmer 2009, 275–276).

## Knowing the successful expatriate

In this section, I look at compartmentalisation as a calculative practice of the GMI. I draw upon Callon's (1998) framework of how calculative practices operate as described above. The first subsection explores ways in which expatriate migration becomes compartmentalised, drawing up a list of what expatriate migration should look like. The second subsection looks at the production of two different states of expatriate migration – success and failure, as the ranking of the states of expatriate migration. The third subsection looks at the actions that are identified to produce success and failure, with the GMI both benchmarking knowledge and claiming expertise in knowing successful expatriate management. Therefore, the industry as a collective draws up the 'state' of expatriate migration, ranks this as successful and then identifies how this can be achieved – through using their services. Collectively, this section will show how knowing the successful expatriate works to produce a need for the GMI. That is, in commodifying the knowledge of how to successfully manage the expatriate as an economic resource, the GMI creates and legitimises a need for expatriates and their managers to use their services.

### *Compartmentalisation: identifying expatriate migration*

The 'state' of corporate expatriate migration is closely tied with IHRM, which as an academic discipline and practice within transnational organisations focuses on the transnational management of people: 'the way in which international organisations manage their human resources across different national contexts' (Brewster, Sparrow, and Vernon 2007, 6). Within this, the main way in which the management of the expatriate is expressed is through a compartmentalised 'life cycle' of the expatriate, which shows the different stages of the expatriate within the transnational organisation: selection, preparation, relocation, adjustment, performance and repatriation (Figure 1). The utilisation of this expatriate assignment cycle illustrates a way through which we can visualise the journey of this type of migration, from a beginning through the selection of the employee, to an assumed end when they return back to where they started from. Significant research

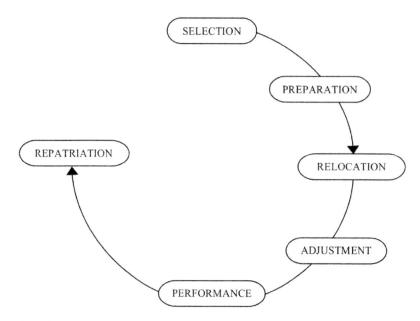

**Figure 1.** Expatriate assignment cycle.

within expatriate management is directed at producing effective strategies for managing each stage of the cycle, and the cycle as a whole: 'the complexities of managing this cycle have been the focus of sustained academic research over many years' (Brewster, Sparrow, and Vernon 2007, 242).

The expatriate assignment cycle is a 'textbook' account (Harzing and Christensen 2004, 619) of expatriate migration, where the person relocating is seen to 'experience a predictable series of stages in transferring from a domestic to a global assignment and back home again' (Adler 1997, 236). For example, Black et al. write about this in terms of the responsibilities of the organisation, 'we feel that companies are not only economically wise but, perhaps more importantly, duty-bound to offer sufficient support to expatriate employees throughout the international assignment cycle' (1999, 275). A consultant in a seminar, displaying the assignment cycle in a figure form, discussed with her participants about 'creating a no-fail environment expat life-cycle' (Webinar, September 2011). Or a senior global mobility manager when talking about how her assignees are managed suggested that:

> so in terms of the what happens once it is decided, we do follow an international assignment life-cycle and that is fairly typical across the whole of the industry, or the whole of the industries I have ever worked for, from start to being on assignment to repatriation. (Alice, Interview, August 2012)

The use of its cycle in its variant forms can be seen to be a hegemonic interpretation of expatriation, one whose original authorship is no longer acknowledged. It is one that utilises a process-based view of expatriation, focusing on the practices of managing migration rather than the individual moving. This process-based viewed of migration is a crucial way in which migration becomes known through the GMI. It illustrates that corporate expatriate migration is not just visualised as a movement from A to B, but within it there remains an expectation of return. It is therefore a key way in which expatriate migration as a 'state' is drawn up.

IHRM, in both theory and practice, works to organise and categorise the expatriate through the assignment cycle. It is a way in which expatriate migration becomes known, acting as a calculative practice in itself. However, importantly, the GMI has adapted the expatriate assignment cycle into a further compartmentalised form of how to manage the expatriate. This is the breaking down of, into a step by step format, of all the processes associated with relocation, described as the 'expatriate assignment flow', shown in Figure 2. A version of this diagram was used as part of a meeting explaining and selling the role of the GMI to potential IHRM clients. Like the expatriate assignment cycle, this is a further distillation of a process-based view of the 'state' of expatriate migration, that turns the management of the expatriates relocation into a set of smaller steps.

The compartmentalisation of how corporate expatriates are moved clearly illustrates a way in which the GMI makes this type of mobility known. Figure 2 then illustrates how

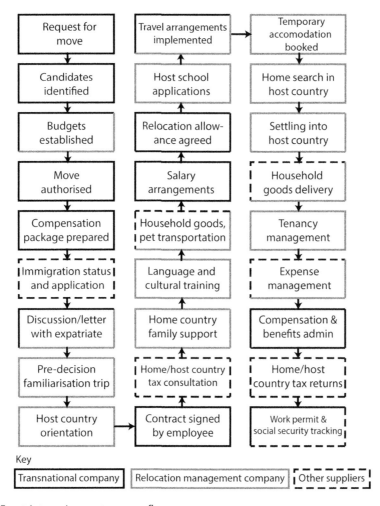

**Figure 2.** Expatriate assignment process flow.

compartmentalisation works as a qualitative calculative practice, as it works to order expatriate migration. It shows the ways through which migration is visualised as a series of steps that the organisation and the individual relocating move through. It contributes to the ways through which we understand how 'rather than being a means to an end, the journeys migrants make are their migration projects' (Burrell 2008, 360); how the ways through which people move, and are moved, are central to the ways in which migration is understood as a practice in itself. While not assuming a linearity in all migrants following this flow, it shows how a conceptualisation of steps becomes important in thinking about how the migration industry intersects with the journey of migrants. Some of these steps can be seen as universal in legal international migration: applying for immigration status, the movement of possessions, school applications and so on. The expatriate assignment process flow therefore provides a way in which migration can be understood as a series of steps as part of a wider process – how migration in itself becomes known. However, as the next section will show, looking at the component parts of the expatriate assignment flow, works to 'rank' different states of expatriate management – success and failure.

### *Ranking the successful expatriate*

The discussions on effective expatriate migration are discussions about the success of the transnational organisation. IHRM is intertwined with the strategic success of transnational organisation, in that IHRM becomes a strategy in itself: 'the effective management of HR is seen as a major determinant of success and failure in international business' (Tayeb 2005, 8). This strategy then is directed at the end product of IHRM, the success or failure of the expatriate. Success and failure are the two ways in which expatriate migration as a state becomes ranked.

The failure of expatriation is regularly used to frame and support global mobility authors arguments about best practices (Harzing and Christensen 2004). For example, Dowling, Festing, and Engle (2008) describe failure as being:

> the premature return of an expatriate (that is, a return home before the period of assignment, or expatriate management cycle, is completed). In such a case, an expatriate failure represented a selection error, often compounded by ineffective expatriate management policies. (Dowling, Festing, and Engle 2008, 112)

The failure of the expatriate then is seen as not completing the steps from the beginning to the end of the expatriate journey, from relocation to return. This failure is disastrous to the organisation in terms of the significant cost of expatriate assignments, which in terms of direct cost is estimated at 1–3.5 million dollars for a four-year assignment (Black et al. 1999, 15). The financial risks associated with a failed expatriation also becomes a key way through which the GMI operates, with this migration industry constructing themselves as risk managers (c.f. Faulconbridge et al. 2009). This point is discussed in more detail below.

The definition of success is often debated within expatriate management circles without a clear conclusion being reached. Therefore, success becomes understood as not being failure. The successful expatriate is one who is first selected properly and second managed effectively. Selection criteria will obviously vary between roles, sector and organisation, but have a number of common factors – technical ability, cross-cultural suitability, family requirements, country or cultural requirements, language skills and company requirements (Dowling, Festing, and Engle 2008). In the interviews I carried out with IHRM managers, 'flexibility' was identified as an ideal characteristic for success, defined in terms of culture and family: 'is this person flexible, are they culturally sensitive, do they have a complicated home situation' (Beth, Senior Global Mobility Manager, Interview, February 2012). While flexibility is hard to define, one of the ways in which Beth suggested it could be defined was by looking at the expatriate's family situation. This supports the notion that an inability to adjust to a new cultural environment is the most commonly cited reason for the failure of expatriates (Black et al. 1999) – they fail at the adjustment stage and therefore do not complete the assignment. Success therefore becomes understood as the expatriate who is managed effectively round the expatriate assignment cycle, completing all of the steps. This is clearly the desirable state of expatriate management, ranked the highest.

### Identifying actions: the GMI

Both the failed expatriate migration and the successful expatriate migration become ways in which expatriate migration as a state become ranked. In this section, I look at how the GMI works to produce their services as being part of the way in which 'success' can be achieved. This is the identification and description of the actions required to produce the state of the successful expatriate, by utilising the advice provided by the GMI. This happens despite the fact that the GMI's concern is with the day-to-day management of the expatriate's move and management – they are not directly involved in discussions about how to manage expatriates effectively. The industry itself argues that it operates as the 'activity end of the policy' (Elizabeth, Relocation Management Consultancy, Interview, October 2011), enacting the transnational organisation's directions and facilitating the expatriate's move, they are 'transnational rather than strategic ... we are not involved in that debate, just waiting on instruction to move Joe Bloggs from A to B' (Evan, Relocation Management Company, Interview, October 2011). While this shows the way in which the GMI acts to facilitate the movement of corporate expatriates, it does not illustrate why transnational organisations use their services. However, it is through knowledge that the industry places itself as being part of the strategic success of corporate expatriate migration. This is enacted through three interlinked practices of knowledge – the designation of steps, claiming expertise and benchmarking.

The first practice of knowing that works to identify how successful expatriate migration can be achieved is the designation of each step of managing the expatriate between the transnational organisation, relocation management company and specialist provider (as shown by Figure 2). This compartmentalisation of expatriate migration means the GMI legitimises a need for their services at various stages of the process – it is a way in which successful expatriate migration becomes realised. On the expatriate assignment flow, various stages are claimed as being provided by the GMI. It is through claiming their services as contributing to the success of the steps of expatriate migration that the industry produces themselves as a solution to failure. By telling the client how to achieve a state of success, the industry produces themselves as being strategically involved in successful expatriate management – identifying the actions through which successful expatriate management can be achieved. However, although compartmentalisation illustrates a division of labour between the transnational organisation and the GMI in managing the processes of expatriate migration, other practices of knowing – claiming expertise and benchmarking – discursively act as a way through which transnational organisations are persuaded to use the GMI services in order to achieve a successful expatriate migration.

The second practice of knowledge that identifies a need for the GMI's services to produce the state of successful expatriate migration is through the self-portrayal of the industry as being expert. This is another way in which we can see how the industry acts as a form of the knowledge economy, in that it is through the cultural packing of knowledge that the industry produces and sells the need for its services. Drawing on work on the internationalisation of the headhunting industry, we can see how this industry packages business knowledge in order to create an economic need for itself, 'the discursive strategies in the engineering of an exclusive role of headhunters in elite recruitment processes' (Faulconbridge et al. 2009, 801). Faulconbridge et al. (2009) look at how companies in the headhunting industry propagate both ideas of the knowledge and skills required to headhunt as being complex, and themselves as risk managers, persuading others to use their services. Following this, I argue that through compartmentalisation as a calculative practice, we can see how the GMI mobilise themselves as being experts in preventing a failed expatriation.

The GMI collectively produces a (self) portrayal of being expert, illustrating the idea that 'business has to become more *knowledgeable* in a turbulent and constantly fluctuating world' (Thrift 1997, 30; emphasis in original). This claim is made through two complimentary types of knowledge. First, is that of empathetic knowledge, that the people who work within the industry often have experience of expatriation themselves: 'Because we've walked in their shoes, we have developed the know-how to provide the best service for our clients' (Advertising Brochure 2012). Second, is the technical know-how of how to manage the different stages of relocation. This is promoted through the idea of the difficulties of managing expatriates: 'the complexities of international assignments have contributed to the growth of outsourcing, which offers an avenue for the company to best serve the needs of the expatriate' (Lockhart in Outsourcing International HR 2004). It is the most technically demanding services, immigration and tax, that are two of the most commonly outsourced services (Forum for Expatriate Management 2011) and are designated as being supplied by the GMI in the expatriate assignment process flow (Figure 2). The advertising materials of companies within the GMI promote complexity, with for example 'transferring employees' being seen as 'more challenging than ever before' (Mercer, Advertising Brochure 2011), or more explicitly with a company saying that they 'guide our clients through thousands of unique and complex programs' (Cartus, Advertising Brochure 2011). How this technical know-how is promoted by individual organisations obviously depends on the primary service that they offer. For example, one company, who specialise in providing software, suggest that 'the expertise is putting the package together, gross to net, so payroll know what to pay' (Robert, Relocation Management Company, October 2011). Others claim this technical expertise in the number of situations and problems associated with corporate relocation they have encountered, that 'you name, we have seen it' (Elizabeth, Relocation Management Consultancy, October 2011). In this way, the GMI is produced as the solution to relocation management problems, because of their know-how and experience. We can see that like the headhunting industry, knowledge of the process of migration acts as a 'device for legitimating the expertise and role' of the industry in migration management (Beaverstock, Faucolnbridge, and Hall 2010, 840). Using the expertise of the industry then becomes a way in which achieving success is identified.

These types of claims to expertise are contrasted with the industry's portrayal of HR managers as being inexperienced. Again this is based on both tacit and technical knowledge. For example, HR managers are seen to be inexperienced because they themselves have not had international experience. They are seen to be focused on technical rather than emotional elements: 'HR is more practical – what is my per diem. Often they don't realise what the issues are, can be an eye opener' (Betty, Relocation Management Consultancy, January 2012). This is part of the lack of length and breadth of experience HR managers are perceived to have: 'HR managers are young and without experience, it's a difficult job ... they are qualified as HR without the background and experience' (Elizabeth, Relocation Management Consultancy, October 2011). Elizabeth is suggesting that the lack of experience that these 'young' HR managers have means that they do not have the needed expertise and therefore 'need to be trained in how the industry works'. This lack of knowledge is a way in which failure is seen to occur. For example, the lack of expertise was attributed as one of the main reasons that companies choose to outsource some functions of expatriate management to the GMI, with Beth when asked why she outsources replying 'to take advantage of their expertise' (Global Mobility Manager, February 2012). Hence, whilst using the GMI's services becomes a way in which how to achieve success is identified, how to achieve failure is also produced – by not using the GMI's knowledge.

Third, while the compartmentalisation of expatriate management is in itself a calculative practice of how the successful expatriate becomes ordered and known as whole, this is also carried out through the benchmarking of the individual steps of expatriate migration. Benchmarking is the comparison of one company's international assignment policy to another, where 'their world states' become known, measured and comparable into a 'common language for communication' (Larner and Le Heron 2002, 760). By looking at how the GMI facilitates benchmarking we can see how the industry produces themselves as being part of how success is ranked. There are different ways in which the GMI facilitates benchmarking, for example, through events (see Cranston 2014 for a discussion of this) and through surveys and reports which will be the focus of the rest of this section.

Benchmarking through surveys is again discursively produced as being a means by which to achieve a successful expatriation. For example, one company suggests that 'aligning your company's expatriation practices with best practices in the marketplace is critical to your expatriation program's success' (Mercer, Advertising Brochure, 2011). It is a way in which actions are identified to achieve the state of 'successful' expatriation. The production, dissemination and circulation of surveys are a way in which the GMI directly sells knowledge. Companies within the GMI, such as *Brookfield GRS*, *Santa Fe Relocation*, *Cartus*, *Deloitte*, *PwC*, and Global Mobility groups like the *Forum for Expatriate Management* and *RES*, produce a variety of surveys and reports which are a way in which to 'explore some of the most pertinent questions asked by HR/Global Mobility Directors worldwide for establishing and maintaining their global mobility teams according to global best and next practices' (Forum for Expatriate Management 2011). The output from these surveys are quantitative which allows for easy comparison between organisations. For example, referring back to the process flow shown in Figure 2, one of the stages is language or cultural training, whereby the individual, and their family, are taught how to culturally adapt their behaviour in the destination that they are going to, hence improving their cultural 'flexibility'. The RES annual report in 2011 suggests that 68% of organisations offer some form of 'cultural training', the Brookfield 2010 Global Relocation Trends survey highlights that 27% of organisations offer this for all assignments, and 53% for some assignments, depending on where the individual is moving to. These figures are presented through pie charts, bar charts and text, often with quotes from survey respondents. The numbers presented are a material manifestation of benchmarking practices, they allow for the comparison between companies, the production of an industry norm, and the potential adaptation to fit. The production of surveys offers a way through which often confidential expatriate assignment policies can become known to others.

However, although many of the statistics and 'facts' are not standard in surveys, as they differ from one another depending on the make-up of their respondents, they do portray themselves as offering a comprehensive picture of expatriate assignment policies. As Wilson suggests in his look at how data was produced for a community project in Seattle, 'data are products resulting from specific practices, and in the affective sense … data are imaginative, generative and evocative' (2011, 857). Using the concept of transduction, that is practices that produce space, Wilson shows how indicators about the urban quality of life are made legitimate through standardisation and objectification. Drawing upon this, I argue that surveys work to make certain characteristics of global mobility programmes legitimate, as they become a standard interpretation of what a 'successful' global mobility programme should look like. They therefore work to legitimise and objectify in a numerical form the idea of what successful expatriate migration should look like within transnational organisations. This illustrates two practices of knowledge in the GMI that work to identify how success can be achieved. The first of these is through the direct use and commodification of the knowledge of success, with for example, the Forum for Expatriate Management annual report costing £1250 in 2011. The second, is the placing of the services offered by the GMI as part of achieving a successful expatriate migration. For example, cross-cultural training can be seen as the industry norm, especially if the expatriate is being moved to a location that is deemed to be difficult. Offering cross-cultural training then becomes a way through which successful expatriate migration can be achieved, a service, which as Figure 2 illustrates, is one offered by the GMI.

This use of benchmarking is something that is articulated as a common practice for IHR managers, meaning that there is an active take-up of the actions identified by the GMI to achieve success:

> … we very much monitor what's happening within our industry sector and our policy team undertake regular benchmarking processes to ensure that we remain competitive within our own industry and again that is something that I, you know, have experienced as being very typical across the various sectors that I have worked in as well, the whole benchmarking exercise. (Alice, Senior Global Mobility Manager, August 2012)

Alice, in describing benchmarking as a practice that enables her company to remain competitive, highlights its performativity, that they might change their expatriate assignment policies in order to fit the norm. This shows how transnational organisations change their policies as an action designed to achieve a successful expatriate migration, as Beth also highlighted:

> For example we opened an office in [location] recently and I needed to find some information out … and then when the business came back to me and said we have been challenged on x, y, z, then I can respond and say well 'I've reached out to some other, you know, other professionals, who worked at different organisations and [company] who have offices, or, you know, [company] who have offices in [location] also say that we don't do this, blah, blah, blah' there is no need to do it and then when assignees are challenging the business on additional help, additional support, we can go back and say 'well nobody else does this', or we can go back and say 'well everybody else does this, we need to start offering this'. (Global Mobility Manager, Finance, February 2012)

Beth is suggesting that benchmarking offers the IHR manager an additional level of knowledge that enables her to offer what she perceives as a suitable level of support. If something is not being offered by her company, that is offered by others in the same location, then she will think about, and have justification to support, changing the policy. This is viewed from every step of the expatriate assignment process flow, shown in Figure 2, where each action taken by the transnational organisation in assisting expatriate migration can be broken down and compared between companies. It is a way that we can directly see how knowledge is performative, how people use what is seen as best practices and change their policies to fit the norm. For our understanding of migration, this acts as a way in which migration processes are produced, working to shape the services that move migrants (Cranston 2016a).

Therefore, we can see the way in which the GMI not only makes expatriate migration known, but also works to produce its services as being part of a successful expatriate migration. This is the way in which it identifies how successful expatriate migration can be achieved – by using its services. This is produced through knowledge, the benchmarking of the steps of expatriate migration, identifying which steps of expatriate migration involve using the industry's expertise. This works to produce the industry as expert in the knowledge of how to achieve success. Knowing expatriate migration is therefore the GMI's market. It is the production, circulation and reproduction of knowledge about the successful expatriate which legitimises a need for this industry within expatriate migration.

## Conclusions

The GMI can be seen as a facilitator of expatriate migration, by providing services which facilitate this type of mobility. This means we can see the ways in which exploring this industry contributes to our understandings of migration more widely. For example, looking at the way in which the GMI facilitates expatriate migration contributes to closing the gap where 'mainstream migration theory … has been notably reluctant to engage with corporate forms of human mobility' (Millar and Salt 2008, 28). It tells us ways in which expatriate mobility is theorised from a labour market perspective by thinking through the ways in which the industry assists with relocation, from a mobilities perspective by exploring the ways through which these migrants move and from a social and cultural perspective in looking at how industries contribute towards the production of an 'expatriate' identity (Cranston 2016a). In this way, this paper contributes to a growing body of research that looks at how labour market intermediaries function as part of the migration industry, looking at the mechanisms through which organisations seek employees abroad (van den Broek, Harvey, and Groutsis 2015; McCollum and Findlay 2018). For research on East European recruitment agencies, this has looked at the ways in which they produce the category of the 'good migrant', illustrating 'hiring practices that draw socially constructed boundaries around migrant bodies – those that are deemed "ideal" relative to images of the "good worker"' (Findlay 2013, 163). These are practices that are produced and justified through knowledge. The 'successful expatriate' similarly is a figure within corporate relocation, where a norm of the expatriate is produced and labelled. It helps us to understand how entrenched understandings of privilege are within this type of mobility, for example, with the discussions over the best housing allowances. It is through understanding these knowledge practices, that we can see how migration industries work to produce migration in particular ways.

However, through this paper, I have argued for a need to explore migration industries more widely, to think about how we understand their economy. In the paper, I have shown how the GMI operates as part of the knowledge economy, how they produce a space for themselves within migration processes. Successful expatriate migration as a state of migration is not self-evident, but becomes known, with the GMI identifying the use of their services and expertise as a way in which this state can be achieved. This knowledge is therefore performative in that it produces a need for the GMI. It orders and categorises expatriate migration into a step-by-step process, ranks success and identifies using its services as the way to achieve success. This is how the GMI legitimises a need for its services, as the organisation are told that they are mitigating the risk of a potential failed assignment (Faulconbridge et al. 2009). Therefore, we can see how the different practices of knowing, compartmentalisation and benchmarking, work to produce the need for the GMI. This exploration of why organisations use the GMI is important for understanding the recent growth in migration industries. While political economy accounts of migration industries highlight our understanding of both industries and migration within a neoliberal context, this does not account for how they operate in practice. The paper has shown that we cannot solely reduce the operation of migration industries to the logics of neoliberal retrenchment from the perspective of states reinforcing their borders by outsourcing their services. Utilising a cultural economy approach means investigating the way in which the practices of knowing migration work to produce migration and migration industries in certain ways. We cannot fully understand the ways in which migration is produced by migration industries, without first understanding the industry itself.

This highlights the importance of asking 'small questions' in order to address the 'big questions' at hand when researching migration industries (Berndt and Boeckler 2009). The small questions here are the ways in which migration industries operate, and the big questions are those looking at to what end this happens. It does not involve separating ourselves from the political, it involves utilising a different lens to 'examine the relationship between migration industry and the political, economic and social structures' (Nyberg–Sørensen and Gammeltoft-Hansen 2013, 14). It involves thinking about how migration industries, their economy, and the political more widely are produced through practice, giving us the 'theoretical capacity to better understand how everyday micro-social practices influence and can embody the complexities, contingencies, and meanings that constitute most social-economic and political-economic phenomena'

(Jones and Murphy 2011, 367). Through practices of knowing, we can explore how migration industries function, and through this, develop our understanding and theorisation of the intersections between migration industries and other domains of migration. It shows how we need to ask how industry produces migration, as well as how migration produces industry.

## Note

1. Expatriate is also a loaded term, often used to refer exclusively to white, privileged migrants more widely (see, for example Cranston 2017). However, in this paper I refer to 'expatriate' in the way that transnational organisations have traditionally utilised this term, although there is evidence to suggest that this is changing (Cranston, 2016b).

## Acknowledgements

Thanks to Dan Swanton and Allan Findlay for all of their advice and assistance when writing an earlier draft of this paper. Also to Matt Baddock for his help with the figures.

## Disclosure statement

No potential conflict of interest was reported by the author.

## Funding

This work was supported by the ESRC [grant number ES/I018670/1].

## ORCID

*Sophie Cranston* ⓘ http://orcid.org/0000-0001-7068-7029

## References

Adler, N. 1997. *International Dimensions of Organizational Behaviour*. Cincinnati, OH: South Western College.
Amin, A., and N. Thrift. 2003. "Introduction." In *The Blackwell Cultural Economy Reader*, edited by A. Amin, and N. Thrift, i–xxx. Oxford: Blackwell.
Andersson, R. 2014. *Illegality, Inc*. Oakland: University of California Press.
Barnes, T. 2008. "Making Space for the Economy: Live Performances, Dead Objects and Economic Geography." *Geography Compass* 2 (5): 1432–1448.
Beaverstock, J. 2004. "'Managing Across Borders': Knowledge Management and Expatriation in Professional Service Legal Firms." *Journal of Economic Geography* 4: 157–179.
Beaverstock, J. 2012. "Highly Skilled International Labour Migration and World Cities: Expatriates, Executives, Entrepreneurs." In *International Handbook of Globalization and World Cities*, edited by B. Derudder, M. Hoyler, P. Taylor, and F. Witlox, 240–250. Cheltenham: Edward Elgar.
Beaverstock, J., J. Faucolnbridge, and S. Hall. 2010. "Professionalization, Legitimization and the Creation of Executive Search Markets in Europe." *Journal of Economic Geography* 10 (6): 825–843.
Berndt, C., and M. Boeckler. 2009. "Geographies of Circulation and Exchange: Constructions of Markets." *Progress in Human Geography* 33 (4): 535–551.

Berndt, C., and M. Boeckler. 2010. "Geographies of Markets: Materials, Morals and Monsters in Motion." *Progress in Human Geography* 35 (4): 559–567.

Black, J., H. Gregerson, M. Mendenhall, and L. Stroh. 1999. *Globalizing People Through International Assignments*. Harlow: Addison Wesley Longman.

Brewster, C., P. Sparrow, and G. Vernon. 2007. *International Human Resource Management*. London: Chartered Institute of Personnel and Development.

Burrell, K. 2008. "Materialising the Border: Spaces of Mobility and Material Culture in Migration from Post-Socialist Poland." *Mobilities* 3 (3): 353–373.

Callon, M. 1998. *Laws of the Markets*. Oxford: Wiley-Blackwell.

Crampton, J., and S. Elden. 2006. "Space, Politics, Calculation: An Introduction." *Social and Cultural Geography* 7 (5): 681–685.

Cranston, S. 2014. "Reflections on Doing the Expat Show: Performing the Global Mobility Industry." *Environment and Planning A* 46: 1124–1138.

Cranston, S. 2016a. "Producing Migrant Encounter: Learning to be a British Expatriate in Singapore Through the Global Mobility Industry." *Environment and Planning D: Society and Space* 34 (4): 655–671.

Cranston, S. 2016b. "Imagining Global Work: Producing Understandings of Difference in Easy Asia." *Geoforum* 70: 60–68.

Cranston, S. 2017. "Expatriate as a 'Good' Migrant: Thinking Through Skilled International Migrant Categories." *Population, Space and Place* (Online First).

Cranston, S., J. Schapendonk, and E. Spaan. 2018. "New Directions in Exploring the Migration Industries: Introduction to Special Issue." *Journal of Ethnic and Migration Studies* 44 (4): 543–557. doi:10.1080/1369183X.2017.1315504.

Dittmer, J. 2009. "Textual and Discourse Analysis." In *SAGE Handbook of Qualitative Research in Human Geography*, edited by D. DeLyser, S. Herbert, S. Aitken, M. Crang, and L. McDowell, 274–286. London: SAGE Publications.

Dowling, P., M. Festing, and A. Engle. 2008. *International Human Resource Management*. Andover: Centage Learning EMEA.

Faulconbridge, J., J. Beaverstock, S. Hall, and A. Hewitson. 2009. "The 'War for Talent': The Gatekeeper Role of Executive Search Firms in Elite Labour Markets." *Geoforum* 40 (5): 800–808.

Fechter, A. 2007. *Transnational Lives: Expatriates in Indonesia*. Aldershot: Ashgate.

Findlay, A. M., D. McCollum, S. Shubin, E. Aspite, and Z. Krisjane. 2013. "The Role of Recruitment Agencies in Imagining and Producing the 'Good' Migrant." *Social and Cultural Geography* 14 (2): 145–167.

Gammeltoft-Hansen, T., and N. Nyberg-Sørensen. 2013. *The Migration Industry and the Commercialization of International Migration*. Abingdon: Routledge.

Harzing, A., and C. Christensen. 2004. "Expatriate Failure: Time to Abandon the Concept?" *Career Development International* 9 (7): 616–626.

Jones, A. 2014. "Geographies of Production I: Relationality Revisted and the 'Practice Shift' in Economic Geography." *Progress in Human Geography* 38 (4): 605–615.

Jones, A., and J. Murphy. 2011. "Theorizing Practice in Human Geography: Foundations, Challenges and Possibilities." *Progress in Human Geography* 35: 366–392.

Knowles, C., and D. Harper. 2009. *Hong Kong: Migrant Lives, Landscapes, Journeys*. Chicago, IL: University of Chicago press.

Larner, W., and R. Le Heron. 2002. "The Spaces and Subjects of a Globalising Economy: A Situated Exploration of Method." *Environment and Planning D: Society and Space* 20 (6): 753–774.

Larner, W., and R. Le Heron. 2005. "Neo-Liberalizing Spaces and Subjectivities: Reinventing New Zealand Universities." *Organization* 12 (6): 843–862.

Leonard, P. 2010. *Expatriate Identities in Postcolonial Organizations: Working Whiteness*. Farnham: Ashgate.

Lindquist, J., B. Xiang, and B. Yeoh. 2012. "Opening the Black Box of Migration, Brokers, the Organization of Transnational Mobility and the Changing Political Economy in Asia." *Pacific Affairs* 85 (1): 7–19.

MacKenzie, D. 2006. *An Engine, not a Camera: How Financial Models Shape Markets.* London: MIT Press.

McCollum, D., and A. Findlay. 2018. "Oiling the Wheels? Flexible Labour Markets and the Migration Industry." *Journal of Ethnic and Migration Studies* 44 (4): 558–574. doi:10.1080/1369183X.2017.1315505.

Menz, G. 2013. "The Neoliberalized State ad the Growth of the Migration Industry." In *The Migration Industry and the Commercialization of International Migration,* edited by T. Gammeltoft-Hansen, and N. Nyberg–Sørensen, 108–127. Abingdon: Routledge.

Mercer. 2010. *How Do You Define Global Mobility?* s.l.: Mercer.

Millar, M., and J. Salt. 2008. "Portfolios of Mobility: The Movement of Expertise in Transnational Corporations in Two Sectors – Aerospace and Extractive Industries." *Global Networks* 8 (1): 25–50.

Miller, P. 2001. "Governing by Numbers: Why Calculative Practices Matter." *Social Research* 68 (2): 379–396.

Nyberg–Sørensen, N., and T. Gammeltoft-Hansen. 2013. "Introduction." In *The Migration Industry and the Commercialization of International Migration,* 1–24. Abingdon: Routledge.

Schapendonk, J., and G. Steel. 2014. "Following Migrant Trajectories: The Im/mobility of Sub-Saharan Africans en Route to the European Union." *Annals of the Association of American Geographers* 104 (2): 26–270.

Schwartzman, H. 1993. *Ethnography in Organizations.* London: Sage.

Spaan, E., and F. Hillmann. 2013. "Migration Trajectories and the Migration Industry: Theoretical Reflections and Empirical Examples from Asia." In *The Migration Industry and the Commercialization of International Migration,* edited by T. Gammeltoft-Hansen and N. Nyberg Sorensen, 64–86. Abingdon: Routledge.

Tayeb, M. 2005. *International Human Resource Management: A Multinational Perspective.* Oxford: Oxford University Press.

Thrift, N. 1997. "The Rise of Soft Capitalism." *Cultural Values* 1 (1): 29–50.

Thrift, N. 2005. *Knowing Capitalism.* London: Sage.

van den Broek, D., W. Harvey, and D. Groutsis. 2015. "Commercial Migration Intermediaries and the Segmentation of Skilled Migrant Employment." *Work, Employment, Society* 30 (3): 523–534.

Wilson, M. 2011. "Data Matter(s): Legitimacy, Coding and Qualifications-of-Life." *Environment and Planning D: Society and Space* 29: 857–892.

Xiang, B., and J. Lindquist. 2014. "Migration Infrastructure." *International Migration Review* 48 (S1): S122–S148.

# Intermediaries and destination reputations: explaining flows of skilled migration

William S. Harvey, Dimitria Groutsis and Diane van den Broek

**ABSTRACT**

Governments have increasingly commercialised their migration services, which has fuelled a mushrooming migration industry creating a ripe context for the central role of migration intermediaries. It is therefore timely to explore the new actors responsible for shaping contemporary flows of skilled migration. Drawing on the work of existing studies and a wide variety of secondary data, we argue that the range of intermediaries who have emerged as a result of the commercialisation process, have been poorly understood in the skilled migration and migration industries literatures. Discussion of these actors sheds important theoretical light on how intermediaries, destination reputations and skilled migration flows intersect. Accordingly, we outline six propositions that identify the interconnected relationship between migration intermediaries, reputation and skilled migration flows.

## Introduction

The commercialisation of migration services has led to a proliferation of non-state actors and there has been a subsequent growth of literature on the so called 'migration industries' (Findlay et al. 2013; Gammeltoft-Hansen and Nyberg Sørensen 2013; Cranston 2014, 2016; Cranston, Schapendonk, and Spaan 2018). At the same time, there has been a lack of discussion of skilled migration flows, despite the fact that they represent an important talent pool for countries (Harvey 2014; Silvanto, Ryan, and McNulty 2015). The migration literature identifies the factors that shape migration decisions, by examining different scales of analysis (e.g. immigration policy at the macro-level; network contacts at the meso-level and individual decisions at the micro scale). Social network theory has been an important framework to understand how these networks connect individuals at the micro-level to immigration policies at the macro-level and to job opportunities and integration experiences at the meso-level (Lindquist, Xiang, and Yeoh 2012). However, surprisingly there has been little consideration in the migration industries literature of social networks or the interconnecting factors at the macro-, meso- and micro-levels which influence skilled migration flows.

To date, there has been limited research on how intermediaries shape the flows of skilled migrants, reinforcing and reproducing the commercial interests within the migration industries. Skilled migrant intermediaries are actors operating at the intersection between skilled migrants and the destination or origin country (Groutsis, van den Broek, and Harvey 2015; van den Broek, Harvey, and Groutsis 2016). They are similar to what the international labour organisation (ILO 2005) refer to as a 'triangular employment relationship' when the intermediary (rather than the employer) engages directly with the migrant. These intermediaries are also referred to as 'brokers', 'middlemen' and 'autonomous enterprises', and represent an essential part of the migration industries in the global labour market. There has also been little analysis of how intermediaries service skilled migrants (cf. Groutsis, van den Broek, and Harvey 2015; van den Broek, Harvey, and Groutsis 2016) and how the migration industry impacts on migration patterns and networks (Gammeltoft-Hansen and Nyberg Sørensen 2013; Spaan and Van Naerssen 2018). Given changes to both the scale of skilled migration and the nature of intermediaries, it is timely to analyse how intermediaries impact on skilled migration flows. One of the contributions of this paper is to highlight the variety of intermediaries beyond those who are already well-known in the skilled migration industries literature such as migration, recruitment and global mobility firms (Findlay et al. 2013; Cranston 2016; McCollum and Findlay 2018) to provide a broader understanding of how these disparate actors are impacting on skilled migration flows.

A second important contribution of the paper is to show that different forms of destination reputations, which are often addressed in isolation such as country reputations, city reputations and organisational reputations, influence skilled migration flows in different and salient ways. While there have been many attempts to define reputation (Fombrun 1996, 2012; Walker 2010), this research develops the important work of Fombrun (2012) and Walker (2010) to define reputation as the collective positive or negative assessment of destinations among skilled migrants. In addition to our narrow understanding of intermediaries, there is arguably even less understanding of how reputation impacts on skilled migration flows. This paper provides clarity around how destination reputations impact on skilled migration flows.

Given the gaps in our understanding from the migration industries literature on social networks, intermediaries, skilled migration flows and reputation, the paper focuses on addressing this neglect while also connecting these different strands of literature.

## Skilled migration flows and social networks

There has been a surge of cross-disciplinary interest in skilled migrants in the last decade (Harvey 2011; Van Riemsdijk 2014). The focus on skilled migration in the literature has been matched by a growth of coverage in the media, government and supranational policies and reports as well as in the business press (Chaloff and Lemaître 2009; Boxell 2010; PwC 2010; The Economist 2010). There are many definitions of skilled migrant and it is not our intention to problematise existing definitions (see Boucher and Cerna 2014; Findlay and Cranston 2015). Instead, we follow Andresen et al. (2014, 2307), and use the term skilled migration broadly to encompass a wide spectrum of workers, including intra self-initiated expatriates (e.g. individuals looking for global opportunities through their existing organisational employers), inter self-initiated expatriates (e.g. dependent workers such as foreign recruits and independent workers such as entrepreneurs), assigned expatriates (e.g. traditional organisational expatriates) and drawn expatriates (e.g. top global executives approached by organisations).

The literature on skilled migration has argued that flows of skilled migration are driven by considerations at the macro-, meso- and micro-level. At the macro-(country) level, factors such as the political, economic and legal climate may determine whether people stay in their home country or move to a destination country (Massey et al. 1993; Regets 2001). Immigration policy and the allocation of particular visas, for example, will impact upon the volume of skilled migrants. At the meso-level, there is a wealth of research on how various forms of individual and organisational networks affect migration decisions (Vertovec 2002; Harvey 2011). For instance, migrant networks have historically influenced the migration flows of skilled migrants. At the micro-level, there is extensive research on individual migration decisions, including but not limited to the importance of economic, professional, political and environmental factors (Borjas 1999; Hardill and MacDonald 2000). Skilled migrants, for example, may move based on their predictions of where they can maximise their return in the labour market or where they can increase their quality of life. What is absent, however, is an explanation of flows of migration which cross-sects the macro-, meso- and micro-level (de Haas 2010) in what Xiang (2012, 68) describes as the 'complex structure of the middle ground'. The literature on migrant social networks has responded by adopting a multi-level analysis to bridge macro- and micro-level approaches to migration (Lindquist, Xiang, and Yeoh 2012), which has been somewhat absent from the migration industries literature.

Although the migration industries literature highlights new actors in the migration process (Gammeltoft-Hansen and Nyberg Sørensen 2013), there has been little exploration of new social networks which emerge as a result of these nascent actors, despite an extensive literature on social networks and migration flows (Curran and Rivero-Fuentes 2003). Massey et al. (1993, 448) argue that migrant networks are the social ties that connect potential and former migrants as well as non-migrants in sending and destination countries through family, friendship, ethnic origin and workplace ties. Social networks are important for facilitating flows of skilled migration because the contacts migrants have with different actors provide them with valuable information about their likely experiences of moving to another country (de Haas 2010) and therefore reduce the cost burden of migration. They are also the means by which workers in sending countries find work in destination countries through connections to various forms of intermediaries (Pittman 2016), which highlights the links between social networks and commercially driven migration intermediaries. Ryan (2015) shows the complexity surrounding skilled Irish migrants forming trusted networks in Britain, which significantly impacts upon their experiences of mobility. The above literature highlights that social networks, if available, are important for helping skilled migrants to both migrate and integrate into destination countries.

## Skilled migrant intermediaries

Turning attention to intermediaries and how they shape migration flows shifts the starting point of migration decision-making from social networks to intermediary relations (Lindquist, Xiang, and Yeoh 2012; Groutsis, van den Broek, and Harvey 2015; van den Broek, Harvey, and Groutsis 2016). While there is an established literature on how social

networks impact the flow of skilled migrants, we know little about new forms of social networks that have emerged between skilled migrants and various intermediaries. From the
perspective of skilled migrants, there has been an absence of detailed labour market information around the practicalities and realities of immigrating to destination countries. This
information vacuum stymies a developed understanding of new market opportunities for
intermediaries and what the reputational implications of that may be for migration
destinations.

Despite a growing literature on skilled migration and labour market intermediaries
(Forde and MacKenzie 2010; Lindquist, Xiang, and Yeoh 2012), there has been an
absence of discussion of what we refer to as 'skilled migrant intermediaries' (see Table 1).
These intermediaries use social networks to connect skilled migrants in sending countries,
provide them with information and services related to labour market opportunities, and
mediate between migrants, client organisations and sending and destination countries
at critical stages of the migration process (Lindquist, Xiang, and Yeoh 2012; Xiang
2012). There is a 'grapevine of intermediaries' (Krissman 2005, 6) and a 'complex articu-
lation of individuals, associations, and organizations' (Goss and Lindquist 1995, 319),
which has intensified the increasingly dependent relationship between migrants and intermediaries (Groutsis, van den Broek, and Harvey 2015). Consequently, there is a need for
'middle-level theory' and 'meso-scale understanding' (Findlay and Li 1998, 682, 683), particularly in the context of the migration industries, so that we can better understand this
complex web of relationships (Xiang 2012) and their impact on flows of skilled migration.

Given the changing nature of international migration, which is marked by a rise in
skilled mobility and a demand-driven approach to attracting such migrants (Saxenian
2006; Harvey 2011), it is important to understand who these different skilled migrant intermediaries are and how they affect skilled migration flows through social networks, particularly given the proliferation of new forms of online and social media. Despite some
emerging literature on reputation and skilled migration (Harvey and Groutsis 2015),
there is a scarcity of understanding around how intermediaries influence and are influenced by destination reputation among skilled migrants, and the implication this has on
skilled migration flows. This represents a further body of literature and provides important
insights for the migration industries which has given less focus to skilled migration flows.

## Reputation

While absent from the migration industries literature, there is an extensive literature on
reputation that has been applied in the context of organisations. Fombrun and Shanley
(1990) argue that the reputation of organisations will impact upon the job and career
choices of potential employees. For example, Glückler (2007) argues that management
consulting firms may win new client work to further build their reputations, which has
implications for attracting both clients and employees. Aula and Harmaakorpi (2008)
established that firms are more attracted to locating in regions which are strongly networked and which hold high levels of social capital. Building on this literature is the intersection of migration and mobility. Harvey and Groutsis (2015), for example, have argued
that skilled migrants are both influenced by origin and destination country reputations
when making migration decisions, but are also producers of the reputation of origin
and destination countries, based on their direct experiences, which shapes their own

**Table 1.** Examples of skilled migrant intermediaries.

| Proposition | Type of skilled migrant intermediary | Financial cost | Examples | Related references |
|---|---|---|---|---|
| Proposition 1: The activities of skilled migrant intermediaries impact upon the reputation of destinations among skilled migrants. | Recruitment agents | High | Manpower Inc.; Employment Expos; | Boyle et al. (1996); Buchan, Jobanputra, and Gough (2005); Connell and Stillwell (2006); Coe, Johns, and Ward (2009); Findlay et al. (2013); McCollum and Findlay (2018) |
| Proposition 2: The reputation of destinations among skilled migrants impact on the activities of skilled migrant intermediaries. | Government | Medium | Department of Health; NHS; Kea New Zealand | Goss and Lindquist (1995); Larner (2007); Bludau (2011); Sporton (2013) |
| Proposition 3: The activities of skilled migrant intermediaries impact on skilled migration flows. | Executive search firms | Low | Egon Zehnder; Korn Ferry; Spencer Stuart | Salt (1992); Findlay and Li (1998); Khoo, McDonald, and Hugo (2005); Tasker and Jimenez (2010); van den Broek, Harvey, and Groutsis (2016) |
| Proposition 4: Skilled migration flows impact on the activities of skilled migrant intermediaries. | Migration agents | High | Barlow & Company; Offshore migration agents | Salt and Stein (1997); Hardill and MacDonald (2000); Buchan, Jobanputra, and Gough (2005); Coe, Jones, and Ward (2010); Connell (2010); Collins (2012) ; Groutsis, van den Broek, and Harvey (2015); Pittman (2016) |
| Proposition 5: Destination reputations among skilled migrants impact on skilled migration flows. | Ranking agents | Low | Mercer; The Economist | HSBC (2014); InterNations (2014); The Economist (2014); Harvey and Groutsis (2015); Mercer (2015); |
| Proposition 6: Skilled migration flows impact on destination reputations among skilled migrants. | Online and offline forums and media sources | Low | American Expats in the UK; Forbes | Chacko (2007); Montgomery (2008); Moriarty et al. (2011); Harvey and Groutsis (2015) |

perceptions as well as those of other skilled workers. This is important because it provides a new theoretical lens to understand skilled migration flows to destination countries.

We build on the reputation literature and ask how flows of skilled migration are shaped by destination reputations. We deliberately use the phrase 'destination reputations' rather than 'destination country reputations' because we recognise that the country may not be the only or the most salient unit of analysis in the context of reputation among skilled migrants. Destination reputation is arguably important in the context of understanding flows of skilled migration because how countries, cities and/or organisations are perceived will determine mobility decisions among skilled migrants. Skilled migrants often have limited experience and/or information about moving to destinations and in such instances they use reputation as a proxy for judging their likely experience of moving to a destination.

As such, social networks, skilled migrant intermediaries and reputation should be important components of existing theories of skilled migration flows, and yet these themes are not well-understood or connected in the migration industries literature. This leads to a series of propositions that relate to the following research question:

How do migration intermediaries, destination reputations and skilled migration flows interact, reinforce and reproduce the migration industry?

Drawing-upon a wide range of examples, we outline six propositions, which explore the two-way interaction between intermediaries, destination reputations among skilled migrants and depictions of skilled migration flows to destinations (see Figure 1). We believe that this provides a more holistic understanding of skilled migration flows and represents a significant contribution to both the skilled migration and the migration industries literatures.

Proposition 1: The activities of skilled migrant intermediaries impact on the reputation of destinations among skilled migrants.

An emerging body of labour market research highlights the centrality of intermediaries such as recruitment agencies across a range of countries and economic sectors (Samaluk 2016). While valuable for understanding the nature of different labour market sectors, by overlooking how these intermediaries may shape the reputation of destinations

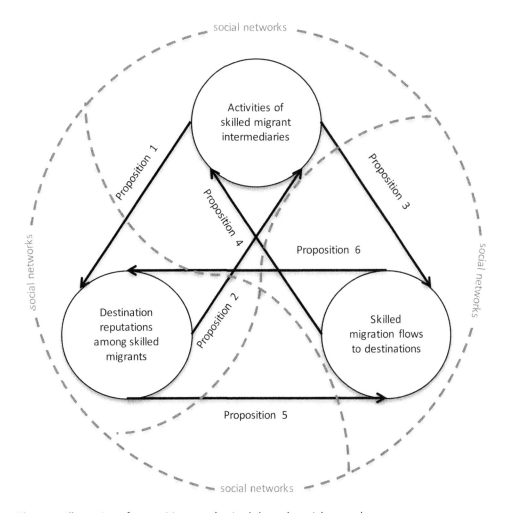

**Figure 1.** Illustration of propositions mechanised through social networks.

among skilled migrants (Coe, Jones, and Ward 2010; Findlay et al. 2013), we miss important implications on the talent pipeline of destinations. A sector where one type of intermediary: recruitment agents, has become commonplace for placing skilled migrants in work, is in healthcare where employers need to quickly fill shortages with skilled migrants (Connell and Stillwell 2006). While the state has significant influence here, as detailed further on in our discussion, private sector employers are increasingly playing a significant role in the recruitment of skilled labour through employer-sponsored programmes. In Canada, for example, the Federal Skilled Worker Program assesses skilled migrants on the basis of their education, work experience and knowledge of English and French. Canadian employers can significantly improve the likelihood of a potential skilled migrant having their application approved through making them a job offer in a skilled occupation. These developments have underscored the proliferation of individual private recruitment firms, temporary staffing and migration agents (Connell and Stillwell 2006; Coe, Johns, and Ward 2009; Cangiano and Walsh 2014; McCollum and Findlay 2018) and the internationalisation of labour markets as employers struggle to source talent from local and national labour pools. Such an emphasis on the demand side of skilled (migrant) labour, which is apparent throughout OECD (2008) member nations, highlights the economic incentive for recruitment agents to act as conduits for both domestic employers and skilled migrants abroad.

The transactional relationship between intermediaries and skilled migrants, is an outcome of macro-level transitions from the 'hollowing out' of government to network governance models (Groutsis, van den Broek, and Harvey 2015). As a consequence, intermediaries are strategically placed to shape the reputation of destination countries among skilled migrants, which historically would have been managed more directly by national governments. The challenge is if promises are made by intermediaries, but not fulfilled at the point of migration and employment then this will disengage skilled migrants. For instance, more than '1.3 million college-educated immigrants are unemployed or working in unskilled jobs such as dishwashers, security guards, and taxi drivers-representing one of every five highly skilled immigrants in the US labor force' (Batalova and Fix 2008, 1). If intermediaries are channelling skilled migrants into destination countries where they subsequently cannot find work commensurate with their skills and training then this will have a negative impact on the reputation of destinations (and intermediaries) among skilled migrants.

One type of recruitment agency that typically enables the mobility of skilled workers at the high end of the labour market is executive search firms (Boyle et al. 1996) or 'elite labour market intermediaries' (Faulconbridge, Hall, and Beaverstock 2008). Examples of these firms include Egon Zehnder, Korn Ferry and Spencer Stuart, who operate on a global scale, connecting applicants who hold and/or are looking to move into senior management positions. Typically, the search for such highly skilled workers operates across international borders and frequently leads to the global mobility of workers, particularly in areas where certain leadership and technical skills are not readily available in the destination country. These types of intermediaries rely on very close social networks between the client organisation and the executive search firm as well as between the potential candidates and the executive search firms. Because many high level executive appointments receive significant media coverage (e.g. Mark Carney, the Governor of the Bank of England moving from Canada to the U.K.), the success or failure of such appointments, which can be considerably costly for clients of executive search firms, will heighten the reputational benefits or deficits for destinations due to the professional and personal networks of skilled migrants.

> Proposition 2: The reputation of destinations among skilled migrants impact on the activities of skilled migrant intermediaries.

Counter-intuitively, government departments also act as intermediaries for skilled migrants because their policies and communication impact upon migration decisions and behaviour. However, marketisation of government has 'fragmented service delivery, multiplied networks and diversified membership of those networks' (Rhodes 2007, 1248), at a time when migration is a highly emotive public discourse. Public concerns around immigration, for example, was at the centre of the outcome of the U.K.'s referendum vote in June of 2016, which has major repercussions for skilled migration flows to and from the U.K. within the EU. Governments in the destination country also implement policies that determine how many and what types of skilled migrants are able to enter a country, and under what conditions. They collate skills shortages lists, actively market professional vacancies and hold expo events abroad to target workers with particular skills. In addition, they set the conditions for particular types of relationships between migrants, employers and labour markets (Rodriguez 2009). This has significant repercussions for employers who are looking to employ skilled migrants and for skilled migrants, many of who are looking to move for work purposes. Sporton's (2013) research on Eastern European migration finds how international recruitment agents are able to identify demand for workers in particular under-performing local labour markets, while Bludau's (2011) research finds that recruitment firms in the Czech Republic provide a supply of skilled migrant nurses, who are seeking employment abroad. The destination reputations among skilled migrants impacts on the demand for talent from employers and the potential supply of talent from skilled migrants interested in moving, both of which influence the activities of intermediaries.

The Prime Minister of Singapore, Lee Hsien Loong has made many public statements and supported the recruitment of professionals and business workers through government policy as part of a strategy of growing the city-state's knowledge-based economy (Ho 2011). These policies create a positive reputation among potential skilled migrants around the value the Singaporean government places on their human capital. This has meant that there are a variety of intermediaries, including but not limited to migration and recruitment agents, who enable skilled migration flows into Singapore. This is in stark contrast with rhetoric in the U.S. where there have been discussions of a reduction in the country's H-1B visa allocation, culminating in high-profile business leaders such as Microsoft's Chairman Bill Gates (Broache 2008) and News Corporation's Executive Chairman Rupert Murdoch (Murdoch 2014) warning of the damage that this could cause to the country's competitiveness because skilled migrants would be put off applying for visas and less would be admitted each year. Here, restrictive immigration policies around the country's skilled H-1B visa will reduce the capacity of different intermediaries such as migration agents to operate. This argument has knock-on effects for other kinds of skilled workers because restrictive and bureaucratic visa requirements impact on the flow of tourists, business workers and temporary migrants (The Economist 2016).

Proposition 3: The activities of skilled migrant intermediaries impact on skilled migration flows.

A number of organisations in the destination country attempt to adopt a direct approach to recruiting skilled migrants (Pittman 2016). Multinational corporations with offices in overseas locations are particularly well placed to do this because they can transfer employees to other locations as assigned expatriates (Salt 1992). While some organisations are successful at convincing skilled migrants directly of the benefits of living and working in a destination, the engagement of particular intermediaries is not even across different migrant groups. Khoo, McDonald, and Hugo (2005), for instance, found that 83% of Korean skilled migrants in Australia preferred to use a migration agent, compared to only 23% of German skilled migrants. They found that Asian migrants in particular used agents because they felt that they might attain 'a high rate of approval' which facilitates their ability to gain access to the Australian labour market (Khoo, McDonald, and Hugo 2005, 30). Havergal (2015) reports that there has been an unprecedented growth of agents commissioned by universities in the U.K. to recruit non-EU students, implying that these intermediaries are important for influencing the flow of skilled migrants into the U.K.

Organisations that are sourcing executive and specialist roles often do not have the internal expertise and capacity to source this talent and therefore frequently utilise the services of executive search firms (Faulconbridge et al. 2009), as discussed above. Many medium and large organisations are outsourcing recruitment and selection work to other intermediaries such as recruitment and migration agents for efficiency and competitive purposes so that they can focus their resources on their core services. Importantly, this is not simply a labour market intermediary argument of organisations outsourcing services to a specialist service provider. They are also relying on these intermediaries to convince potential talent, many of whom are skilled migrants, of the positive benefits of living and working in a particular country. Hence, they play a valuable role in shaping the destination reputation for skilled migrants.

Proposition 4: Skilled migration flows impact on the activities of skilled migrant intermediaries.

Approximately half of overseas-qualified nurses in the U.K. gain posts through specialist migration agents, with the remainder recruited directly through individual hospitals, which have an international profile and points of overseas contacts (Hardill and MacDonald 2000). At the time of Hardill and MacDonald's (2000) study, a fee of £2000 was paid for an agent's service and typically employees would be offered a one-year contract. This use of migration agents in the health-care sector is a direct response to high market demand for skilled migrants and the knowledge and image of such opportunities among this group in different parts of the world.

Migration agents play an important intermediation role for overseas students looking to enter the higher education market (Collins 2012). Although international students are not always defined under the category of skilled migrants, they are in the process of becoming skilled migrants through their education and training. A report by the Observatory on Borderless Higher Education (2014) found that 32% of first-year international students at 48 universities in the 3 largest destination countries (the U.S., U.K. and

Australia) used a migration or recruitment agent: a 10% increase in the last five years. As such, intermediaries are shaping skilled migration flows in powerful ways, channelling students into particular tertiary institutions in certain countries (see Beech 2018).

> Proposition 5: The reputation of destinations among skilled migrants impact on skilled migration flows.

There has been a surge of reputational rankings in the last decade. One of the conceptual challenges of these rankings in the context of skilled migration flows is that there is a disconnect between different forms of reputation such as corporate reputations, country reputations and city reputations. Yet, we suggest below that they all impact on skilled migration flows in different and salient ways. Many rankings have focused on the reputations of organisations across different sectors such as *Fortune*'s (2015) Most Admired Companies, or have focused on one sector in particular such as the *Times Higher Education* (2015) World University Rankings. Notwithstanding the considerable methodological limitations of measuring reputation, these formal and informal reputation benchmarks enable reputable firms to accrue significant benefits from high rankings, including the ability to attract and retain talent (Fombrun 1996). Hence, we suggest that reputation is important for attracting skilled migrants, who are an important part of an organisation's talent pool. Samsung, for example, has successfully sourced high-quality software engineers to move from India to South Korea because of the company's high reputation (Harvey and Groutsis 2015). Saxenian (2006) has documented a similar phenomenon in the U.S. with large volumes of skilled migrants in the ICT sector moving to Silicon Valley because of the presence of nearby elite universities (e.g. Stanford and UC Berkeley) and IT firms (e.g. Apple and Google). Samaluk (2016) has found that workers are attracted to move to particular places (often misguidedly) because their reputations may grant them particular social capital or economic returns. In short, organisational reputation has a strong influence on the mobility of talent, including but not limited to skilled migrants.

Reputation is also important at a national and regional level and there are a growing number of high-profile and widely distributed survey rankings, which also influence skilled migration. HSBC's (2014) Expat Explorer Survey, for instance, commissioned YouGov to survey over 9000 expatriates in more than 100 countries, asking questions on economics, work and social experiences, and raising children. The InterNations (2014) annual survey targets thousands of expatriates and skilled migrants, and it highlights the best and worst places to live, with questions focusing on quality of life, ease of settling in, working abroad, family life (if applicable), personal finance and general satisfaction. The experiences of skilled migrants living abroad can vary markedly not only between but also within countries, and there are a number of influential surveys of global cities. The Economist's (2014) annual liveability survey presents safety and environmental factors in 140 global cities. Similarly, Mercer's (2015) quality of living survey looks at a range of factors, including climate, disease, sanitation standards, ease of communication, the political and social environment, and crime.

The above reputational rankings (corporate, country and city) are important because they reach a wide, skilled and influential audience, providing skilled migrants with information about moving to potential destinations. Yet, they have not been recognised in the skilled migration or migration industries literatures as having an impact upon skilled migration decisions. Importantly, these ranking agents will portray positive, negative or sometimes ambivalent representations of different places, which will influence skilled migration flows because skilled migrants will typically consider the pros and cons of living in multiple destinations. The implication is there are multiple forms of reputation, all of which act in tandem rather than in isolation when skilled migrants make migration decisions. These operate together because in reality skilled migrants will use all the information available to them, which entails aggregating these reputations, rather than evaluating them individually. This does not mean that all reputations are treated equally because skilled migrants will weigh factors differently depending on the degree of importance to them.

Proposition 6: Skilled migration flows impact on destination reputations among skilled migrants.

There is an extensive literature on the effect that migrant networks have on shaping decisions to migrate to a particular destination country (Massey et al. 1993; Goss and Lindquist 1995). Chacko (2007) found that many Indian professionals moved to the U.S. because of the positive stories they had heard from skilled migrants who had successfully moved. Surprisingly, there has been relatively little understanding of how different experiences of moving to destination countries may impact upon the destination reputation among skilled migrants. Much of the literature on skilled migrants has overlooked the impact of media, online content and social media in shaping destination reputation for skilled migration flows. Montgomery (2008) is one of the few exceptions in her discussion of Indian and Taiwanese engineers using their social ties with fellow alumni by e-mail to share their perceptions of destination country experiences. With increasing advancements in IT and the prevalence with which people are engaging with different forms of media, it is not surprising that there has been rapid growth in informal migrant intermediaries such as online expatriate forums and social media groups. American Expats in the UK, for example, is an online forum for American expatriates planning to move to the U.K., or for those who have already moved to the country, to discuss a range of topics with other members such as migration and relocation issues, finding work, healthcare, schooling as well as participating in sports and social activities (American Expats in the UK 2011). Such online resources provide a range of migration information from skilled migrants or from skilled migration experts, which shape the destination reputations among potential skilled migrants. However, there has been a dearth of research or media coverage of how information shared through such channels can explicitly and implicitly shape destination reputations among skilled migrants.

To date, there has been very little research conducted on how information on skilled migration emerges and is shared on online forums or different media, and in particular social media (e.g. SnapChat, Facebook, Twitter and LinkedIn), which in turn impacts on the destination reputations among skilled migrants. This is a major oversight because we know in social and business contexts, such forums can play a valuable role in communicating reputations (Jøsang, Ismail, and Boyd 2007). So it would be reasonable to predict that such online forums where migratory experiences are shared play an important role in shaping destination reputations among skilled migrants.

## Discussion

Based on existing studies and a wide range of secondary data, we have formulated six propositions that seek to better understand flows of skilled migration today. Returning to our research question, we argue that there are important interaction effects between skilled migrant intermediaries, destination reputations among skilled migrants, and skilled migration flows. This is an important contribution to the migration industries literature which has hitherto given less attention to skilled migration flows and social networks which cut across different scales of analysis, or to the reputational effects of these interactions. We also argue that there is a growing group of intermediaries who are influencing the migration flows of skilled migrants. The implication is that national governments may lose both control and responsibility of their reputation among skilled migrants, particularly if such intermediaries are invisible (Xiang 2012). This is salient given our multidimensional argument of reputation which incorporates not one but multiple forms of reputation and cross-sects at the macro-, meso- and micro-levels.

The literature on social networks has an important role to play in these propositions because social networks influence each relationship. In particular, important information is exchanged between skilled migrants and intermediaries, which influences destination reputations and ultimately flows of skilled migrants. For example, the social ties between intermediaries and skilled migrants will impact upon the destination reputations among skilled migrants through information exchanged between both groups (proposition 1). Such networks create and shape destination reputations among skilled migrants. However, we recognise that social networks are neither the same, nor operate in a uniform way in relation to the six propositions (see also Curran and Rivero-Fuentes 2003).

There is only partial evidence from the migration industries literature on the different types of skilled migrant intermediaries and one of the contributions of this paper is to highlight the broad ranging nature of intermediaries beyond the well-known influence of migration and recruitment agents. There is also little analysis of how intermediaries shape the destination reputations among skilled migrants, or how the reputations of destinations among skilled migrants impact on the activities of intermediaries (proposition 2). This is another important contribution of this paper because current theories of skilled migration have not adequately captured the importance of intermediaries despite their prevalence in the skilled migration labour market, nor have they captured the impact of social networks between intermediaries and skilled migrants. This is at the very time that the outsourcing of migration and its commercialisation has become more prevalent, meaning that traditional network ties with government have become fragmented (Rhodes 2007), attracting new intermediaries into the field (Lindquist, Xiang, and Yeoh 2012; Gammeltoft-Hansen and Nyberg Sørensen 2013; Groutsis, van den Broek, and Harvey 2015; van den Broek, Harvey, and Groutsis 2016). It is these visible and invisible actors and the interactions that they are forging that are reinforcing and reproducing the migration industry. It is timely to understand the different social ties that exist between intermediaries and skilled migrants, not least because it impacts upon destination reputations among skilled migrants.

Figure 1 shows the complex nature in which networks intersect with skilled migrant intermediaries and the destination reputations among skilled migrants. We suggest that there is no clear cause/effect binary between these dimensions, but instead they are bound by mutual but by no means equal interdependencies. The behaviour of skilled migrant intermediaries will impact upon the destination reputation and skilled migration flows. This is a process facilitated by the information that is transferred from intermediaries to potential skilled migrants (proposition 3). At the same time, the perceptions of skilled migration flows will affect the demand for intermediaries and therefore their subsequent activities (proposition 4).

Social networks are critical because information is disseminated through information channels, which can be online (e.g. mass media, popular media, social media or gaming), or offline (e.g. through face-to-face interaction). Significantly, because new intermediaries and technologies have emerged in the last decade, many new offline and online social networks between skilled migrants and intermediaries have arisen which have yet to be explored in the migration industries literature. The destination reputations among skilled migrants are shared through social networks, which will impact upon the skilled migration flows to destination countries (proposition 5). Intermediaries can shape destination reputations among skilled migrants in a positive way and therefore constitute 'reputation builders' for countries, or in a negative way as 'reputation damagers' (Harvey and Groutsis 2015). This represents both an opportunity and a risk for destination countries and therefore cannot be ignored because of the direct impact of reputation on flows of skilled migration. At the same time, prior experiences of moving to destination countries also shape migration flows, with migrants following each other along the 'beaten track' (de Haas 2010, 1589). This will impact on destination reputations among skilled migrants through experiences of skilled migration flows to destinations (proposition 6).

## Conclusions and future research

This paper has argued that the relationship between skilled migrant intermediaries and destination reputations among skilled is central for understanding today's flows of skilled migrants. We have highlighted that intermediaries are common and more wide-ranging than the literature has acknowledged and comprise a key part of the actors in the migration industry, which to date has provided less analysis of skilled migration flows and new forms of social networks. According to Cangiano and Walsh (2014), employers in the U.K. and Ireland are using intermediaries because of the excessive burden of keeping up-to-date with immigration regulation, but it is less clear how aware various organisations and migrants are of the extent to which intermediaries are, or should be, regulated. Arguably increased regulation of various forms of intermediaries will help to reduce misconduct towards skilled migrants and also ensure that governments and organisations are more aware of how these actors shape the flows of skilled migrants (see Cranston 2018 for an example). A failure to acknowledge and analyse the function of intermediaries will entrench misunderstanding of a major and disparate stakeholder group who are increasingly shaping skilled migration flows today.

At present, we do not know whether the experience for skilled migrants has changed in light of these new forms of intermediaries, either positively or negatively. Hence, we encourage scholars to pursue more fine-grained research into the different intermediaries that exist, including those discussed above as well as others (e.g. NGOs and trade unions).

We need to understand the activities of these various intermediaries and ascertain what the reputational outcomes are. This will affect not only future flows of skilled migrants, but also future levels of business partnerships and investments, which are often harnessed through the social networks of skilled migrants (Saxenian 2006).

We have also argued that destination reputations among skilled migrants plays a major role in explaining flows of skilled migrants. In particular, the destination reputations among skilled migrants will influence and be influenced by skilled migration flows to destinations by third parties and a multitude of intermediaries. One aspect, which could be further developed, is that of reputation contagion, which we define as the means by which one form of reputation impacts upon another form of reputation, either positively or negatively. If a group of skilled migrants, for instance, have encountered negative experiences with migration agents then this will not only impact upon the reputation of migration agents (intermediaries) at a local level, but also the reputation of the organisation (e.g. corporate reputation). The logic for this is their experiences of work in the destination have also been tarnished because of their negative experiences of moving to another country (Harvey and Groutsis 2015). This 'reputational spillover' effect (Glückler 2007) between the intermediary, organisation and country, can be a positive or a negative force and can be long term and enduring. However, we know very little about the interplay of various forms of reputation and what implications they have for flows of skilled migrants. This is theoretically important because we need a holistic understanding of the impact of reputation, and practically important because there are arguably various actors who influence the flows of skilled migrants who interest groups such as NGOs, trade unions and the media are starting to question. In addition, given that the perceptions of migrants are strongly shaped by their early experiences and can often be filled with unrealistic expectations (Bhattacharya and Schoppelrey 2004), destination countries should pay particular attention to the experiences of early arrivals, which is difficult when many migration services are outsourced to third parties amid varying levels of regulation and monitoring. This is a similar challenge that organisations face in other contexts when their reputation now depends not only on their own activities, but also on the activities of others (Tate, Ellram, and Kirchoff 2010; The Economist 2014; Schapendonk 2018). Arguably this makes them more vulnerable to the 'reputation commons' when all organisations suffer in a given sector when the actions of one organisation negatively impact upon the reputation of the industry as a whole (Barnett and King 2008).

This paper provides an important contribution to the migration industries literature by highlighting that a range of intermediaries and reputation are important for theorising flows of skilled migration today, particularly through different forms of social networks. We also explain that intermediaries, reputation and skilled migration flows do not operate in isolation, but interact with one another, which provides a more holistic understanding of skilled migration flows. We encourage scholars to deepen the empirical evidence of the relationship between intermediaries, reputation and skilled migration flows, and in particular explore how social networks enable (or disable) these relationships. Now is a timely moment to expand our research and analysis of these new actors and relationships, particularly given their relative invisibility in the migration industries literature.

## Disclosure statement

No potential conflict of interest was reported by the authors.

## References

American Expats in the UK. 2011. "Bringing the American Community Together Around the UK." http://www.americanexpats.co.uk/forum/index.php.

Andresen, M., F. Bergdolt, J. Margenfeld, and M. Dickmann. 2014. "Addressing International Mobility Confusion-Developing Definitions and Differentiations for Self-initiated and Assigned Expatriates as Well as Migrants." *The International Journal of Human Resource Management* 25 (16): 2295–2318.

Aula, P., and V. Harmaakorpi. 2008. "An Innovative Milieu – A View on Regional Reputation Building: Case Study of the Lahti Urban Region." *Regional Studies* 42 (4): 523–538.

Barnett, M. L., and A. A. King. 2008. "Good Fences Make Good Neighbors: A Longitudinal Analysis of an Industry Self-regulatory Institution." *Academy of Management Journal* 51 (6): 1150–1170.

Batalova, J. and Fix, M. (2008). *Uneven Progress: The Employment Pathways of Skilled Immigrants in the United States.* With Peter A. Creticos. Washington, DC: Migration Policy Institute. www.migrationpolicy.org/pubs/BrainWasteOct08.pdf.

Beech, S. E. 2018. "Adapting to Change in the Higher Education System: International Student Mobility as a Migration Industry." *Journal of Ethnic and Migration Studies* 44 (4): 610–625. doi:10.1080/1369183X.2017.1315515.

Bhattacharya, G., and S. L. Schoppelrey. 2004. "Preimmigration Beliefs of Life Success, Postimmigration Experiences, and Acculturative Stress: South Asian Immigrants in the United States." *Journal of Immigrant Health* 6 (2): 83–92.

Bludau, H. 2011. "Producing Transnational Nurses: Agency and Subjectivity in Global Health Care Labor Migration Recruitment Practices." *Anthropology of East Europe Review* 29 (1): 94–108.

Borjas, G. J. 1999. "The Economic Analysis of Immigration." *Handbook of Labor Economics* 3 (1): 1697–1760.

Boucher, A., and L. Cerna. 2014. "Current Policy Trends in Skilled Immigration Policy." *International Migration* 52 (3): 21–25.

Boxell, J. 2010. "Skilled Migrants Face Tougher Rules." http://www.ft.com/intl/cms/s/0/6c8c0754-e201-11df-a064-00144feabdc0.html#axzz1YNdQmFxQ.

Boyle, M., A. M. Findlay, E. Lelievre, and R. Paddison. 1996. "World Cities and the Limits to Global Control: A Case Study of Executive Search Firms in Europe's Leading Cities." *International Journal of Urban and Regional Research* 20: 498–517.

Broache, A. 2008. "Bill Gates to Congress: Let us Hire More Foreigners." *CNET.* http://www.cnet.com/news/bill-gates-to-congress-let-us-hire-more-foreigners/.

Buchan, J., R. Jobanputra, and P. Gough. 2005. "Should I Stay or Should I Go?" *Nursing Standard* 19 (36): 14–16.

Cangiano, A., and K. Walsh. 2014. "Recruitment Processes and Immigration Regulations: The Disjointed Pathways to Employing Migrant Carers in Ageing Societies." *Work, Employment and Society* 28 (3): 372–389.

Chacko, E. 2007. "From Brain Drain to Brain Gain: Reverse Migration to Bangalore and Hyderabad, India's Globalizing High Tech Cities." *GeoJournal* 68: 131–140.

Chaloff, J., and G. Lemaître. 2009. "Managing Highly Skilled Labour Migration: A Comparative Analysis of Migration Policies and Challenges in OECD Countries." OECD Social, Employment and Migration Working Papers, No. 79. OECD Publishing. https://doi.org/10.1787/225505346577.

Coe, N. M., J. Johns, and K. Ward. 2009. "Agents of Casualization? The Temporary Staffing Industry and Labour Market Restructuring in Australia." *Journal of Economic Geography* 9 (1): 55–84.

Coe, N. M., K. Jones, and K. Ward. 2010. "The Business of Temporary Staffing: A Developing Research Agenda." *Geography Compass* 4 (8): 1055–1068.

Collins, F. L. 2012. "Organizing Student Mobility: Education Agents and Student Migration to New Zealand." *Pacific Affairs* 85 (1): 137–160.

Connell, J. 2010. *Migration and the Globalisation of Health Care: The Health Worker Exodus?* Cheltenham: Edward Elgar.

Connell, J., and B. Stillwell. 2006. "Merchants of Medical Care: Recruiting Agencies in the Global Health Care Chain." In *Merchant of Labour*, edited by C. Kuptsch, 239–253. Geneva: International Labour Organization (Institute for Labour Studies).

Cranston, S. 2014. "Reflections on Doing the Expat Show: Performing the Global Mobility Industry." *Environment and Planning A*, 46 (5): 1124–1138.

Cranston, S. 2016. "Producing Migrant Encounter: Learning to be a British Expatriate in Singapore through the Global Mobility Industry." *Environment and Planning D: Society and Space* 34 (4): 655–671.

Cranston, S. 2018. "Calculating the Migration Industries: Knowing the Successful Expatriate in the Global Mobility Industry." *Journal of Ethnic and Migration Studies* 44 (4): 626–643. doi:10.1080/1369183X.2017.1315517.

Cranston, S., J. Schapendonk, and E. Spaan. 2018. "New Directions in Exploring the Migration Industries: Introduction to Special Issue." *Journal of Ethnic and Migration Studies* 44 (4): 543–557. doi:10.1080/1369183X.2017.1315504.

Curran, S. R., and E. Rivero-Fuentes. 2003. "Engendering Migrant Networks: The Case of Mexican Migration." *Demography* 40 (2): 289–307.

de Haas, H. 2010. "The Internal Dynamics of Migration Processes: A Theoretical Inquiry." *Journal of Ethnic and Migration Studies* 36 (10): 1587–1617.

Faulconbridge, J. R., J. V. Beaverstock, S. Hall, and A. Hewitson. 2009. "The 'War for Talent': The Gatekeeper Role of Executive Search Firms in Elite Labour Markets." *Geoforum* 40 (5): 800–808.

Faulconbridge, J. R., S. J. E. Hall, and J. V. Beaverstock. 2008. "New Insights into the Internationalization of Producer Services: Organizational Strategies and Spatial Economies for Global Headhunting Firms." *Environment and Planning A* 40 (1): 210–234.

Findlay, A. M., and S. Cranston. 2015. "What's in a Research Agenda? An Evaluation of Research Developments in the Arena of Skilled International Migration." *International Development Planning Review* 37 (1): 17–31.

Findlay, A. M., and F. L. N. Li. 1998. "A Migration Channels Approach to the Study of Professionals Moving to and from Hong Kong." *International Migration Review* 32 (3): 682–703.

Findlay, A. M., D. McCollum, S. Shubin, E. Apsite, and Z. Krisjane. 2013. "The Role of Recruitment Agencies in Imagining and Producing the 'Good' Migrant." *Social and Cultural Geography* 14 (2): 145–167.

Fombrun, C. J. 1996. *Reputation. Realizing Value from the Corporate Image.* Boston, MA: Harvard Business School Press.

Fombrun, C. J. 2012. "The Building Blocks of Corporate Reputation: Definitions, Antecedents, Consequences." In *The Oxford Handbook of Corporate Reputation*, edited by M. L. Barnett, and T. G. Pollock, 94–113. Oxford: Oxford University Press.

Fombrun, C. J., and M. Shanley. 1990. "What's in a Name? Reputation Building and Corporate Strategy." *Academy of Management Journal* 33 (2): 233–258.

Forde, C., and R. MacKenzie. 2010. "The Ethical Agendas of Employment Agencies Towards Migrant Workers in the UK; Deciphering the Codes." *Journal of Business Ethics* 97 (1): 31–41.

Fortune. 2015. "World's Most Admired Companies 2015." http://fortune.com/worlds-most-admired-companies/apple-1/.

Gammeltoft-Hansen, T., and N. Nyberg Sørensen. 2013. *The Migration Industry and the Commercialization of International Migration.* Abingdon: Routledge.

Glückler, J. 2007. "Geography of Reputation: The City as the Locus of Business Opportunity." *Regional Studies* 41 (7): 949–961.

Goss, J., and B. Lindquist. 1995. "Conceptualizing International Labor Migration: A Structuration Perspective." *The International Migration Review* 29 (2): 317–351.

Groutsis, D., D. van den Broek, and W. S. Harvey. 2015. "Transformations in Network Governance: The Case of Migration Intermediaries." *Journal of Ethnic and Migration Studies* 41 (10): 1558–1576.

Hardill, I., and S. MacDonald. 2000. "Skilled International Migration: The Experience of Nurses in the UK." *Regional Studies* 34 (7): 681–692.

Harvey, W. S. 2011. "British and Indian Scientists Moving to the U.S." *Work and Occupations* 38 (1): 68–100.

Harvey, W. S. 2014. "Winning the Global Talent War: A Policy Perspective." *Journal of Chinese Human Resource Management* 5 (1): 62–74.

Harvey, W. S., and D. Groutsis. 2015. "Reputation and Talent Mobility in the Asia Pacific." *Asia Pacific Journal of Human Resource Management* 53 (1): 22–40.

Havergal, C. 2015. "Agents Paid an Average of £1,767 per non-EU recruit." *Times Higher Education*. https://www.timeshighereducation.co.uk/news/agents-paid-an-average-of-1767-per-non-eu-recruit/2018613.article.

Ho, E. L. E. 2011. "'Claiming' the Diaspora: Elite Mobility, Sending State Strategies and the Spatialities of Citizenship." *Progress in Human Geography* 35 (6): 757–772.

HSBC. 2014. "Expat Explorer Survey." https://expatexplorer.hsbc.com/survey/?HBIB_dyn_lnk=hme_nav_t4_col1_lnk_1.

ILO. 2005. "Global Alliance Against Forced Labour." *International Labour Organisation*, Geneva.

InterNations. 2014. "The Best & Worst Places for Expats." http://www.internations.org/expat-insider/2014/the-best-and-worst-places-for-expats.

Jøsang, A., R. Ismail, and C. Boyd. 2007. "A Survey of Trust and Reputation Systems for Online Service Provision." *Decision Support Systems* 43 (2): 618–644.

Khoo, S., P. McDonald, and G. Hugo. 2005. "Temporary Skilled Migrants in Australia: Employment Circumstances and Migration Outcomes." Australian Centre for Population Research, Australian National University and University of Adelaide, Department of Immigration and Multicultural and Indigenous Affairs.

Krissman, F. 2005. "*Sin Coyote Ni Patrón*: Why the "Migrant Network" Fails to Explain International Migration." *International Migration Review* 39 (1): 4–44.

Larner, W. 2007. "Expatriate Experts and Globalising Governmentalities: The New Zealand Diaspora Strategy." *Transactions of the Institute of British Geographers* 32 (3): 331–345.

Lindquist, J., B. Xiang, and B. S. Yeoh. 2012. "Opening the Black Box of Migration: Brokers, the Organization of Transnational Mobility and the Changing Political Economy in Asia." *Pacific Affairs* 85 (1): 7–19.

Massey, D. S., J. Arango, G. Hugo, A. Kouaouci, A. Pellegrino, and J. E. Taylor. 1993. "Theories of International Migration: A Review and Appraisal." *Population and Development Review* 19 (3): 431–466.

McCollum, D., and A. Findlay. 2018. "Oiling the Wheels? Flexible Labour Markets and the Migration Industry." *Journal of Ethnic and Migration Studies* 44 (4): 558–574. doi:10.1080/1369183X.2017.1315505.

Mercer. 2015. "Newsroom. Vienna tops latest Quality of Living rankings." http://www.uk.mercer.com/content/mercer/europe/uk/en/newsroom/2015-quality-of-living-survey.html.

Montgomery, A. F. 2008. "Virtual enclaves: the influence of alumni email lists on the workspaces of transnational software engineers." *Global Networks* 8 (1): 71–93.

Moriarty, E., J. Wickham, T. Krings, J. Salamonska, and A. Bobek. 2011. "Taking on Almost Everyone?' Migrant and Employer Recruitment Strategies in a Booming Labour Market." *The International Journal of Human Resource Management* 23 (9): 1871–1887.

Murdoch, R. 2014. "Immigration Reform Can't Wait." *Wall Street Journal*. http://online.wsj.com/articles/rupert-murdoch-immigration-reform-cant-wait-1403134311.

Observatory on Borderless Higher Education. 2014. "The Agent Question: Insights from Students, Universities and Agents." http://www.obhe.ac.uk/documents/view_details?id=953.

OECD. 2008. "The Global Competition for Talent: Mobility of the Highly Skilled." http://www.oecd.org/innovation/inno/theglobalcompetitionfortalentmobilityofthehighlyskilled.htm#howto.

Pittman, P. 2016. "Alternative Approaches to the Governance of Transnational Labor Recruitment." *International Migration Review* 50 (2): 269–314.

PwC (PricewaterhouseCoopers). 2010. "Managing Tomorrow's People. Talent Mobility 2020. The Next Generation of International Assignments." http://www.pwc.com/gx/en/managing-tomorrows-people/future-of-work/pdf/talent-mobility-2020.pdf.

Regets, M. C. 2001. "Research and Policy Issues in High-Skilled International Migration: A Perspective with Data from the United States." IZA Discussion Paper 366.

Rhodes, R. A. 2007. "Understanding Governance: Ten Years On." *Organization Studies* 28 (8): 1243–1264.

Rodriguez, R. M. 2009. *Migrants for Export: How the Philippine State Brokers Labor to the World.* Minneapolis: University of Minnesota Press.

Ryan, L. 2015. "Friendship-Making: Exploring Network Formations through the Narratives of Irish Highly Qualified Migrants in Britain." *Journal of Ethnic and Migration Studies* 41 (10): 1664–1683.

Salt, J. 1992. "Migration Processes Amongst the Highly Skilled in Europe." *International Migration Review* 26: 484–505.

Salt, J., and J. Stein. 1997. "Migration as a Business: The Case of Trafficking." *International Migration* 35 (4): 467–494.

Samaluk, B. 2016. "Migrant Workers' Engagement with Labour Market Intermediaries in Europe: Symbolic Power Guiding Transnational Exchange." *Work, Employment and Society* 30 (3): 455–471.

Saxenian, A. 2006. *The New Argonauts. Regional Advantage in a Global Economy.* Cambridge, MA: Harvard University Press.

Schapendonk, J. 2018. "Navigating the Migration Industry: Migrants Moving Through an African-European Web of Facilitation/Control." *Journal of Ethnic and Migration Studies* 44 (4): 663–679. doi:10.1080/1369183X.2017.1315522.

Silvanto, S., J. Ryan, and Y. McNulty. 2015. "An Empirical Study of Nation Branding for Attracting Internationally Mobile Skilled Professionals." *Career Development International* 20 (3): 238–258.

Spaan, E., and T. van Naerssen. 2018. "Migration Decision-making and Migration Industry in the Indonesia-Malaysia Corridor." *Journal of Ethnic and Migration Studies* 44 (4): 680–695. doi:10.1080/1369183X.2017.1315523.

Sporton, D. 2013. "'They Control My Life': The Role of Local Recruitment Agencies in East European Migration to the UK." *Population, Space and Place* 19 (5): 443–458.

Tasker, S., and K. Jimenez. 2010. "Skills Crisis Risks $150bn Worth of Projects." http://www.theaustralian.com.au/business/skills-crisis-risks-150bn-worth-of-projects/story-e6frg8zx-1225967252748.

Tate, W. L., L. M. Ellram, and J. F. Kirchoff. 2010. "Corporate Social Responsibility Reports: A Thematic Analysis Related to Supply Chain Management." *Journal of Supply Chain Management* 46 (1): 19–44.

(The) Economist. 2010. "Skilled Immigration. Green-Card Blues." http://www.economist.com/node/17366155.

(The) Economist. 2014. "The Best Places to Live." http://www.economist.com/blogs/graphicdetail/2014/08/daily-chart-13.

(The) Economist. 2016. "Travel Visas. A Strange Sort of Welcome." http://www.economist.com/news/business/21684791-governments-are-deterring-business-travellers-and-tourists-cumbersome-visa-requirements.

The Times Higher Education. 2015. "World University Rankings." https://www.timeshighereducation.co.uk/world-university-rankings/.

van den Broek, D., W. S. Harvey, and D. Groutsis. 2016. "Commercial Migration Intermediaries and the Segmentation of Skilled Migrant Employment." *Work, Employment and Society* 30 (3): 523–534.

Van Riemsdijk, M. 2014. "International Migration and Local Emplacement: Everyday Place-Making Practices of Skilled Migrants in Oslo, Norway." *Environment and Planning A* 46 (4): 963–979.

Vertovec, S. 2002. *Transnational Networks and Skilled Labour Migration: Transnational Communities Programme*. Oxford: University of Oxford.

Walker, K. 2010. "A Systematic Review of the Corporate Reputation Literature: Definition, Measurement, and Theory." *Corporate Reputation Review* 12 (4): 357–387.

Xiang, B. 2012. "Predatory Princes and Princely Peddlers: The State and International Labour Migration Intermediaries in China." *Pacific Affairs* 85 (1): 47–68.

# Navigating the migration industry: migrants moving through an African-European web of facilitation/control

Joris Schapendonk

**ABSTRACT**
This paper approaches the African-European migration industry as a complex web of relations in which different actors liaise, objectives oppose each other, and roles overlap. Starting from this notion, the question emerges: How do migrants navigate this fuzzy web of migration facilitation/control? To answer this question, this paper uses a 'trajectory ethnography' that follows the im/mobility processes of migrants from West – and Central Africa to, and inside, Europe. In so doing, it particularly focuses on two practices that are related to the concept of social navigation. First, it concerns *débrouillardise*, a term that points to the power of improvisation, creativity and hustling. Second, it regards social negotiation, a term referring to the process of *how* migrants 'massage' their relations with important actors in the field. The findings stress the relational dimension of the migration industry in the sense that the functioning of one actor depends so much on the intentions and efforts of others. I conclude that we could enhance our knowledge on migration industries with studies that constantly shift between the perspective of the migrant, the social network, the facilitator and controller. Such a dynamic approach unpacks further the multiple efforts that produce migrant im/mobility.

## Introduction

In April 2014, I sit together with Yahya, Omar and Shakur in a little Italian bar. The three young men from the Gambia belong to a group of six informants who, together with approximately 80 other migrants, have embarked the same boat in Libya to reach Lampedusa. After three transfers, Yahya, Omar and Shakur are now living in a relatively closed reception centre that is run by Caritas – the charity organization that reflects the social mission and core values of the Catholic church. While they appreciate the way the 'Caritas people' take care of them and assist them in their asylum procedures, they feel frustrated about the way 'the camp' controls their daily mobility by having strict time schedules and by giving migrants the obligation to report their whereabouts, every day again. In this particular bar, the three men share their past experiences related to their trans-Saharan passage that started in their country of origin and brought them through Senegal, Mali, Burkina Faso, Niger and Libya. Although they did not travel together at this stage of their journeys, their collective memory tells me that they have faced many moments whereby state officials, soldiers, drivers or bandits have asked for their money. Out of frustration, Shakur raises his voice and states: 'They are making money from us, they are making money from us! The drivers and the police officers and the soldiers.' The conclusion of the three men about the facilitators and controllers of migration is straightforward: 'They are all the same mafia!' (Reconstruction based on diary notes, Italy, April 2014)

Migration is booming business. This reality is particularly emphasised in reports on human smuggling and trafficking. In the context of irregular migration to Europe, Europol framed human smuggling as the 'fastest growing criminal market in Europe'.[1] As a response to this, the EU and its member states increasingly shift their migration management practices towards a military combat against the facilitation of migration. The general rationale behind this is: If we cut off the business networks of smugglers, we stop migrants from entering Europe and, in so doing, we prevent humanitarian dramas. This rationale, however, remarkably bypasses the argument raised by critical researchers that firmer border controls actually create a market for human smuggling (Gammeltoft-Hansen and Nyberg-Sørensen 2013), and when barriers for migration are heightened, migrants pathways are likely to become even deathlier than they have been (Carling 2007). Markets for border control actually reinforce markets for migration facilitation, and vice versa.

The 'absurdity' of this reinforcing relationship is convincingly unpacked by Ruben Andersson's book *Illegality, Inc.* In his attempt to locate the migration industry of African migration and European borders, he came across a migration apparatus that binds together humanitarianism and violence, policemen and *passeurs,* security forces and aid workers (Andersson 2014). Following his observations, this paper approaches the migration industry not as a homogeneous field of actors sharing a certain goal, but rather as a networked entity in which objectives oppose each other, roles overlap and responsibilities shift over time. In this field, smugglers and state officials may indeed appear to the migrants as similar actors, as suggested by Shakur. Furthermore, the practices of charity organisations like Caritas may indeed liaise with the agenda of state apparatuses when it concerns the control of migrant's mobility.

However, if the migration industry is considered to form a complex landscape with diverse actors and shifting roles, an important question is: How do migrants make sense out of this fuzzy web of migration control and facilitation? How do migrants navigate the migration industry? To answer these questions, this paper concentrates on migration trajectories of migrants from West – and Central Africa to and inside the European Union. It thereby particularly aims to understand the various ways how migrants create rooms for manoeuvre during their im/mobility processes. In so doing, I focus on two interrelated practices that can be subsumed under Vigh's notion of social navigation (2006, 2009). These practices are *débrouillardise* – a term that points to the power of improvisation, creativity and hustling – and social negotiation, a term referring to the process of *how* migrants mediate their relationships with relevant actors of the migration industry.

The first section defines the migration industry and relates it to the conceptual debate on migrant trajectories. After a brief methodological note, three subsequent sections illustrate how the African-European industry functions and how migrants navigate this complex landscape. I thereby distinguish three intersected fields: the industry of facilitation/control in Africa, the industry of reception/asylum in Italy and the industry of detention/removal in the Netherlands. The empirical findings include the risky journey of six men from Senegambia through Africa and Europe as well as the struggle of an undocumented Congolese man with the migration authorities in the Netherlands. The analysis starts in Africa and moves gradually to the European continent.

## Migration industry and migrant trajectories: im/mobility and navigations

In contrast with some of the other papers in this volume – that strictly divide the realms of migration facilitation and control (see Cranston (2018) as well as Yee Koh and Wissink (2017) for a focus on migration facilitation) – I argue that it is of vital importance to analyse the opaque boundaries and shifting roles between the same. Consequently, I follow the argument of Nyberg-Sørenson and Gammeltoft-Hansen (2013, 6) that the migration industry encompasses migration facilitation, migration control as well as the rescue industry. However, I do not consider these domains of facilitation, control and rescue as 'different subcategories' of the industry per se, as suggested by the same authors. By only looking at the smuggling industry or the role of security guards, for instance, we would create a very fragmented picture of what it means for African migrants to be on the road to Europe. It is, in fact, the interplay of migrants, smugglers and border guards (as well as the interplay between security companies and asylum authorities; the International Organization for Migration (IOM) and local NGOs; and commercial airlines and deportation agencies, to name but a few actors) that affect so profoundly the experiences of African migrants towards and inside Europe. In other words, it is the 'coming-togetherness' of all sorts of migration facilitators and migration controllers that create a 'force field of relationalities' (Ingold 2011, 93) that I call the migration industry. Approaching the industry as a complex web of relations, helps us to understand better the evolvement of migrant trajectories, with all its ups and downs.

Migrant trajectories are understood as dynamic processes that involve mobility as well as intervening periods of rest, blockage and re-orientation (Schapendonk and Steel 2014; Mainwaring and Brigden 2016). Although individual decision-making is relevant in this context, migration trajectories cannot be explained by focusing solely on migrant agency as a form of autonomous power. In fact, the evolvement of individual pathways depends so much on social networks, brokering services, helping hands, un/expected encounters and policy interventions. With a focus on migrant positionality vis-a-vis actors of the migration industry we are able to articulate how individual practices relate to, and are entangled with, a wider web of relations. This creates an insightful lens to understand the courses of migrant trajectories and the related politics of mobility (Adey 2006). To give the analysis some more focus, I concentrate on the concept of social navigation – a concept that refers to the way people 'move in social environments of actors, actants, individuals and institutions' (Vigh 2009, 419) and the effects it has on 'possible positions and trajectories' (Vigh 2009, 425). Two particularities of Vigh's notion of social navigation add specific value to the analysis of migration trajectories from Africa to Europe. First, it emphasises the instability of the social environment in which 'spaces of possibility' may emerge unexpectedly and disappear rapidly.[2] This implies that migrants are 'on the move', but so too are the environments (rules, institutions and networks) they are moving in. Second, it entangles aspired to distant futures with instant decision-making. To phrase it in Vigh's own words (2009, 425): '[navigation] is constantly attuned to the way we move in the here and now as well as to the way we move in relation to social goals and prospective positions'. In this paper, I further operationalise the concept of social navigation in two practices with which migrants creates room to manoeuvre: *débrouillardise* and social negotiation. Both notions are briefly discussed below.

*Débrouillardise* is a French term with various English translations (varying from 'getting by' to ingenuity). It points to the power of improvisation, creativity and hustling (e.g. Vigh 2006; Waage 2006; Homaifar 2008) and it is predominantly used in studies on African urban economies and insecure environments. As Homaifar's (2008) argues, the notion of débrouillardise fits a de Certeauian approach since it refers to the art of the marginalised to invert the logics of an oppressive system in order to use it to their own advantage (see Vigh 2009 for a similar argument). It might point to the ingenuity of individuals but also to the flexibility of livelihoods and production systems (Müller-Koné 2015). As such, the notion of débrouillardise has important links with broader discussions on informality and mobility in urban studies (Simone 2001), and it appears in migration studies occasionally (e.g. Bakewell and Jónsson 2011; Terreta 2015).

The second concept of social negotiation emerges from recent criticism towards static conceptualisation of social networks in migration studies. The criticism implies two arguments (see Schapendonk 2015). First, it is stated that the social network is too easily perceived as a grid-like entity consisting of a fixed set of strong and weak ties (as if migrants do not build new networks) (Somerville 2015). Second, it is argued that conventional network approaches neglect the efforts and investments that are needed to mobilise social capital. In this regard, the notion of social negotiation refers to migrant's 'network work' (Pathirage and Collyer 2011) that is needed to mobilise social connections in such a way that it helps them to achieve personal objectives. The efforts and energies that migrants put in network*ing* their relations can be easily subsumed under the header of social navigation. In this paper, the term social negotiation goes beyond the domain of family and friends, as it may also appear at moments migrants meet the smuggler, the lawyer or the border guard. In so doing, social negotiation refers to the process of *how* migrants 'massage' their relation with relevant actors of the migration industry. It follows that the concepts of débrouillardise and social negotiation are not mutually exclusive. A migrant might need to improvise to get the right thing from his/her social contact, and on his/her turn the social contact may help the migrant to find instant or future solutions for emerging problems.

## Methodological note

This paper is based on my recent empirical findings regarding the im/mobility of African migrants to and inside Europe. In my current research,[3] I take three methodological steps that together form a trajectory ethnography (Schapendonk and Steel 2014). First, I reconstruct migrants' pathways through my ethnographic engagements in three European countries: Spain, Italy and the Netherlands. These practices include informal conversations, in-depth interviews and observations and they allow me to gain in-depth insights into migrants' mobility histories and future aspirations. These in-place practices form the entry point for my second step, which is staying in contact with a selection of my informants to gain longitudinal insights into the un/expected twists and turns of migration processes. Hereby I rely on telephone and internet conversations. It is important to note this 'translocal' element varies over time in terms of the intensity of the connection. In some cases I connect to the same individual several times a week, but I may lose track of him/her soon afterwards. However brittle the connection may be, the translocal element enables me to put my third methodological step into practice, namely, the re-visiting of my informants in the different places they end up in. During my re-visits I combine again interviews, informal conversations and observations to understand migrants' changing, and sometimes remarkably unchanging, situations. The trajectory cases that are reconstructed in this paper are based on my longitudinal ethnographic engagements with informants that I first met in, respectively, Italy and the Netherlands. It concerns a group of six young men from Senegambia (five Gambians and one Senegalese) who all embarked the same inflatable boat in Libya in 2013 in order to reach Italy. I have followed this group from early 2014 until the moment of writing (January 2017) (see also Schapendonk 2017).[4] Two of them have stayed in Italy in this period of time, the four others moved to other European countries where I have been able to re-visit them. Next to this group, the analysis includes the struggle of a Congolese man with the migration bureaucracy in the Netherlands. I met him a few days after he was released from a migrant detention centre, and from that moment onwards we have seen each other almost on a weekly basis. Our countless informal conversations, in combination with some recorded interviews, have given me in-depth insight into how he navigates the Dutch migration industry in the context of his potential repatriation to Congo DRC. To protect the identity of my respondents, pseudonyms are used and exact living places or important locations are not mentioned.

The next three sections focus on the ways migrants navigate the diverse actors, the opaque boundaries and shifting roles at play in the African-European migration industry. The analysis starts in sub-Saharan Africa and moves along the trans-Saharan passage gradually to the European border. From there it continues to discuss reception and asylum procedures in Europe and it ends with a case on deportation.

## Navigating facilitation/control in Africa

Although human smuggling and trafficking are often articulated in public discourses regarding African migration, it is important to note that there are numerous brokering services assisting would-be migrants with their migration process in the countries of origin, and most notably with their travel papers. Travel papers are one of the most desirable objects for African youngsters in West Africa, including the Gambia (Gaibazzi 2014), Cameroon (Alpes 2011) and Ghana (Lucht 2012). However, the default situation is that Europe's visa regime excludes these would-be emigrants from conventional mobility channels. As a result, 'bureaucratic slaloms' (Gaibazzi 2014, 39) and 'mediation' (Alpes 2011, 110) are needed to realise one's dream. In her detailed description of the migration brokerage sector in Cameroon, Alpes (2011) identifies a whole range of services, varying from well-established offices specialised in the facilitation of study migration to individual agents who are considered to have 'just the right contacts'. This sector, as Alpes so clearly illustrates, does not work outside the domain of the state. Quite to the contrary, it is rather its connectivity with local government officials, embassies and consulates that characterises it.

My six informants from Senegambia, however, did not use any brokering services for a visa application. Yahya highlighted the reason for this during an African dinner at his work place. At that moment, he received a phone call from one of his younger family members in the Gambia who is in touch with a broker. This broker has promised him to deliver a visa for Europe, in this case, for Cyprus. Yahya started to comment on this situation:

> This boy, he wants to come, but he does not have a visa. One man is telling this boy, I CAN DO IT! I can bring the visa. … So I tell him [his family member], if you give this guy the money, maybe he cheats on you, maybe you are lucky. [But] before you give this man the money, he has to bring the visa first!

With his advice, Yahya attempted to prevent that his younger family member becomes subject to misleading practices of this brokering service. The fact that Cyprus (an EU member state that is not part of the Schengen agreements) was the targeted European country made us concerned about the promises and practices of this dubious actor. But, according to Yahya, even with the help of a trustworthy broker, the chances on a successful passage to Europe are rather limited:

> The visa system is still like gambling. So you can have luck sometimes, but many times you lose your money for nothing.

This reflection of Yahya reflects well Belloni's (2016a) work that portrays Eritrean refugees as gamblers (see also Gaibazzi and Gardini 2015 for a discussion on luck in West Africa; see Gladkova and Mazzucato 2015 for an interesting paper on 'chance' in the light of migration trajectories). The notion of gambling does not only imply that one may be more or less fortunate, it also touches upon the fact that migrants may have various attempts at different times to reach their destination. For instance, Omar told me that he has tried to reach Europe in four different ways. In 2008, he tried to reach the Canary Island (Spain) from the Senegalese coast. His neighbour arranged his boat journey but due to some 'boat problems' he ended up in Mauritania. In 2009, he tried the same way, but his 'connection man ran with the money'. In 2011 he tried to cross the Libyan desert, but he stranded in Agadez due to the Libyan conflict, so he returned again to the Gambia. Only the fourth time, in 2013, he managed to reach European grounds by following the same trans-Saharan pathway to Libya.

Regarding the overland journey, my six informants more or less followed the same route by crossing the Gambia, Senegal, Mali, Burkina Faso, Niger and Libya. Only the Senegalese man, Amat, had passed through Mali, Algeria and Morocco before he took off for Libya. The first legs of these overland journeys are mostly embedded in conventional mobility systems, consisting of bus companies and collective taxis that facilitate cross-border mobility in Africa (Carling 2016). These facilitators are liaised (against their will or not) with border guards and police officers who stop and control the mobility at the countless checkpoints in the region. At these checkpoints, individuals are often selected on the basis of their appearance and are asked to pay some extra (Choplin and Lombard 2010). This issue was particularly highlighted by Omar when I asked him about the border between Mali and Burkina Faso:

> O: Between the border, those policemen ask money too much. When they see Gambian people they are very happy, and then they say HEEY GAMBIAN PEOPLE, PRESIDENT JAMMEH, YOU ALWAYS PARTY, ALWAYS FIESTA!

JS:    Always party?

O:    Yes always party, always fiesta. They do programme! They say Gambian people they get money … When for example Senegalese people come they will ask him like 1000CFA … for example just only 1 euro. When Gambian people come they will ask you 5 euro. If you don't pay! They tell you GO, and they will search you pocket and take money from your pocket.

JS:    So this is the police, not the trafficker?

O:    Yea, is the police or the border police … sometimes, every three kilometre you see a checkpoint.

Further up North, migrants pass important transport hubs where the trans-Saharan passage is arranged, such as Agadez (Niger), Gao (Mali) and Nouakchott (Mauritania). In these places, the image of the migrant changes from a usual regional traveller to a candidate for a clandestine passage (Andersson 2014). This change of status is accompanied by an intensified vulnerability, since transporters and state officials know that they profit from the presence of clandestine migrants (Brachet 2012). A Dutch journalist estimated that about one-third of the expenditure of migration facilitators in Agadez is spent on bribing policemen and convoy protection services provided by the Nigerien military (Vermeulen 2016). This leaves the state as one of the most important beneficiaries of irregular migration in the region (Bensaad 2007). Furthermore, transporters easily turn into robbers once migrants find themselves in the desert. The existence of this double role is tellingly described by Triulzi in the context of Ethiopian journeys through Libya:

> The long journey in fact, was broken into continually negotiated tracts, travelling migrants being retained and freed alternatively by different 'captors' and 'saviours', under the changeable guise of guide, mediator or policeman. (Triulzi 2012, 224)

These practices of migration facilitators induce the incentive of the EU to intervene in this trans-Saharan mobility landscape. In this context, the EU and its member states invest heavily in transit – and detention centres in Africa to transform important transit places into holding places (Bensaad 2007). There are, for example, four transit centres in Niger, being located in Arlit (close to Algeria), Dirkou (close to Libya), Agadez (the main transit hub in Niger) and Niamey (the capital city). These centres are mostly run by the IOM and the Red Cross and they provide temporary shelter, food and medical assistance to expelled and stranded migrants (UNHCR 2015). Moreover, these centres manage the return of expelled and stranded migrants to their countries of origin (Brachet 2012). The latter includes the task of acquiring the right travel papers. Thus, some of the activities of these transit centres do not differ very much from the brokering services in Cameroon, being discussed above (Alpes 2011). Concerning the issue of detention along the trans-Saharan journey, my Gambian informants were rather explicit about the Nigerien-Libyan borderland. They considered this a 'prison-place' and they portrayed this place is an important node for the previously discussed *saviours/captors* markets where migrants are beaten and migrant families are contacted to pay extra money (Triulzi 2012; Belloni 2016b). As Omar phrased it: 'that place is human trafficking'.

In different settings, my informants explained me how different social connections are of crucial importance for their navigation of the overland passages. A first important source of trustworthy information is formed by co-travellers. Omar, for example, explained me how he consulted his friend on Facebook, 'who passed the same way' to gain information on who to contact in Agadez for the Sahara crossing. Upon arrival, he only mentioned the name he had received from his friend to a taxi driver who brought him immediately to the *ghetto* – a place where migrants prepare for the next step of the journey. The ghetto is another resource of information as the latest prices, risks and travel plans are discussed there.

However, social connectivity is not per definition very helpful for the migrants in question. Much depends on migrant's *timing* of their social negotiation. The best illustration here comes from Yahya, whose older brother is my friend in the Netherlands. Yahya did not inform his brother about his departure because he knew his brother would not agree with this adventurous and risky plan. He only contacted his brother when he really was in trouble. Due to the many road blocks, he totally ran out of money when he reached Agadez and only there he decided to call his brother for help. Although reluctantly (as he indeed got angry with him), his brother sent him money through Western Union, which enabled Yahya to pay the transport to Libya. In the meantime, his brother in the Netherlands feared that Yahya would get in trouble again once he would reach Libya. For that reason, he started a process that reflects well the notion of débrouillardise. He shipped a second-hand car from the Netherlands to the Gambia. The car was handed over to the wife of a Gambian man. This particular Gambian man – who Yahya's brother knew in person – worked in Tripoli as a 'connection man', recruiting potential candidates for the boat journey to Italy. The latter indicates that migrants themselves may become important figures in the migration industry (Lucht 2012). This specific second-hand car that was shipped to the Gambia functioned, at the end, as the payment for Yahya's 'connection' from Libya to Lampedusa. Consequently, Yahya had only a very brief stay in Tripoli, while some of his friends had to wait more than a year before they could afford the boat ticket.

It would be problematic, however, to consider migrants during the overland passage as being 'connected' permanently. In fact, migrants can be very isolated from any social connection at certain points of time, especially in the middle of the desert. The art of improvisation is then an important tactic to avoid extra payments and/or exploitation. Shakur told me how his convoy of trucks was put to a halt in the desert by the truck drivers in order get more money from the migrants. After the migrants were off-loaded, a heated debate followed between migrants and the migration facilitators/robbers. In this hectic situation, Shakur asked permission to pray. He pretended to pray, while he was watched by two armed facilitators/robbers. At the moment a new truck of the convoy arrived the scene, the gunmen were distracted and in this split second Shakur ran to jump onto the truck that had continued his overland journey. He escaped without paying extra money.

Once migrants manage to arrive in Tripoli and they are connected to a connection man, they have to wait for the actual boat trip to Europe. The actual moment of entry of the boat is a process that is heavily controlled by the migration facilitators, as Saihou – the youngest of the six African men – lively explained:

> [Y]ou have to bring [the boat] into the water, and at that time it is night time, so you don't see anything, and you feel the water … those people [the facilitators], they give you instructions, and they don't care about you. They have guns, so you must act. They give instructions *YOU HERE, YOU SIT THERE < YOU SIT HERE, QUIET < SHUT UP …* and the only thing you can do is listen to these wicked people.

During this process, there was one African man trying to enter the boat 'without the ticket'. When the facilitators noticed the intruder, he was seriously beaten with a gun. This unfortunate African man did not belong to the approximately 80 boat passengers who took off for Italy that night. Thus, not every act of improvisation leads to an important breakthrough. Or, as Vigh puts it, 'not all situations are navigable' (Vigh 2009, 432).

## Navigating reception/asylum in Italy

During the crossing of 'the river' (a frequently used euphemism for the Mediterranean) the boat ran out of fuel and 'the captain' (a migrant himself) lost track until the moment they encountered a Maltese ship. The Maltese crew helped the captain to get on track again and they were finally saved by the Italian coast guard. Interestingly, while Frontex operations and border controls are often criticised by migration scholars (including myself), many of the migrants I spoke to were very grateful for their presence. They mainly see them as safeguards instead of border guards. In order to sketch the migration industry, it is important to note that, next to the Frontex operations and national border guards, there are also several humanitarian organisations active in the rescue industry at EU's outer borders. This includes established international organisations like *Medecins Sans Frontieres* as well as relatively new initiatives such as the Malta-based Migrant Offshore Aid Station (a private search-and-rescue operation) and Watch the Med alarm phone (an activist platform that identifies emergency situations at sea). In the same context, there has been a remarkable initiative launched in the Eastern Mediterranean by the tour operator Sunweb, the airline Transavia and the aid organisation Movement on the Ground. This alliance offers fully organised refugee aid trips to the Greek island of Lesvos for people who wish to assist migrants at the first moment of their arrival.[5] The aid group involved promotes this trip on their website as follows: 'Lesvos Volunteers! Super cheap flights and accommodation by MOTG, Transavia & Sunweb'. Commercialisation and rescue seems to go hand in hand with each other.

After the moment of rescue, the six men from Senegambia were brought to Lampedusa and they stayed there approximately for a week before they got transferred to the Italian mainland. There the asylum labyrinth started. In this procedure, there is a thin line between 'reception' and 'removal', and hence, it is not always clear for the migrant who is there to trust. One of the crucial players in the migration industry is the lawyer, whose role in this Italian context becomes particularly important in the stage of appeal. The role of the lawyer is to turn the often complex migration stories of their clients into 'legally effective stories' (Berger et al. 2015). This was tellingly described by Saihou:

> You need to tell the story from beginning to end, but the judge might start in the middle … So before the court, you need to learn your story very very good. … [T]he judge also asks you questions about things you forget. All the things on the road to Libya, they challenge your mind. They ask, OK, how long did you stay there, and when did you move from that place, and what place was next. … And the difficult thing is, you don't know where the judge will start. So me and my lawyer, we practice this.

Saihou's lawyer made an appeal on the basis of the presence of another actor in this asylum labyrinth: the translator. According to Saihou and his lawyer, fundamental mistakes entered his narrative through the misinterpretations of his words by his translator during his first case. Therefore, they looked for another translator, as he explained:

> [During the first application] they give me a boy from Mali, he does not speak Madinka too good, you see … he made mistakes … So this time she [the lawyer] arranged a translator from Senegal, he is a Madinka boy, so he knows how to speak [my language]. My lawyer called him, and she give me the phone, and say: can you speak to this man? I say yes, I can speak with him, he speaks the same language. Then we say OK, we take him with us to court. I even paid him [the translator] myself for this, maybe like 40 euro.

After the hearing, the Italian migration court took Saihou's appeal in consideration, which finally led to a five years residence permit. Saihou was very grateful for his 'good lawyer'. However, the legal power is not the only criterion of my respondents to judge the quality of their lawyers. Equally important is the social bonding involved. Saihou's say in choosing the translator is not trivial here. It is part of a rather strong alliance between him and this Italian woman. He once told me how his lawyer invited him to her home and paid some train tickets for him. Most important for him, however, was the fact that his lawyer allowed him to travel to other European countries during his procedure. This granting of freedom to a client was not a common practice among lawyers. Shakur, for example, asked for the same mobility opportunity, but his lawyer said to 'break the contract' when he would move across borders.

In terms of the legal outcome of the asylum process it is worth noting that there are remarkable discrepancies between the six men from Senegambia (see Schapendonk 2017). Lamin, Saihou and Amat received a five years residence permit after waiting periods of different length, whereas Omar and Yahya received documents that are valid for shorter periods of time. Shakur has until the moment of writing (January 2017) not seen any progress in terms of his legal status. This discrepancy was well noticed by Lamin, who labelled the Italian system as 'funny' since 'they don't know what they are doing'. To clarify his words, he referred to Shakur's situation: 'Shakur and me for instance, we come from the same area, we don't differ too much. But his situation [here in Italy] is so different'. Lamin's reflection resembles the perception of many migrants that the Italian asylum procedure is a lottery as the outcome depends so much on one's luck (Lucht 2012; Schapendonk 2017).

When migrants obtain their Italian permits, however, a next step of the navigation of their movements commences. Four of my six informants have moved to other European countries to 'try their luck' there. Saihou, for instance, moved to Switzerland after his first asylum application was rejected in Italy. He lived some time as an undocumented migrant close to Lausanne, until the moment he faced a police control 'just on the streets'. He ended up in a detention centre from where the authorities returned him to Italy. Soon after, however, he left Italy again in order to 'try his luck' in Germany. His mode of transport is an interesting form of débrouillardise as he used an online hitchhiking site to arrange his travel.

After having spent some months in Germany, Saihou received the phone call from his Italian lawyer that his documents will arrive soon. That message was a big relief, as he was 'tired' about his living conditions in Germany. In several occasions he compared the situation in Germany with the situation in Italy, and he praised Italy as there are always opportunities for 'raba raba' – a term that has a mixed connotation of hustling, struggling and business. He tried to hitchhike back to Italy (the '*raba raba*' way), but there were no rides offered in that direction. Therefore, he opted for the bus, but this led to another confrontation with the facilitation/control dimension of the migration industry. During his ticket purchase he was asked for his ID card. Although he expected this question, he acted to be very surprised:

> I tell them: ohhh, you say what!? They say pass your ID, I say ooh fuck, definitely I don't have it. That time I had nothing, but I say yes I have some paper. So I present that [German asylum] paper.

A long negotiation followed in which Saihou emphasised the urgency of his move, and the desk worker finally gave him a ticket. She warned him that the bus driver could still refuse him for travelling without documents. Saihou decided to 'just try it'. The bus arrived late, hence the bus driver allowed the passengers to enter quickly. Without any further control, Saihou crossed Switzerland and reached Italy. Such escape routes reinforce the notion shared by my respondents that you can always 'try your luck'.

## Navigating detention/removal in the Netherlands

With the final empirical case I aim to illustrate how migrants are confronted with harsh apparatuses of deportation, and how they try to navigate this process of removal. The example comes from a Congolese man, called Maggis, whose asylum application has been rejected twice since his moment of arrival in the Netherlands. The asylum process in the Netherlands is mainly coordinated by three key partner organisations which are directly linked to the Dutch government. These main parties are the IND (the immigration and naturalisation service), COA (the central organisation for the reception of asylum seekers) and DT&V (the repatriation and departure service). IND processes the asylum claims, COA coordinates the accommodation of asylum seekers and DT&V implements the repatriation policy of the Netherlands. Through subcontracts, subsidies and work relations, these asylum organisations have important linkages with, among others, the national police, asylum lawyers, international organisations, translation agencies, security companies and refugee support organisations. COA, for instance, started to sign agreements in 2015 with holiday villages and event halls to accommodate the higher number of asylum seekers in the Netherlands. This indicates that the privatisation of migration management goes beyond the matter of security companies being placed in detention centres (Mountz et al. 2012). DT&V also grants subsidies to NGOs and international organisations helping to implement the expulsion agenda of the Dutch government. Their most important partner is, undoubtedly, the IOM,[6] but they also engage with smaller organisations and, in so doing, the Dutch state produces a 'cozy consensus' around the politically sensitive topic of migrant deportations (Andeweg 2000, in Kalir and Wissink 2016, 37).

After the IND rejected his asylum application for the second time, Maggis has been put in detention for a period of nine months. Inside the detention centre, Maggis was confronted with soft and rather aggressive approaches to return him to Africa. The DT&V (the repatriation service) had put particularly pressure on him to accompany them to the Congolese embassy in Brussels in order to arrange the necessary laissez-passer.

After having kindly asked for his cooperation, the DT&V started to 'push him', as Maggis explained by reconstructing his dialogue with the authorities:

> M: The first time he [the DT&V staff member] comes, he tells me, you have to go to the embassy. And then [the second time] they say, if you don't go to the embassy then, we send you by force. You understand? … And then, one day they come to me and say [Maggis started to talk with a seductively kind voice]: 'Ohhh, the IND wants to see you … They want to talk to you about your problem again!' I said: ah, but, I talk to IND four times, the IND did not give me anything … He says: 'Oh nooo they will give you a chance' … I said no man, I am not crazy, I am not stupid. He says: 'Oh no, just try, maybe you get [your] paper.' I say noooo I don't want that paper anymore. I only want my freedom … He says: 'So you don't want to speak to IND anymore?' I say no! I don't want to speak to IND. If IND wants to see me, I am here, in this place! The IND knows that I am here. They can come … so why do they want to take me [out] from here? And then, when I spoke to somebody [another detained migrant], he say aaaahhhh you make something good, if you go … the IND always bring some people from you government, your embassy.
>
> JS: To arrange [the laissez-passer]?
>
> M: Ya! … If you come there, then the people see you, and say: Ah. He is from Congo! Allez! And then paff!

In this power play, Maggis resisted this form of cooperation, and in this way he negotiated his relations with DT&V staff. While the DT&V staff member had its own strategy, Maggis also tried to massage this relation, as he reflected: "I was also trying to get him. I was trying to act like being one of his people he like." During his period of detention, he received legal support from a lawyer and mental support (during visiting hours) from a volunteer of a migrant support organisation. With regard to the latter, Maggis has been a 'client' of this organisation for some years, and they helped him with legal advice and assisted him in his basic living conditions. Nevertheless, he is sometimes frustrated about the 'clientisation' involved in the organisation, especially among the older volunteers 'treading the clients sometimes as children'. Hospitality practices are therefore not free from tensed social negotiations.

The nine months of detention ended only after a judge prohibited the IND to detain Maggis any longer. Thereupon, the IND gave him an expulsion order – a document that says he is no longer allowed to be in the Netherlands. This resulted in a legal deadlock: Maggis is obliged to leave the Netherlands, but the Dublin regulation forbids him to move to another European country. A two months period of doubt, exploration and discussion followed that did not only concern Maggis, but also his partner. At the end, they decided to move to Germany, where Maggis could live under the radar. This decision had profound consequences for Maggis, as his social-economic life takes place at the Dutch side of the border. Consequently, and despite his legal status, he started to become a border-commuter with weekly visits to the migrant support organisation, his friends and the people he worked for in the Netherlands.

His border mobility has remained unnoticed for some weeks. It is telling that the first problems arose, not during any border crossing, but at a random control in his German living place. His unfamiliar face in this small village caught the attention of a police officer, asking Maggis for his papers. As he could not hand over any document, he was brought to the police station. There his fingerprints were checked, and according to the Dublin regulations, he was handed over to the border police at the Dutch side of the border. A

Kafkaesque situation followed when the Dutch border police told Maggis that he is not allowed to be in the Netherlands. Maggis replied by saying that he did not find himself in the Netherlands at the moment he was caught. Quite to the contrary, the German police *brought* him to the Netherlands. Nevertheless, an official warning followed and the Dutch authorities articulated Maggis' *inreisverbod* (entry ban). With this entry ban in his pocket, he moved back to Germany. This unpleasant encounter, however, did not stop Maggis from commuting the border, and there is a cruel logic behind that. For him, the border is everywhere, as any police control in any location (be it close to the border or not) would again confront him with migration-related bureaucracies, a forced return to the Netherlands and, possibly, another period of detention.

## Synthesis

The empirical cases have illustrated that through practices of débrouillardise, my informants are able to bind together different passages of their trajectories and find escape routes where necessary. This notion encompasses more than just a daily survival strategy. It indicates a certain openness towards new opportunities. In this context, Abdoumaliq Simone (2001, 18) states that one of the specificities of African livelihoods in times of globalisation is that Africans are constantly prepared to 'switch gears'. In times of dwelling they are at the same time ready to move, change scenes and transcend borders. This preparedness is reflected in many expressions of the six migrants from Senegambia, such as 'trying your luck', and 'raba raba'. This cocktail of mobility, readiness and improvisation is very hard to control through repressive measures. In fact, the omnipresence of borders and control may be an important explanatory factor why migrants continuously 'try their luck', as it is also illustrated by Maggis' mobility between Germany and the Netherlands. For him, borders are everywhere, so why should he not move between different European countries?

The empirical cases also underline that, however harsh the apparatuses of facilitation/control appear to be, specific moments and encounters emerge that allow for social negotiation. This may imply stressing the urgency of your move to staff members of a bus company (in the case of Saihou), but also maintaining some level of stubbornness as shown with the dialogue between Maggis and the DT&V official in the Dutch detention centre. Even in cases where migrants encounter the European asylum bureaucracy, there is often some space for negotiation, reframing and other forms of 'legal gymnastics' (Berger et al. 2015). This argument does not simply lead to the emphasis of migrant agency. In fact, it articulates the *relational* dimension of the situations at play. Whether migrants' efforts and negotiations actually help them to get ahead depend so much on the intentions and efforts of those people the migrants (attempt) to connect with or are confronted with. This relationality is what my respondents most probably would call 'luck'.

The notion of the migration industry as a relational force field (Ingold 2011) blurs the line between the migration industry on the one hand and migrants' social networks at the other (see Cranston, Schapendonk, and Spaan 2018; McCollum and Findlay 2018). As it is illustrated by the empirical cases, and as put forward by several studies, family ties are of crucial importance in migrant's smuggling processes (Belloni 2016b) and actors of the migration industry, be it a smuggler (Khosravi 2011) or lawyer (see the case of Saihou) may (soon) belong to a migrant social network. As Belloni rightly argues (2016b), rather than isolating the migration industry from its social context we may actually find better ways to connect them. In other words, migrant trajectories can be best approached as a 'navigational continuum' (Vigh 2006, 48) of a social environment that includes migrants social networks and a diverse set of actors of the migration industry that are closely connected to migrant's spatial navigation across borders. However, mobility is not only the end goal of navigation per se. The fact that Saihou, Maggis and others move across European borders illustrate that geographical mobility itself can become an important tactic to navigate social environments (Schapendonk 2017). This cross-border mobility intensifies the uncertainty and shifting context that is so central to Vigh's concept of social navigation.

## Conclusion

In this migrant-centered sketch of the African-European migration industry, we have seen that seemingly opposed actors (state vs. civil society, facilitators vs. controllers) work in a continuum of practices. In some cases, migration facilitators appear to block migrant mobility, and in other cases seemingly repressive actors of migration control secure migrant's passages. Whereas violence and force are so often emphasised in public discourses on irregular migration from Africa to Europe, this paper shows that it is actually the winning of migrant's trust that forms a common interest for many parties involved. This counts for the brokers in the country of origin, the connection man in Tripoli, the DT&V worker in a detention centre, but also for me, the researcher whose work is to make sense of migrants' travel experiences.

The relational component that is emphasised in the synthesis leads to a new direction in research on migration industries. Where many studies focus on how different actors (be it recruitment offices, smugglers or visa brokers) deal with different migrants, we could be more sensitive to the different ways the same actors mediate their relations with other relevant actors in the migration industry. Even more so, we could enhance our knowledge on migration industries with studies that constantly shift between the perspective of the migrant, the social network, the facilitator and controller. Such a dynamic approach could help us to identify the synergies and frictions at play and the efforts that are needed to produce migrant im/mobility. After all, not only migrants have to navigate the industry and mediate relations, so too do different actors of migration facilitation and control.

## Notes

1.  http://mashable.com/2016/02/22/migrant-refugee-smugglers-europe/#kNdAx82PUZqq, accessed on 9-3-2016.
2.  Vigh argues that the instability of social environments is articulated in, but not unique to, West African societies (in his case Guinea Bissau). As he states: 'all social environments are in perpetual motion, yet some move at a slower pace than others, so that people have time to internalize and routinize change' (Vigh 2009, 430).
3.  This project entitled Fortress Europe as a Mobile Space is funded by the Netherlands Organisation for Scientific Research (NWO), and it runs from 2014 until mid-2018.
4.  I initially met three of them in early April 2014 (see opening vignette), but through my networking practices I was able to find two of their friends in Italy and one of them in Switzerland.

5. See: http://zon.sunweb.nl/lesbos-extra and http://movementontheground.com/, accessed on 2-3-2016.
6. In 2014, the Dutch department of IOM spent more than €23 million on diverse migrant return programmes. The main funder of these programmes was DT&V and the European Return Fund (IOM 2015).

## Disclosure statement

No potential conflict of interest was reported by the author.

## References

Adey, Peter. 2006. "If Mobility Is Everything Then It Is Nothing: Towards a Relational Politics of (Im)mobilities." *Mobilities* 1 (1): 75–94.
Alpes, Jill. 2011. *Bushfalling. How Young Cameroonians Dare to Migrate*. Amsterdam: University of Amsterdam.
Andersson, Ruben. 2014. *Illegality Inc. Clandestine Migration and the Business of Bordering Europe*. Oakland: University of California Press.
Bakewell, Oliver, and Gunvor Jónsson. 2011. *Migration, Mobility and the African city*, IMI Working Paper Series, No. 50. Oxford University. https://www.imi.ox.ac.uk/pdfs/wp/wp-50-11.pdf.
Belloni, Milena. 2016a. "Refugees as Gamblers: Eritreans Seeking to Migrate Through Italy." *Journal of Immigrant & Refugee Studies* 14 (1): 104–119.
Belloni, Milena. 2016b. "My Uncle Cannot Say "No" if I Reach Libya: Unpacking the Social Dynamics of Border-Crossing Among Eritreans Heading to Europe." *Human Geography* 9 (2): 47–56.
Bensaad, Ali. 2007. "The Mediterranean Divide and Its Echo in the Sahara. New Migratory Routes and New Barriers on the Path to the Mediterranean." In *Between Europe and the Mediterranean*, edited by T. Fabre and P. Sant-Cassia, 51–69. New York: Palgrave MacMillan.
Berger, Iris, Benjamin N. Lawrance, Tricia Redeker Hepner, Meredith Terretta, and Joanna Tague. 2015. *African Asylum at a Crossroads. Activism, Expert Testimony and Refugee Rights* Athens, OH: Ohio University Press.
Brachet, Julien. 2012. "Stuck in the Desert: Hampered Mobility Among Transit Migrants in Northern Niger." In *The Challenge of the Threshold. Border Closures and Migration Movements in Africa*, edited by J. Streiff-Fénart and A. Segatti, 73–88. Lanham, MD: Lexington Books.
Carling, Jørgen. 2007. "Migration Control and Migrant Fatalities at the Spanish-African Border." *International Migration Review* 41 (2): 316–343.
Carling, Jørgen. 2016. "West and Central Africa." In *Migrant Smuggling Data and Research, A Global Review of the Emerging Evidence Base*, edited by M. McAuliffe and F. Lackzo, 25–54. Geneva: International Organization for Migration.
Choplin, Armelle, and Jérome Lombard. 2010. ""Suivre la route". Mobilités et Échanges entre Mali, Mauritanie et Sénégal." *EchoGéo* 14: 1–21. http://echoeo.revues.org/12127.
Cranston, Sophie. 2018. "Calculating the Migration Industries: Knowing the Successful Expatriate in the Global Mobility Industry." *Journal for Ethnic and Migration Studies* 44 (4): 626–643. doi:10.1080/1369183X.2017.1315517
Cranston, Sophie, Joris Schapendonk, and Ernst Spaan. 2018. "New Directions in Exploring the Migration Industries: Introduction to Special Issue." *Journal of Ethnic and Migration Studies* 44 (4): 543–557. doi:10.1080/1369183X.2017.1315504
Gaibazzi, Paolo. 2014. "Visa Problem: Certification, Kinship, and the Production of 'Ineligibility' in the Gambia." *Journal of the Royal Anthropological Institute* 20 (1): 38–55.
Gaibazzi, Paolo, and Marco Gardini. 2015. "The Work of Fate and Fortune in Africa." *Critical African Studies* 7 (3): 203–209.
Gammeltoft-Hansen, Thomas, and Ninna Nyberg-Sørensen, eds. 2013. *The Migration Industry and the Commercialization of International Migration*. Oxford: Routledge.

Gladkova, Nataliia, and Valentina Mazzucato. 2015. "Theorising Chance: Capturing the Role of Ad Hoc Social Interactions in Migrants' Trajectories." *Population, Space and Place*. doi:10.1002/psp1988.

Homaifar, Nazaneen. 2008. "The African Prostitute: An Everyday débrouillard in Reality and African fiction." *Journal of African Cultural Studies* 20 (2): 173–182.

Ingold, Tim. 2011. *Being Alive. Essays on Movement, Knowledge and Description*. London: Routledge.

IOM. 2015. *Annual Report 2014, The Hague*. http://www.iom-nederland.nl/images/AR2014/Annual%20Report%20IOM%202014%20with%20Summary.pdf.

Kalir, Barak, and Lieke Wissink. 2016. "The Deportation Continuum: Convergences Between State Agents and NGO Workers in the Dutch Deportation Field." *Citizenship Studies* 20 (1): 34–49.

Khosravi, Shahram. 2011. *'Illegal' Traveller. An Auto-ethnography of Borders*. Basingstoke: Palgrave Macmillan.

Koh, Sin Yee, and Bart Wissink. 2018. "Enabling, Structuring and Creating Elite Transnational Lifestyles: Intermediaries of the Super-Rich and the Elite Mobilities Industry." *Journal of Ethnic and Migration Studies* 44 (4): 592–609. doi:10.1080/1369183X.2017.1315509.

Lucht, Hans. 2012. *Darkness Before Daybreak. African Migrants Living on the Margins in Southern Italy*. Berkeley: University of California Press.

Mainwaring, Ċetta, and Noelle Brigden. 2016. "Beyond the Border: Clandestine Migration Journeys." *Geopolitics* 21 (2): 243–262.

McCollum, David, and Allan Findlay. 2018. "Oiling the Wheels? Flexible Labour Markets and the Migration Industry." *Journal of Ethnic and Migration Studies* 44 (4): 558–574. doi:10.1080/1369183X.2017.1315505

Mountz, Allison, Kate Coddington, Tina Catania, and Jenna Loyd. 2012. "Conceptualizing Detention. Mobility, Containment, Bordering and Exclusion." *Progress in Human Geography* 37 (4): 522–541.

Müller-Koné, Marie. 2015. "Débrouillardise: Certifying 'Conflict-Free' Minerals in a Context of Regulatory Pluralism in South Kivu, DR Congo." *The Journal of Modern African Studies* 53 (2): 145–168.

Nyberg-Sørenson, Ninna, and Thomas Gammeltoft-Hansen. 2013. "Introduction." In *The Migration industry and the Commercialization of International Migration*, edited by Thomas Gammeltoft-Hansen, and Ninna Nyberg-Sorenson, 1–24. Oxford: Routledge.

Pathirage, Jagath, and Michael Collyer. 2011. "Capitalizing Social Networks: Sri Lankan Migration to Italy." *Ethnography* 12 (3): 315–333.

Schapendonk, Joris. 2015. "What if Networks Move? Dynamic Social Networking in the Context of African Migration to Europe." *Population, Space and Place* 21 (8): 809–819.

Schapendonk, Joris. 2017. "The Multiplicity of Transit. The Waiting and Onward Mobility of African Migrants in the European Union." *International Journal of Migration and Border Studies* 3 (2/3): 208–227.

Schapendonk, Joris, and Griet Steel. 2014. "Following Migrant Trajectories: The Im/mobility of Sub-Saharan Africans en Route to the European Union." *Annals of the Association of American Geographers* 104 (2): 262–270.

Simone, Abdoumaliq. 2001. "On the Worlding of African Cities." *African Studies Review* 44 (2): 15–41.

Somerville, Kara. 2015. "Strategic Migrant Network Building and Information Sharing: Understanding 'Migrant Pioneers' in Canada." *International Migration* 53 (4): 135–154.

Terreta, Meredith. 2015. "Fraudulent Asylum Seeking as Transnational Mobilization. The Case of Cameroon.." In *African Asylum at a Crossroads. Activism, Expert Testimony and Refugee Righ*, edited by Iris Berger, Benjamin N. Lawrance, Tricia Redeker Hepner, Meredith Terretta, and Joanna Tague, 58–74. Ohio: Ohio University Press.

Triulzi, Allesandro. 2012. "'Like a Plate of Spaghetti': Migrant Narratives from the Libya-Lampedusa Route." In *Long Journeys. African Migrants on the Road*, edited by A. Triulzi and R. L. McKenzie, 213–232. Leiden: Brill.

UNHCR. 2015. *Asylum, Refugees and Migration in Niger*, May. https://data.unhcr.org/SahelSituation/download.php?id=1287 accessed on 31-1-2017.

Vermeulen, Bram. 2016. De Veermannen van de Sahara, *NRC Handelsblad*. Accessed January 31, 2017. http://www.nrc.nl/handelsblad/2016/02/20/de-veermannen-van-de-sahara-1589973, accessed on 31-1-2017.

Vigh, Henrik. 2006. "Social Death and Violent Life Chances." In *Navigating Youth Generating Adulthood: Social Becoming in an African context*, edited by C. Christiansen, M. Utas, and H. Vigh, 31–60. Uppsala: Nordiska Afrikainstitutet.

Vigh, Henrik. 2009. "Motion Squared. A Second Look at the Concept of Social Navigation." *Anthropological Theory* 9 (4): 419–438.

Waage, Trond. 2006. "Coping with Unpredictability. Preparing for Life in Ngaoundéré, Cameroon." In *Navigating Youth Generating Adulthood. Social Becoming in an African Context*, edited by C. Christiansen, M. Utas, and H. Vigh, 61–87. Upssala: Nordiska Afrikainstitutet.

# Migration decision-making and migration industry in the Indonesia–Malaysia corridor

Ernst Spaan and Ton van Naerssen

**ABSTRACT**
This paper explores the involvement of migration industry (MI) in the migration system of Indonesia and Malaysia. The two countries share an extensive border and have much in common in culture and history but they are very different in geographical size, population and economic development, the latter being a main cause for labour migration from Indonesia to Malaysia. The changing context of government policies generates new niches for migration services taken up by formal and informal intermediaries, thereby confronting migrants with a varied migration-decision field and thresholds during their migration process. Much of the migration is legal, but a large part of it also takes place outside the control of the national governments. While taking mental processes in migration decision-making as starting point, we analyse how the MI, by way of fostering, facilitating and controlling geographic mobility and localised employment, connects to the production and negotiating of three migration decision thresholds faced by migrants.

## 1. Introduction

In this contribution, we aim to assess the interplay between governmental migration management, migration industry (MI) and migrant decision-making. The three actors, government institutions, private sector and migrants, are involved in a complex network of mutual relations, of which the MI is the core. The decision-making of Indonesian labour migrants to leave for Malaysia or not serves as an example to demonstrate the interplay between the three actors.

Southeast Asia is a highly dynamic region in terms of population mobility, as manifested in large-scale population movements within these countries but also in the existence of international migration corridors, including that between Malaysia and Indonesia. The two countries share an extensive border and have much in common in culture and history but are very different in geographical size and economic development. Since the 1970s, Malaysia's sustained economic growth led to considerable labour shortages and estimates of the number of migrant workers currently varies between 20% and 30% of the total labour force. They are found in four main sectors: agriculture and forestry, construction, electronic industry and services, especially domestic work (ILO 2016). Due to cultural, linguistic and historical relations and an active Indonesian labour export policy, the greatest share of migrants consists of Indonesians. The number of labour migrants placed in Malaysia through the Indonesian Ministry of Manpower increased from a few thousand per annum in the early 1980s to an average of 100,000 in the 1990s. After 2000 their numbers more than doubled. The Malaysian Ministry of Finance in 2010 reported 1.9 million legal migrants of which two thirds from Indonesia (Devadason and Chan 2014). Unofficial sources suggest there are probably an equal number of undocumented Indonesians in the country and although accurate data are not available, it seems safe to estimate the total number of all Indonesian migrant workers at over two million (IOM 2010). Legal migrants are mostly female, the irregular ones predominantly male (Adi 2003, 142; IOM 2010, 9).

Both the Indonesian and Malaysian Governments have stepped up management of labour migration. Foreign labour recruitment became legalised by the bilateral Medan agreement of 1984, aimed at promoting and regularising labour migration, while countering undocumented migration. Nevertheless, the fact remains that many aspects of the regularly frameworks are arranged nationally. In response to rapidly rising labour demand and the mushrooming of contractors recruiting migrant workers for companies and domestic services, the Malaysian Government policy to regulate immigration consists of four major components: By way of the *Employment Restriction Act 1968* access to the labour market for non-citizens is legalised and restricted by issuing work permits, with a system of quotas and restriction by economic sector. Second, to ensure temporary labour immigration, the number of years immigrants are allowed to work is limited as stipulated in the work permits (maximum is five years), and by prohibiting entry of migrant dependents, the marriage to citizens and applications for permanent residency. The core of Malaysia's policy is a temporary guest-worker programme (Kaur 2015). The intent is to maintain a strict insider–outsider distinction: the stipulations render such outsiders simply ineligible for citizenship (Chin 2008). Third, recruitment agencies play an active role and since 2006 were labelled as 'outsourcing companies', responsible for recruitment and employment of migrant workers in Malaysia (Ahsan et al. 2014; Brandström 2014; Garcés-Mascareñas 2012, 71–72). Finally, stricter control takes place both at and behind the porous borders. The amendments 1997 and 2002 to the *Immigration Act* made work of foreign workers without a permit or visa a criminal offence and subject to punitive judicial measures, including jail sentences, caning, and fines for illegal migrants and their employers. This involves a state-sponsored civil volunteer corps called RELA (*Ikatan Relawan Rakayat Malaysia*, or Volunteers of the Malaysian People), which carries out raids and assists in managing Malaysia's immigration detention centres.[1] However, irregular migration continues due to undocumented migrants or their employers bribing immigration officers and the police (Wong and Anwar 2003; Ford and Lyons 2011), to let them pass or refrain from raids on worksites (Wong and Anwar 2003). Malaysian authorities have sought to cope with irregular immigration alternately by mass raids and brief amnesty periods, during which undocumented migrants can leave the country without facing criminal charges under the *Immigration Act* (Government of Malaysia n.d.). Garcés-Mascareñas characterises the response of the Malaysian government to the large-scale immigration as contradictory (2012, 64) and Devadason and Chan (2014) as chaotic.

In Indonesia, the system of migration management has shifted from a laissez-faire approach to a more state-managed system, with regulation of private enterprise providing migration services. Despite government attempts to control migration, regularise recruitment agencies and streamline the recruitment and placement of Indonesian labour in Malaysia, Indonesia has had to accommodate the growing migration pressure and commercial interests of employers and labour recruiters. The devolution of regulatory authority under decentralisation of government after 2000 contributed to a lack of coordination and clarity regarding jurisdiction and responsibilities at local level. Policies implemented left ample room for the private sector to acquire a large part of the migration services market, thereby influencing volume and directionality of labour migration. The division between the public and private actors in this field is not clear-cut, and involves a mutual dependency, flexibility in roles and often the transgressing of regulations in pursuit of efficiency and profit (Spaan 1999; Jones 2000; Palmer 2013). As a result, significant numbers of migrants make use of unlicenced agents, actively looking for loopholes in regulations and resorting to illegal practices, including facilitating illegal border crossing and faking documents (Lindquist 2010; Ford and Lyons 2011, 2013). An important reason for irregular migration and continuous involvement of brokers are the intricate, costly and time-consuming requirements and regulations set-up by government.[2]

To demonstrate how MI influences the migration decision-making and behaviour of migrants, in the next sections we explain the various functions of the MI (enticement, facilitation, and control) and distinguish three stages in the migration process, using the threshold approach (Van der Velde and van Naerssen 2011, 2015). By taking the thresholds (indifference, locational, and trajectory thresholds), as analytical starting points, we explain the relationship between various MI actors and the thresholds in migrant decision-making, within the context of government policy and regulatory frameworks. By embedding the mental decision-making process in a context of MI, we provide further insights into how migrants react on MI actors, and how MI is actually influencing migration in different stages.

## 2. MI and migrant decision-making

The structure of labour recruitment in the migration corridor between Indonesia and Malaysia is characterised by the central role of the MI. The exact nature of what constitutes MI has been subject to debate and there is no consensus as to its scope and function. Nyberg-Sørensen and Gammeltoft-Hansen (2013, 6–7) define MI as 'the array of non-state actors who provide services that facilitate, constrain or assist international migration'. This is a useful starting point but we argue that state actors are part of MI when they provide services to migrants in collusion with recruiters outside the official regulatory framework (see also Harvey, Groutsis, and van den Broek 2018). Simultaneously, while states are important in the governance of labour migration, an evolving market for migration services has fostered the involvement of various non-state actors (Spaan and Hillmann 2013). The actors constituting MI bear heavily on direction, timing and composition of migration flows. During the process of migration, migrants require knowledge, skills and financial investments, assets many prospective migrants lack, thus creating a market for services that MI is able to fulfil. On the other hand, MI may encourage labour migration if only through publicity around its mere existence.

Migrants are seen here as active individuals, weighing and choosing alternative strategies and pathways, during the different phases of migration. These choices are influenced by their social networks but restricted by spatial, socio-cultural, economic and political factors. A decision for migration is based on 'bounded rationality' and limited by incomplete information, risk and uncertainty (Simon 1972). Choice then is (partially) contingent on (information on) the political, social and economic conditions in the country of origin and destination, as well as on entrance and employment regulations. It furthermore hinges on access to (transnational) social networks and brokers providing information, supportive products and services along the spatial migration trajectory (Lindquist, Xiang, and Yeoh 2012; Schapendonk 2009). The importance of social networks (Gurak and Caces 1992; Haug 2008) and brokers in fostering labour migration in origin areas and at destination (Spaan 1994; Fee and Rahman 2006; Lindquist 2012) has been recognised. Less is known about how these actors impact on the actual migration trajectory including transit and return (Kloppenburg and Peters 2012; Schapendonk 2011).

In the political debate, MI is often reduced to its informal and irregular dimensions and is seen as part of the smuggling and trafficking networks (Salt and Stein 1997). We argue for a broader conceptualisation of MI, in that it includes an array of formal and informal/illegal actors and institutions, functioning as inducer, facilitators and controllers of migration (Spaan and Hillmann 2013). Although prospective migrants often seek alternatives to legal trajectories in the face of increasingly restrictive immigration policies, many services related to migration are part of the regular economy, for example, in the case of licenced recruitment agencies and governmental coordinating institutions such as the Bangladesh Overseas Employment and Services Limited. Governments outsource certain functions related to labour recruitment, visa regulations and border control to private entities (Gammeltoft-Hansen 2013; Kaur 2015), thus externalising costs and risks connected to the matching of supply and demand of migrant labour. Both Indonesia and Malaysia have devolved labour recruitment management to non-state actors, while simultaneously following a policy of securitisation and centralising migration and border control (Lindquist 2010, 118).

In anticipation and reaction to stricter governmental regulation and control, MI actors (including representatives of state institutions) can also function as countervailing force in providing alternative pathways and circumventions of existing regulations and laws. In the context of a shifting policy domain, MI actors manoeuvre and create space to capitalise on the changing market for migration services: providing information, documentation, travel and financial services needed for migration; they also offer strategies for circumventing formal administrative requirements and regulations, to make migration more rapid and efficient. Migration brokers, considered facilitators, equally take on a control function by constraining migration and determining temporality and directionality of migration if that fits their interests and profits. Brokers have a varying degree of professionalism (Lindquist, Xiang, and Yeoh 2012) and many have been migrants themselves, having entered the migration brokerage business with varying motives, on a continuum from altruism, profit-seeking entrepreneurship to outright exploitation (trafficking) (Spaan

1999; Asis 2004; Molland 2012). The association between personal migrant networks and altruism on the one hand, versus migration brokerage and profit, on the other, is not straightforward and needs further scrutiny (Faist 2014). The *modus operandi* and profit extraction along gender lines can differentiate and therefore needs to be taken into account as well (Lindquist 2010).

In our analysis below, we discern various functions of MI, namely (1) enticement, (2) facilitation and (3) control. As promoters, facilitators, organisers and controllers of migration flow, MI sets the conditions and boundaries of action. The question is how this relates to the decision-making and behaviour of (potential) migrants. Many theories and models on international migration concern the structural macro-context of human mobility and international migration (Hoerder 2002, 1–21; Castles and Miller 2009, 20–49). Such are various push–pull models and (transnational) social network theories. Other approaches centre on the decision-making of the migrant actor. The New Economics of Labour Migration takes the household as an entity influencing who within the context of the household livelihood strategy will migrate (Stark and Bloom 1985). We focus more on the mental process of migration decision-making (Koikkalainen and Kyle 2016), and, in analysing the various steps taken by migrants during their sojourn and the role, function and impact of MI actors on the different phases in the decision-making process, we draw on the Threshold Approach (Van der Velde and van Naerssen 2011, 2015). Thresholds represent geographical barriers to international migration. Three crucial thresholds can be distinguished shaping migration decisions and conditions for action. First of all, Van der Velde and Van Naerssen outline an *indifference threshold*. Before someone crosses a border, migration must enter the psyche of the individual as a viable option to his or her current position (it makes a difference) and (s)he takes measures to leave. Second, a *locational threshold*, determining the choice of a destination as a safe place and a locus of employment and third, a *trajectory threshold*, referring to how a chosen destination is reached, including legal means and channels as well as illegal ones. In the following, we aim to show how MI actors interact with the mental processes in passing these thresholds and in this way contribute on the migration outcomes. In so doing, we start from the three thresholds and analyse the three different roles of the MI (enticement, facilitation and control).

### 2.1. Indifference to migration and enticement

Enticement involves the informing about opportunities and persuading prospective migrants to migrate. This function of MI impacts on the indifference threshold of migrants; private and State-led recruitment agencies and their sub-agents play a large role in increasing awareness of overseas employment opportunities by active promotion, for example, by way of visiting rural areas and enticing people to migrate by word of mouth[3] or through advertisements (OECD 2001; Higuchi 2003). Where a 'culture of migration' exists and a tradition to work abroad, people will consider to leave especially when they are young, their living and working conditions unfavourable and brokers offer opportunities to go. But even then many prefer to stay in their familiar environment and leaving for another country will not seriously cross their minds.[4] Living abroad must make a real and positive difference with the option to stay before they become actively involved in preparing to live abroad. If people decide to go, this process is considered as passing the indifference threshold.

Although the Indonesian Government admits the economic benefits for the country in the form of remittances, at local level the formal system is not very active in encouraging working abroad; this is rather the terrain for private labour recruiters and their sub-agents. A comparison with The Philippines is enlightening. In the late 1970s, the government initiated an export labour policy and since then the Filipino emigrant population has continued to grow. President Cory Aquino (1986–1992) declared the overseas Filipino workers 'national heroes' who sacrifice their family lives for economic improvement of their kin and their country. The Philippine Overseas Employment Services (POEA) and other government agencies promote, facilitate and protect labour migrants. MI is also embedded in private educational institutions that offer courses in nursing, accounting and ICT for careers overseas. Advertisements in newspapers and billboards suggest that transnational migration belongs to the 'better life'. Besides, various types of migrant NGOs provide services in the migration chain, offering pre-departure courses, counselling and support to 'families left behind', pursuing human rights for migrants, organising re-integration programmes and lobbying (Nah 2012). Thus, governmental and non-governmental institutions are of major importance in establishing a 'culture of migration' (Asis 2006; Gresham, Smit, and Smith 2016) and in this way lower the indifference threshold substantially.

In contrast, the Indonesian MI publicity for jobs abroad is less institutionalised, rather modest and relatively low profile. That does not say that encouragements to work across borders and advertisements in newspapers are lacking but often the traditional and less conspicuous oral means of communication are being used by brokers operating in rural areas (Spaan 1994; Lindquist 2012). Palmer (2013) asserts that licenced recruiters play a significant role in promoting and linking specific source areas with countries of employment, as is shown by the majority of Indonesian migrant workers from Lombok, who end up working in Malaysia and Saudi Arabia (Mantra 1999; Lindquist 2010). Thousands of men and women venture abroad from Lombok each year, an island that only has 2.4 million people in 2010, representing a mere 1% of the total Indonesian population. Despite government efforts to promote regular migration, labour recruitment for the latter country and the Gulf States also occurs informally for example by way of Islamic village schools. After many incidents of sexual abuses of female Indonesian domestic workers abroad, the Indonesian Government became reluctant in sending young women for domestic work abroad and its official policy is discouragement. After the execution of two Indonesian women in 2015, the government announced a moratorium on female migration for domestic work in Saudi Arabia and other Middle Eastern countries. Part of the policy is that recruitment agencies are not allowed to directly approach and recruit women for domestic work abroad. However, *calos* (intermediaries) who are trusted by the villagers use their informal network to approach women and then contact field agents representing recruitment offices (Spaan 1994; Lindquist 2010, 125). This shows how formal and informal are often intertwined.

Once a pool of prospective migrants has been reached, MI has a crucial function in facilitating the actual international migration, by assisting in mobilising necessary resources (capital, networks), obtaining necessary documentation and arranging travel (*facilitation*). In Indonesia, licenced recruitment companies, their field recruiters and informal intermediaries called *calos, tekongs or taikongs* (Spaan 1994; Wong and Anwar 2003) facilitate to obtain main documents such as visa, health certificate and work permit, and arrange pre-departure trainings, transport and employers. In Malaysia, legalised outsourcing agencies are responsible for recruiting migrant workers, organising and supervising their stay, employing them or redistributing them to companies and employers. Thus, Indonesian workers can enter the Malaysian labour market legally while MI will arrange all from pre-departure training till employment and accommodation at destination. The legal way is relatively expensive and due to legal regulations the work permit tie workers to a specific employer, so they are not free to look for better opportunities. Therefore, many migrants make use of the informal MI system. Although by definition undocumented migrants do not have the officially needed documents, this system is basically the same: workers are recruited through agent networks of Indonesian and Malaysian intermediaries. Many workers are hired as day labourers without any kind of written contract or are seasonal workers.

The other side of the coin is the dependency of the migrant on the MI network, and concomitant risk of abuse. Often, MI actors turn out to be exploiters, manipulating information, demanding exorbitant fees or resorting to usury, trafficking and abandonment of migrants. In this informal circuit, abuses take place such as withholding passports and parts of wages. Sometimes people are outright cheated, exploited, imprisoned without being paid or – after paying recruitment fees – are lured into non-existent jobs by outsourcing companies in collusion with government officials (Ahsan et al. 2014). In the Malaysian electronics industry, Indonesian women are often indebted and it is only in Malaysia that they discover that after the deductions the salary they receive is less than the promised (Killias 2009; Das 2015). Moreover, they can be replaced to other factories without having a say in the shift (Bormann, Krishnan, and Neuner 2010). Thus, the MI actors function as organisers and controllers of the migration flows, by determining conditions and setting boundaries for action (*control*). Brokerage creates and perpetuates power asymmetries and social inequalities (Faist 2014).

Thus, both government agencies and (informal) private recruiters play a role in fostering susceptibility to migration through active enticement and facilitation. The provision of services to migrants spans various borders, economic sectors and jurisdictions and constitutes a range of formal and informal actors. It is important however to note here that the number of Indonesians labour migrants abroad constitute a relatively small percentage of the total population of 250 million. Apparently, a large part of the population does not search for employment abroad and by consequence will not pass the *threshold of indifference*.

### 2.2. Locational thresholds and migrant destinations

After the first threshold has been passed and the decision has been taken to search for an overseas job, the (potential) migrant has to pass the *locational threshold*. This threshold concerns the choice of a destination, which is often dependent on the broker or messages from social networks. The choice of a destination involves the comparison and weighting of advantages and disadvantages between the place of residence and the possible destination. Irregular migrants who enter the country through an informal intermediary often use their local social network of family members or friends to arrange work. In a survey of

Wong and Anwar among undocumented workers in West Malaysia, it turned out that the majority found their first job via social networks (2003, 184 and 217), which might provide services without asking for fees but can be considered as part of MI when money is involved. Thus, informal MI and personal social services are regularly working in a chain and the boundaries between the two could be flexible and vague (Adi 2003; Wong and Anwar 2003; Garcés-Mascareñas 2012; Cranston, Schapendonk, and Spaan 2018; McCollum and Findlay 2018). As prospective migrants are often dependent on social networks or labour brokers, the process of deliberation is mostly based on partial or imperfect information, steering to options that might more in the intermediaries interest rather than that of the migrants. Often, migrants who are dependent on private recruiters are misled and end up with lower than expected wages and employment conditions at destination (Wee and Sim 2004; Palmer 2013). When 'keep' and 'repel' factors weigh more than other concerns, the potential migrant will choose to stay or look for another destination.

It is not surprising that Malaysia is the top destination for Indonesian migrant workers, because of the common history of human mobility, its proximity allowing for return visits, widespread social networks and similarities in language, religion and cultural traditions. Although cultural differences should not be underestimated (Hedman 2008, 378–389), they are considerably less compared to other destinations in East Asia such as Taiwan, Hong Kong and Singapore, which offer higher remunerations and also attract many migrant workers (Table 1) but have strong Chinese traditions.

Many Indonesian migrant workers leave for the Middle East, in particular Saudi Arabia. An important pull factor next to the higher wages[5] is its familiarity because of the *hajj*, the annual pilgrimage to Mecca, mandatory for Muslims once in their lifetime. On the other hand, the majority of the Indonesian migrants in Saudi Arabia is female but due to various accounts of abuse and human rights violations, the number of legal migrants substantially declined (Table 1).

The costly and time-consuming formal procedures for securing a legal job act as a push factor to irregular migration. If migrants decide to leave without documentation and assisted by brokers, the choice for Malaysia is obvious. They leave for Malaysia because of its proximity and porous borders, consisting of a maritime one between West Malaysia and Indonesia and a long land 2000 kilometre border with East Malaysia. Such borders are difficult to control and allows for a large influx of irregular migrants from Indonesia. Much of the work is seasonal and circular migration is common. Besides, with the easing of restrictions on visa to encourage tourism, more irregular migrants are entering the country lawfully but become undocumented by overstaying their travel documents

**Table 1.** Indonesian legal migrants' placements, by year and employer countries.

| Country | 2011 | 2012 | 2013 | 2014 | 2015 |
|---|---|---|---|---|---|
| Malaysia | 13,412 | 134,023 | 150,236 | 127,827 | 97,635 |
| Taiwan | 78,865 | 81,071 | 83,544 | 82,665 | 75,303 |
| Saudi Arabia | 137,835 | 40,655 | 45,394 | 44,325 | 23,000 |
| Hong Kong | 50,301 | 45,478 | 41,769 | 35,050 | 15,322 |
| Singapore | 47,786 | 44,556 | 34,655 | 31,680 | 20,895 |
| United Arab Emirates | 39,917 | 35,571 | 44,505 | 7619 | 7619 |
| Oman | 7306 | 8836 | 10,719 | 19,141 | 6766 |

Source: BNP2TKI (Badan Nasional Penempatan dan Perlindungan Tenaga Kerja Indonesia).

(Kassim, cited by Kanapathy 2008). The ethnic and cultural similarities make it easy for the migrants to remain untraced for long. It is clear that the potential migrant has to out-weigh the costs for legally migrating against the risks of penalties and deportation but, as we have seen, at the borders and once in Malaysia there are opportunities for negotiating their way out of sanctions.

From the foregoing, we can conclude that higher wage levels are only one of the reasons resulting in relatively low location thresholds for specific countries. In comparing desti-nations, migrants have to consider other factors such as distance to the area of origin, culture, risks and costs involved in the migration process. The constitution of the net-works, that is, the contacts between recruiters, intermediaries and employers, at destina-tion also impacts on the choice of locations where migrants end up; those involved could be also be local or regional level civil servants in Indonesia (Spaan 1999; Jones 2000) or representatives of Malaysian state-owned companies, for example, oil-palm plantations (Lindquist 2010, 124). In as far as the State is part of the MI, regularly frameworks are of influence, such as bilateral agreements on labour migration. The locational threshold can differ by social categories, such as ethnicity and gender. The latter is of special interest since Indonesia is an Islamic country and 70% of the Indonesian labour migrants consist of women (BNP2TKI 2013). The protective attitude of the government towards women has led to a temporary moratorium on female domestic work in Malaysia in 2009 and Saudi Arabia (Malahayati 2015; Makovec et al. 2016).

### 2.3. Trajectory threshold and migration control

The *trajectory threshold* refers to how to reach the chosen destination, dependent on for example the financial resources one has and the weighing of financial or bodily risks. Again, the outcome could be that the migrant will decide to stay. The relationship between the locational and the trajectory thresholds may differ. The destination often determines the trajectory but it could well be that the trajectory determines the destina-tion, especially when people have only a vague idea of the destination (the USA or the EU but it does not matter where in the USA or EU). Second, when the actual migration process stretches over a long period or covers extensive spatial trajectories, most often each threshold may be (re)visited on a continual yet irregular basis. For example, individuals who wish to reach a particular destination for various reasons may later change that in another one. During actual migration, the influence of intermediaries such as recruitment agencies on the migrants trajectory is significant. In the Indonesian case, as recruiters initially often cover the costs related to migration, the migrants are generally indebted and highly dependent on their recruiters. Many female migrants are coerced into long term stays in 'training centres' or into non or low-paid work in urban centres in Indonesia before actual departure abroad (Spaan 1999; Jones 2000; Wee and Sim 2004).

The flow of Indonesians to Malaysia has evolved into distinctive collective mobility pat-terns and corridors, some of which are long-standing. MI has created routes that both legal and irregular migrants follow to pass the *trajectory threshold*. The major migration routes and corridors of both legal and undocumented migrants are:

- From North Sumatra to Peninsular – Malaysia. Medan is an important transit point where legal migrants can secure the required documents and then take a ferry to

Penang. Undocumented migrants go to the small towns or villages on the coast of Sumatra and clandestinely take a boat.

- A major migration route has developed between Jambi and Riau provinces in southern Sumatra with Singapore and Malaysia, partly due to its proximity and the Growth Triangle strategy, a policy aimed at rapid development, leveraging comparative advantages and economic integration in transnational regions. The region is an attraction pole for migrant workers due to its labour intensive industry, in particular electronics (Van Grunsven and Hutchinson 2014).

- The Riau region has evolved into a major transit hub for undocumented migration, connecting Eastern Indonesia, East and West Java to Singapore and Malaysia (Spaan 1999; Wong and Anwar 2003; Ford and Lyons 2013). Lampung is a popular transit point through Riau province to Peninsular Malaysia.

- On Java, the ports of Jakarta (West-Java) and Surabaya (East Java) are major transit points. Legal migrants can leave from the airports (relatively expensive), while undocumented migrants often travel overland to Riau.

- Movement from the Indonesian provinces on the island of Borneo has a long history and includes circulatory movements of local ethnic groups linked to hunting, shifting cultivation and trade. Nowadays, it also concerns labour migration to the oil palm and construction sectors in Sabah and Sarawak in East Malaysia (Kurus 1998; Kaur 1998). At present, in Sarawak, the only official land transport crossing point is at Entikong (Indonesia) – Tebedu (Sarawak).

- Migrants from the Indonesian island of Sulawesi enter Sabah via the Nunukan – Tawau border crossing but traditionally between Indonesia and East Malaysia there are many informal crossings used for smuggling and migration as well (Wong and Anwar 2003; Idrus 2010).

Although crossing the border without legal documents is relatively easy, the risks could be considerable as illustrated by this newspaper report:

> Local authorities in West Kalimantan have arrested six Indonesian irregular migrant workers heading to Sarawak. They came from Lombok and tried to cross borders but police noticed and arrested them after they failed to provide complete identification papers, such as working visa and the country's migrant workers ID card (KTKLN). According to their statements, they were hired by a guy called Kasim and were going to work at a palm oil plantation in Sibu, Malaysia. One of the migrant workers, said that his group had each paid up to Rp 3.5 million (US $266) to work in Malaysia: 'We were promised that we would work at a palm oil company in Sibu, Malaysia and get a big amount of salary. However, we have not met Kasim,' Salam said. (Jakarta Globe 13-06-2015)

How smooth a long travel can be and how legal and irregular ways of transportation are intertwined, shows the example of an undocumented female migrant from Flores, an island in the eastern part of Indonesia and located at some 3000 kilometres from West Malaysia, where the husband already worked for some years. When the couple decided that his wife would join him, she had to travel from Flores to the central island of Java, then further Northeast to Riau and finally to Malaysia. Since this was a long journey, she was accompanied by a friend of her spouse who organised the public transport: a boat to Surabaya (a three day's journey), where she stayed in transit for two days; a bus to Dumai (Riau), which took five days and where she again stayed in transit two days;

a boat trip (eight hours) to a fishing town in Malaysia facilitated by a *tukong*; a bus from this fishing town to Kuala Lumpur that she reached after five hours travelling (Wong and Anwar 2003, 192–193). In total, the journey took some two weeks and most of the travel was by public transport but the crucial link by which she became an undocumented migrant was the irregularly arranged boat trip between Indonesia and Malaysia. Moreover, she (and her husband) broke the law since it in Malaysia it is forbidden for a migrant worker to have a family member with him/her. This example shows how at specific points in the migrant trajectory, intermediaries played a crucial role in organising travel and (illicit) border crossings, whereby migrants' personal networks and more professional intermediaries are interlinked, as has also been demonstrated elsewhere (Spaan 1994; Jones 2000; Lindquist 2012).

## 3. Final remarks and conclusion

This article has brought out the interplay between the migration management of Indonesia and Malaysia with the MI, the prominent role MI has in the migration corridor between the two countries and its impact on the mobility thresholds. In the course of time, policies and control measures in both countries have changed in reaction to external pressures of employers, trade unions and NGOs, or popular dissent with migrants in Malaysia. Partly due to growing migration pressure, demand for labour in Malaysia and business interests, policy has devolved migration management to non-state actors, creating scope for private recruiters to be involved in promoting, facilitating and controlling labour migration to varying degrees.

In the legal circuit, the Indonesian and the Malaysian Governments give licenced recruitment agencies much space to mediate at the migrant labour market. In Indonesia, the role of the central government changed from an executive one to a regulatory oversight one. In Malaysia, the government changed its liberal policy into one of 'managed migration' (Kaur 2015) but the role of recruitment agencies expanded when they were allowed to act as 'outsourcing companies" and employer of migrant labour. By consequence, the MI system in the Indonesian-Malaysia migration corridor consists of two parallel (but sometimes connected) networks: a formal one with licenced recruitment and outsourcing companies at the core of the network and an informal one consisting of private agencies outside government control.

Undoubtedly, MI actors, whether legal or irregular, loosely connected or entwined, contribute to impact on migration thresholds in the Indonesia–Malaysia migration corridor. This in itself is not surprising, but striking is the substantial share of irregular migrants on the Malaysian labour market. MI makes use of the weak spots in the regularly frameworks of Indonesia and Malaysia. If we consider MI as acting within the limits of economic, political and cultural circumstances that define its playing field, to a large degree it is the Malaysian regulatory framework that allows for and provokes migrants to enter and stay in-country as irregular migrants. This is because the framework, among others, legally prohibits migrant workers to change jobs during their stay and gives space to government officials to negotiate with irregular migrants. In this way, it creates a market for the informal MI to lower the mobility thresholds, more particularly the location threshold.

The operations of MI is characterised by the blurring of legal, geographical, moral and functional boundaries, putting into question analytical dichotomies such as legitimate/

illegitimate, public/private and facilitation/control. As to the latter, MI actors that formally function within migration control can simultaneously covertly facilitate and sustain undocumented migration through corrupt officials working together with brokers. This functional ambivalence depends on the specific actor and vantage point taken. Certain activities can be considered illegal (e.g. by the state) but legal/acceptable by other actors such as migrants. For example, cooperation between the State recruitment agency and private recruiters is a legitimate, regularised operation, but collusion between a recruitment agency and an informal broker, while not officially sanctioned, is deemed acceptable from the viewpoint of a prospective migrant. In this context, the terms licit/illicit are more appropriate, as Van Schendel and Abraham (2005) propose; they refer to overlapping realities, and challenge existing analytical categorisations.

Figure 1 illustrates the overlapping and blurring of categories and functions of MI actors, together with the thresholds we discerned above.

Within the boundaries of a shifting policy domain of securitisation and governmental regulation and control, MI actors reactively manoeuvre and capitalise on the changing market for migration services. Next to providing resources and services, sanctioned by government, they also employ strategies for circumventing formal regulations, making migration more rapid, efficient and profitable. They function as promoters, facilitators, organisers and controllers of the migration flows, by setting the conditions and boundaries of action. The regulatory frameworks contain several rules fostering irregular migration and a blossoming informal MI.

The changing context of government policies, coupled with a lack of accessible, timely migration channels, has created an environment wherein MI can thrive, thereby confronting migrants with a modified migration-decision field and thresholds. During their migration trajectory, prospective migrants have to negotiate various thresholds with regard to decisions to work abroad, the destination country and the route to follow. In

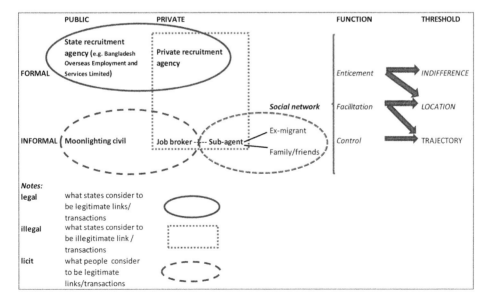

**Figure 1.** MI activities by actor and function. Source: Authors construct.

a context of opaque policies, lack of resources and imperfect information on the part of migrants, the influence of MI is pivotal. Through enticement, advertising and word of mouth, MI increases awareness of overseas employment opportunities and migration channels, thus impacting on the indifference threshold of migrants to move or not. The impact of the operations of intermediaries on the migration trajectory is also significant. The freedom to negotiate location and trajectory thresholds is limited due to indebtedness of migrants, their lack of knowledge and resources and dependent on MI operations. The weighing of advantages and disadvantages of the act of migration and related migration trajectory and destination(s) involves consideration of informational access, costs and financial risk, personal security, legitimacy, duration and social embeddedness. In all domains MI actors have a large influence. Prospective migrants are ever more dependent on intermediaries, in a migration domain characterised by complexity, obscurity and a blurred division between formal and informal actors and actions. Hand in glove, MI actors and migration thresholds remain inextricably linked in dynamic fashion.

## Disclosure statement

No potential conflict of interest was reported by the authors.

## Notes

1. RELA has been criticised for human rights abuses, including excessive use of force and extortion of migrants, during raids (FIDH-SUARAM 2008, 11–13; Hedman 2008).
2. For more details on past and present formal requirements and procedures, see Ananta et al. (1998), Hugo (1995), Spaan (1999) and BNP2TKI (2013).
3. Similar to informal agents (*ronselaars* or *werfagenten*), recruiting labour for work on estates and in mines on Indonesia's outer islands or abroad (Dutch west-Indies, Malaysia, New Caledonia) by persuasion or deceit was part of a system of indentured labour during colonial times (Hugo 1980).
4. Only 3.3% of the world population lives outside the country of birth (UNPFA 2016).
5. For example, in 2014, on the average a domestic worker would earn some US$ 250 a month in Malaysia and US$ 365 in Saudi Arabia; payment to the employment agencies were respectively US$ 1460 and 2200.

## References

Adi, R. 2003. "Irregular Migration from Indonesia." In *Unauthorized Migration in Southeast Asia*, edited by G. Battistella and M. B. Asis, 129–168. Quezon City: Scalabrini Migration Center.

Ahsan, A., M. Abella, A. Beath, Y. Huang, M. Luthria, and T. Van Nguyen. 2014. *International Migration and Development in East Asia and the Pacific*. Washington, DC: World Bank.

Ananta, A., D. Kartowibowo, N. Wiyono, and N. H. Chotib. 1998. "The Impact of the Economic Crisis on International Migration: the Case of Indonesia." *Asian and Pacific Migration Journal* 7 (2-3): 313–338.

Asis, M. B. 2004. "Borders, Globalization and Irregular Migration in Southeast Asia." In *International Migration in Southeast Asia*, edited by Aris Ananta and Evi Nurvidya Arifin, 199–226. Singapore: Institute of Southeast Asian Studies.

Asis, M. 2006. "The Philippines Culture of Migration." *Migration Information Source*. January. Accessed 26 June 2016. http:// http://www.migrationpolicy.org/article/philippines-culture-migration.

BNP2TKI – Badan Nasional Penempatan dan Perlindungan Tenaga Kerja Indonesia (National Authority for the Placement and Protection of Indonesian Overseas Workers, est. 2007). Accessed 14 July 2016. http://www.bnp2tki.go.id/organisasi-mainmenu-176/penempatan-mainmenu-73/g-to-p/7206-pendaftaran-tki-formal-penang-malaysia-2012.html

Bormann, S., P. Krishnan, and M. E. Neuner. 2010. "Migrant Workers in the Malaysian Electronics Industry: Case Studies on Jabil Circuit and Flextronics." Berlin: WEED (World Economy, Ecology and Development). Accessed 30 Jan 2016. http://electronicswatch.org/Migration-in-a-digital-age_3542.pdf.

Brandström, R. 2014. "*Forced Labor and the Migration Industry. Outsourcing Agencies and Migrant Workers in Malaysia.*" M.A. Thesis Global Studies, University of Gothenburg, Gothenburg.

Castles, S., and M. Miller. 2009. *The Age of Migration. International Population Movements in the Modern World*. 4th ed. Basingstoke: Palgrave MacMillan.

Chin, Christine B. N. 2008. "'Diversification' and 'Privatisation': Securing Insecurities in the Receiving Country of Malaysia." *The Asia Pacific Journal of Anthropology* 9 (4): 285–303.

Cranston, S., J. Schapendonk, and E. Spaan. 2018. "New Directions in Exploring the Migration Industries: Introduction to Special Issue." *Journal of Ethnic and Migration Studies* 44 (4): 543–557. doi:10.1080/1369183X.2017.1315504.

Das, R. 2015. "Electrical and Electronics Industry in Malaysia: Present State and Challenges." Accessed 1 February 2016. https://www.linkedin.com/pulse/electrical-electronics-industry-malaysia-present-state-ranen-das.

Devadason, E., and Wai Meng Chan. 2014. "Policies and Laws Regulating Migrant Workers in Malaysia: A Critical Appraisal." *Journal of Contemporary Asia* 44 (1): 19–35.

Faist, T. 2014. "Brokerage in Cross-Border Mobility: Social Mechanisms and the (Re)Production of Social Inequalities." *Social Inclusion* 2 (4): 38–52.

Fee, L., and M. Rahman. 2006. "International Labour Recruitment: Channelling Bangladeshi Labour to East and South-East Asia." *Asia-Pacific Population Journal* 21 (1): 85–107.

FIDH/SUARAM. 2008. *Undocumented Migrants and Refugees in Malaysia: Raids, Detention and Discrimination*. Petaling Jaya: SUARAM.

Ford, M., and L. Lyons. 2011. "Travelling the Aspal Route: Grey Labour Migration Through an Indonesian Border Town." In *The State and Illegality in Indonesia*, edited by E. Aspinall and G. van Klinken, 107–122. Leiden: KITLV.

Ford, M., and L. Lyons. 2013. "Outsourcing Border Security: NGO Involvement in the Monitoring, Processing and Assistance of Indonesian Nationals Returning Illegally by Sea." *Contemporary Southeast Asia* 35 (2): 215–234.

Gammeltoft-Hansen, T. 2013. "The Rise of the Private Border Guard. Accountability and Responsibility in the Migration Control Industry." In *The Migration Industry and the Commercialization of International Migration*, edited by N. Nyberg Sørensen and T. Gammeltoft-Hansen, 128–150. London: Routledge.

Garcés-Mascareñas, B. 2012. *Labour Migration in Malaysia and Spain: Markets, Citizenship and Rights*. Amsterdam: Amsterdam University Press.

Government of Malaysia. n.d. Act 155 Immigration Act 1959/1963 Incorporating all amendments up to 1 January 2006. Kuala Lumpur.

Gresham, Ph., M. Smit, and L. Smith. 2016. "Gender Dimensions of the 'National Script' on Migration and Remittances in The Philippines." In *Women, Gender, Remittances and Development in the Global South*, edited by T. van Naerssen, L. Smith, T. Davids, and M. Marchand, 99–118. London: Routledge.

Gurak, D. T., and F. Caces. 1992. "Migration Networks and the Shaping of Migration Systems." In *International Migration Systems: A Global Approach*, edited by M. Kritz, L. Lim, and H. Zlotnik, 150–176. Oxford: Clarendon Press.

Harvey, W. S., D. Groutsis, and D. van den Broek. 2018. "Intermediaries and Destination Reputations: Explaining Flows of Skilled Migration." *Journal of Ethnic and Migration Studies* 44 (4): 644–662. doi:10.1080/1369183X.2017.1315518.

Haug, S. 2008. "Migration Networks and Migration Decision-making." *Journal of Ethnic and Migration Studies* 34 (4): 585–605.

Hedman, E.-L. 2008. "Refuge, Governmentality and Citizenship: Capturing 'Illegal' Migrants in Malaysia and Thailand." *Government and Opposition* 43 (2): 358–383.

Higuchi, Naoto. 2003. "Migration Process of Nikkei Brazilians." In *Emigración Latinoamericana: Comparación Interregional Entre América del Norte, Europa y Japón*, JCAS Symposium Series, edited by Mutsuo Yamada, 379–406. Osaka: Japan Center for Area Studies, September.

Hoerder, D. 2002. *Cultures in Contact. World Migrations in the Second Millennium.* Durham: Duke University Press.

Hugo, G. 1980. "Population Movements in Indonesia During the Colonial Period." In *Indonesia: Australian Perspectives*, edited by J. J. Fox, R. J. Garnaut, P. T. McCauley, and J. A. C. Mackie, 95–135. Canberra: Research School of Pacific Studies, Australian National University.

Hugo, G. 1995. "Labour Export from Indonesia: An Overview." *ASEAN Economic Bulletin* 12 (2): 275–298.

Idrus, N. I. 2010. *Passports Optional. Inside Indonesia.* No. 100 (April–June).

ILO (International Labour Office). 2016. *Review of Labour Migration Policy in Malaysia.* Bangkok: ILO, Regional Office for Asia and the Pacific.

IOM (International Organization for Migration). 2010. *Labour Migration from Indonesia.* Jakarta: International Organization for Migration.

Jakarta Globe. 2015. "Malaysia Deports Illegal Indonesian Migrant Workers." June 13.

Jones, S. 2000. *Making Money Off Migrants: The Indonesian Exodus in Malaysia.* Sydney: Center for Asia Pacific Transformation Studies, University of Wollongong.

Kanapathy, V. 2008. "Malaysia." Revised Paper after the PECC-ABAC Conference on 'Demographic Change and International Labour Mobility in the Asia Pacific Region: Implications for Business and Cooperation', Seoul, Korea, March 25–26.

Kaur, A. 1998. *Economic Change in East Malaysia: Sabah and Sarawak Since 1850.* London: Macmillan.

Kaur, A. 2015. "Labour Migration, Irregular Movements and Regional Policies." In *Migration and Integration in Europe, Southeast Asia, and Australia. A Comparative Perspective*, edited by J. Pietsch and M. Clark, 75–98. Amsterdam: Amsterdam University Press.

Killias, O. 2009. "The Politics of Bondage in the Recruitment, Training and Placement of Indonesian Migrant Domestic Workers." *Sociologus* 59 (2): 145–172.

Kloppenburg, S., and P. Peters. 2012. "Confined Mobilities: Following Indonesian Migrant Workers on Their Way Home." *Tijdschrift voor Economische en Sociale Geografie* 103 (5): 530–541.

Koikkalainen, S., and D. Kyle. 2016. "Imagining Mobility: The Prospective Cognition Question in Migration Research." *Journal of Ethnic and Migration Studies* 42 (5): 759–776.

Kurus, B. 1998. "Migrant Labor: The Sabah Experience." *Asian and Pacific Migration Review* 7 (2-3): 281–295.

Lindquist, J. 2010. "Labour Recruitment, Circuits of Capital and Gendered Mobility: Reconceptualizing the Indonesian Migration Industry." *Pacific Affairs* 83 (1): 115–132.

Lindquist, J. 2012. "The Elementary School Teacher, the Thug, and his Grandmother: Informal Brokers and Transnational Migration from Indonesia." *Pacific Affairs* 85 (1): 69–89.

Lindquist, J., B. Xiang, and B. Yeoh. 2012. "Opening the Black Box of Migration: Brokers, the Organization of Transnational Mobility and the Changing Political Economy in Asia." *Pacific Affairs* 85 (1): 7–19.

Makovec, Mattia, Ririn S. Purnamasari, Matteo Sandi, and Astrid R. Savitri. 2016. "Intended vs. Unintended Consequences of Migration Restriction Policies: Evidence from a Natural Experiment in Indonesia." Institute for Social and Economic Research, ISER Working Paper, No. 2016-13 (Nov.).

Malahayati. 2015. "Legal Protection on Indonesian Domestic Workers in Malaysia: From Actors' View." *Journal of Law, Policy and Globalization* 43: 75–85.

Mantra, Ida Bagoes. 1999. "Illegal Indonesian Labour Migration from Lombok to Malaysia." *Asia Pacific Viewpoint* 40 (1): 59–68. (April).

McCollum, D., and A. Findlay. 2018. "Oiling the Wheels? Flexible Labour Markets and the Migration Industry." *Journal of Ethnic and Migration Studies* 44 (4): 558–574. doi:10.1080/1369183X.2017.1315505.

Molland, S. 2012. "Safe Migration, Dilettante Brokers, and the Appropriation of Legality: LaoThai 'Trafficking' in the Context of Regulating Labour Migration." *Pacific Affairs* 85 (1): 117–136.

Nah, A. M. 2012. "Globalisation, Sovereignty and Immigration Control: The Hierarchy of Rights for Migrant Workers in Malaysia." *Asian Journal of Social Science* 40 (4): 486–508.

Nyberg-Sørenson, Ninna, and Thomas Gammeltoft-Hansen. 2013. "Introduction." In *The Migration Industry and the Commercialization of International Migration*, edited by Thomas Gammeltoft-Hansen, and Ninna Nyberg-Sørenson, 1–23. Abingdon: Routledge.

OECD. 2001. *International Migration in Asia Trends and Policies: Trends and Policies*, 214–215. Paris: Organisation for Economic Co-operation and Development.

Palmer, W. 2013. "Public–Private Partnerships in the Administration and Control of Indonesian Temporary Migrant Labour in Hong Kong." *Political Geography* 34: 1–9.

Salt, J., and J. Stein. 1997. "Migration as a Business: The Case of Trafficking." *International Migration* 35 (4): 467–494.

Schapendonk, J. 2009. "Staying Put in Moving Sands: The Stepwise Migration Process of Sub-Saharan African Migrants Heading North." In *Respacing Africa*, edited by U. Engel and P. Nugent, 113–138. Leiden: Brill.

Schapendonk, J. 2011. "Turbulent Trajectories. Sub-Saharan African Migrants Heading North." PhD Dissertation, Radboud University Nijmegen, Nijmegen.

Simon, H. 1972. "Theories of Bounded Rationality." In *Decision and Organization*, edited by C. B. MacGuire and R. Radner, 161–176. Amsterdam: North-Holland.

Spaan, E. 1994. "Taikong's and Calos: The Role of Middlemen and Brokers in Javanese International Migration." *International Migration Review* 28 (1): 93–114.

Spaan, E. 1999. *Labour Circulation and Socioeconomic Transformation. The Case of East Java, Indonesia*. The Hague: Netherlands Interdisciplinary Demographic Institute.

Spaan, E., and F. Hillmann. 2013. "Migration Trajectories and Migration Industry. Theoretical Reflections and Empirical Examples from Asia." In *The Migration Industry and the Commercialization of International Migration*, edited by N. Nyberg Sørensen and T. Gammeltoft-Hansen, 64–86. London: Routledge.

Stark, O., and D. Bloom. 1985. "The New Economics of Labor Migration." *The American Economic Review* 75 (2): 173–178.

Van der Velde, M., and T. van Naerssen. 2011. "People, Borders, Trajectories: An Approach to Cross-Border Mobility and Immobility in and to the European Union." *Area* 43 (2): 218–224.

Van der Velde, M., and T. van Naerssen. 2015. *Mobility and Migration Choices. Thresholds to Crossing Borders*. Abingdon: Routledge.

Van Grunsven, L., and F. E. Hutchinson. 2014. *The Evolution of the Electronics Industry in the SIJORI Cross-Border Region*. Economics Working Paper No.2014-2. Singapore: Institute of Southeast Asian Studies (ISEAS).

Van Schendel, A., and I. Abraham, eds. 2005. *Illicit Flows and Criminal Things. States, Borders, and the Other Side of Globalization*. Bloomington: Indiana University Press.

Wee, V., and A. Sim. 2004. "Transnational Networks in Female Labour Migration." In *International Migration in Southeast Asia*, edited by Aris Ananta and Evi Nurvidya Arifin, 166–197. Singapore: Institute of Southeast Asian Studies.

Wong, D. T., and T. A. T. Anwar. 2003. "Migran Gelap: Indonesian Migrants in Malaysia's Irregular Labor Economy." In *Unauthorized Migration in Southeast Asia*, edited by G. Battistella and M. M. B. Asis, 169–227. Quezon City: Scalabrini Migration Center.

# Index

Note: Page numbers in *italics* refer to figures
Page numbers in **bold** refer to tables
Page numbers followed by 'n' refer to endnotes